SCHOOL OF ORIENTAL AND AFRICAN STUDIES
University of London

Please return this book on or before the last date shown

Long loans and One Week loans may be renewed up to 10 times
Short loans & CDs cannot be renewed
Fines are charged on all overdue items

Online: http://lib.soas.ac.uk/patroninfo
Phone: 020-7898 4197 (answerphone)

The Practice of Political Authority

The Practice of Political Authority Authority and the Authoritative

Richard E. Flathman

The University of Chicago Press
Chicago and London

RICHARD E. FLATHMAN is chairman of the
political science department at the
Johns Hopkins University.

The University of Chicago Press, Chicago 60637
The University of Chicago Press, Ltd., London

Library of Congress Cataloging in Publication Data

Flathman, Richard E
  The practice of political authority.

  Includes bibliographical references and index.
  1. Authority.   I. Title.
JC571.E515   301.5'92   79-26431
ISBN 0-226-25319-8

For my family
Superb teachers of the subject

Contents

Acknowledgments

My initial work on the topic of authority was much helped by conversations with Paul Brass, Lance Bennett, Arthur Di-Quattro, and Ruth Horowitz; by the able research assistance of Craig Carr; and by the support (of various kinds) of a superb dean, George M. Beckmann. Funds or research leave were generously provided by the National Endowment for the Humanities and the Johns Hopkins University and research facilities and conditions were afforded by the British Library and the Department of Government of the London School of Economics and Political Science. My thanks to each of these excellent institutions.

Work in London was greatly aided by the many kindnesses of Maurice Cranston and Elie Kedourie and continuously stimulated by conversations with Cranston, Kedourie, Robert Orr, Michael Oakeshott, and especially John Charvet. The book was completed at Johns Hopkins and I hope it shows some of the effects of an intellectual climate that is distinctively supportive of theoretical work.

I have presented parts of the manuscript to a number of scholarly groups, including seminars at King's College, London; the London School of Economics and Political Science; the Foundations of Political Theory Group; the Conference for the Study of Political Thought; the American, Southern, Midwestern, Western, and Southwestern Political Science Associations; and the History of Ideas Club of Johns Hopkins University. My thanks to participants in these sessions for their comments and criticism as well as to the students in my graduate seminar at Hopkins for their patience in working through the argument.

The manuscript has been read in whole or in part by John Charvet, Matthew Crenson, Alan Eade (who contributed some superb editing), Edmund Erde, Richard B. Friedman, Timothy Fuller, Maure Goldschmidt, Nancy Hartsock, Michael Oakeshott, John G. A. Pocock, Gerald Postema, and John C. Rees. The comments of these authorities concerning political authority contributed a great deal to my thinking. Had I been more successful in incorporating and integrating their insights and understandings this would be an authoritative work.

Mrs. Evelyn Scheulen and Mrs. Evelyn Stoller typed the rough drafts with their usual efficiency and good spirit, and Mrs. Joy Pankoff and Mrs. Maria Stewart typed the final version.

Introduction

There is at least one respect in which the author of a work on political authority may draw reassurance from the abundant contemporary literature on the topic. It is all but standard for recent discussions to begin by remarking the great practical and philosophical importance of authority and its complex, multidimensional, and refractory character as a topic of study. Sparing anxiety that his enterprise is trivial or redundant (these opening paragraphs, of course, being the last things their authors wrote), the largely uncontested recurrence of such assertions relieves familiar authorial apprehensions.

For this among other more substantial reasons, I will neither elaborate nor challenge such assertions here. Authority may not be *the* central or defining feature of political life or the foremost topic of political philosophy, but there is no need to belabor its significance; previous students have accomplished a good deal, but it could hardly be claimed that the major issues concerning authority have been conclusively settled. In short, anyone disposed to study political authority need do no more than pass through gates—the gates of political philosophy—over which it is written, "A certain immodesty is a condition of entering here."

Within these portals there are many directions that may be taken, a generous choice of paths to be followed, and, perhaps, some stretches of countryside still suitable for a ramble. Because the better part of the travels taken in the following pages are through familiar regions, detailed maps and itineraries would be an encumbrance to those who choose to follow along. But the most complaisant traveling companions deserve to be informed of major stopping places and the modes of accommodation that can be expected.

In the course of a sensitive exploration of themes in Hegel's thought, George Armstrong Kelly identified three competing "theses" about political authority. According to "the liberal thesis," "public authority is there to facilitate the more or less free transactions of society." The "Marxist or elitist" thesis "is that political authority is there to routinize the domination of one part of society over another through the application of coercive force and the transmission of a public ideology." "A third thesis, shared by Hegel, is that political authority is there to amplify and sustain the solidarity of a people by acting as a focal point of reverence and by superseding particular wills and interests."[1]

However we label them, Kelly's "theses" do encapsulate distinct notions about authority, notions that are undeniably prominent in politics and political thought in our time. For immediate purposes, however, what is most interesting about the theses is what is shared among them, namely, a conception of authority cast in terms of its alleged end or purpose—in terms of what it "is there to" do, accomplish, or bring about. The theses invite us to identify and understand, certainly to assess, authority by looking to its distinctive *telos* or final cause.

In this respect the modern notions that Kelly puts before us continue a mode of thinking about authority that made its first appearance no later than Plato and that has remained prominent ever since. (Specifications of the "that for which" authority exists have of course varied over a quite remarkable range: justice, security and order, a proper distribution of rank and privilege, a duly regulated and reciprocal liberty, social cohesion, and economic efficiency are only the more familiar among them.) Nor will I altogether eschew this approach to the topic here. I deny that there is any single purpose or objective distinctive to authority. But in the concluding justificatory section I do contend that the acceptability or not of political authority should be judged primarily in terms of its compatibility with and potential contributions to the exercise of agency on the part of its subscribers. And my argument that political authority can in principle be accepted by persons who assign due importance to their standing as agents (albeit by this criterion few actual or self-proclaimed practices of authority have in fact deserved such acceptance) is teleological in a somewhat hybrid (perhaps bastard) sense that might be abbreviated by calling it a utilitarianism of agency.

Suppositions have begun to appear that deserve explicit notice before concluding these preliminary remarks. But let me note first—if I may use the going cliché—that it is no accident that teleological argumentation enters our reflections primarily when we reach their most explicitly justificatory moments. If true, the proposition that political or any other type of authority "is there to" promote justice or freedom or social cohesion may be a good reason for instituting and maintaining it as a feature of human affairs. Equally, if Marxists are correct that political authority "is there to" routinize the hegemony of one class over another, we would have an excellent reason for setting ourselves resolutely against its every manifestation. In short, teleological considerations are of undeniable relevance to assessing the merits of political authority.

But we cannot assess the merits of authority unless and until we have ascertained what authority is and is not. True, if investigation showed that what we know to be authority "does" one and only one "thing" (and that authority is the only agency or entity that does that thing), there might be a point to identifying or even defining it exclusively by reference to whatever it is that it distinctively and exclusively does. (As, for example, my dictionary defines "carburetor" as an apparatus "for supplying an internal combustion engine with vaporized fuel mixed with air.") But the several conditions just iterated are without exception patently counterfactual. We may judge that authority plays an especially salient role in effecting, say, justice, and we may cogently conclude that we should value or disvalue it primarily for that reason. Quite clearly, however, the existence of political authority is nothing like a sufficient condition of any mode of justice and—equally clearly—its existence cannot fail to have numerous consequences in addition to the contributions it may make to justice.

Thus quite apart from general objections to purely teleological or functional definitions,[2] it is implausible in the extreme to think that we could give an adequate account of what authority is and is not by reference to its alleged ends or purposes. Kelly's three theses, and indeed the larger array of theories they exemplify (what I will be calling substantive-purposive, or S-P theories), presuppose an understanding of what authority is and is not—of what distinguishes authority from the numerous other phenomena to which it is importantly related and with which it is easily confused— such that we can determine that it is authority and not something else that is playing the role, performing the function, or serving the purpose that the theses pick out as crucial to assessing "its" merits.

In numerous contexts it is entirely reasonable to make this presupposition. Authority has been and is now a feature of the arrangements of a great many societies and associations. Theorists writing in and for such societies have no need to describe and define it as they would some bit of exotica from an alien culture or some invention that they have dreamed up for the edification of themselves or their audiences. Marx, who to my knowledge never paused to analyze or define what authority is and is not, could nevertheless cogently advance the thesis Kelly ascribes to him because he and his intended audiences had the sort of familiarity with authority that comes from living with it—or at least claims to it—on a day-to-day basis. It should be added that such a participant's familiarity is equally a presupposition of the kind of analysis of authority that I attempt in the present work.

Perhaps because of its very ubiquity in human affairs, however, it has proven difficult to translate participant understandings of authority into an articulate, systematic account that commands general acceptance among students of the subject. We generally recognize authority when we encounter it. But philosophical students of the phenomenon continue to dispute basic questions concerning its identification and analysis. And while these disputes have a significance of their own, they are also relevant to intelligent participation in the practice of authority. That practice was not a creation of theorists, and it or something like it may continue or not regardless of the analyses and reflections of theorists. We will have occasion to see, however, that disputes concerning the analysis of authority carry substantial implications for reasoning about conduct in respect to authority.

Readers of my previous studies will recognize in the foregoing remarks elements of the concept of a practice and of the understanding of the theory-practice relationship developed along with that concept.[3] That concept and the attendant understanding of theory and practice provide key orienting and organizing assumptions of the present work as well. Without reiterating the basic features of the "practice" notion, two aspects of its role in the present study require advance notice.

As the concept of a practice is used in this study, we would not apply that concept to an arrangement or set of activities unless rules (of various types) and rule-governed conduct were prominent in it or them. Because it is part of the notion of a rule that it must have been laid down or otherwise established before there can be cases that fall under it or conduct guided by it, the contention that authority should be understood as forming a practice itself asserts that there are at least some aspects of authority that cannot be adequately understood in functional or other teleological terms. Thus a bias against S-P theories is built into my very approach to my subject matter. In terms that are fashionable in much contemporary moral and political philosophy, my approach to authority itself biases me in favor of a deontological account of what it is and is not.

This bias is deepened by two more specific features of the account I will offer. (I also hope, of course, that the bias is justified by the evidence and argumentation presented in support of the account.) According to the first of these features, which I adapt from a tradition of thinking about authority running at least from Hobbes to Michael Oakeshott, I misdescribe the practice of authority if I say no more than that rules and rule-guided conduct are "prominent" in it. If I follow Oakeshott in this regard, I should rather say that insofar as an association possesses genuine authority, that association "begins and ends in the recognition of [a certain kind of] rules."[4] "The authority of rulings and of administrative requisitions is recognized in terms of the rules which permit them to be made and which specify their jurisdiction. The authority of an office lies in the rules which constitute it and endow it with powers and duties and is to be recognized in terms of those rules. The authority of the occupant of an office, his right to exercise its powers, is the license he acquires in coming to occupy it according to the rules of a prescribed procedure of appointment or succession. The authority of legislators to make, to amend, or to repeal *lex* is recognized in the rules which specify the conditions to be subscribed to in order to occupy the office, and the *lex* they declare is recognizable as authentic law in having been enacted in subscription to a prescribed procedure and in the exercise of powers conferred in this procedure."[5]

One might say that for Oakeshott rules of certain kinds and subscription thereto are constitutive of authority, or perhaps that authority consists in rules and subscription to them. Whichever of these or related locutions best renders Oakeshott's thought, it is clear that for him understanding authority consists primarily in understanding rules. If he is correct, it is also clear (as he repeatedly insists in the course of *On Human Conduct*) that notions about what authority "is there to" do can make no contribution to determining what authority is and is not.[6]

Oakeshott's is the best developed and most uncompromising version of a type of theory of authority that insists on interpreting authority as an attribute of rules, procedures, and offices. In my judgment this type of theory (which I will henceforth call formal-procedural, or F-P, theory) offers the best available analysis of what authority is and is not. Accordingly, my attempt to analyze authority will begin with an explication and criticism of leading versions of F-P theory.[7] For reasons already indicated in part, this procedure means that much of the discussion will concern the notion of a rule, of subscription to rules, of rule-guided conduct, of obligations entailed by rules, and so forth.

F-P theory is at its best in showing what authority is and is not; in distinguishing authority from force, power, manipulation, leadership, persuasion, argumentation about merits, and the many other features of political life with which authority is readily confused. But no version of the theory known to me is adequate as an analysis of authority. Its inadequacies, moreover, create serious and unnecessary difficulties for thinking about the time-honored question whether political authority is, in principle, an acceptable feature of human arrangements. My major objections and amendments concern the theory's account of the notion that it itself (correctly) makes crucial to authority, namely, rules (and offices created by rules) and rule following. On both counts the objections are to the effect that, despite being largely correct about the centrality of rules to a practice of authority, F-P theory renders such a practice incomprehensible by giving an excessively formalistic and hence constricted account of rules and rule following.

The first objection is developed primarily in chapter 3 and in the discussion of the so-called surrender of individual or private judgment to authority in chapters 5 and 6. I argue that teleological or consequentialist considerations—considerations of ends, purposes, objectives, and their desirability—are internal to rule making and rule following to an extent well beyond that allowed by most F-P theorists. So far as part 1 is concerned, this argument reaches a kind of culmination in my contention that the mode of action now commonly known as civil disobedience is compatible with genuine and continued subscription to the practice of authority that the agent civilly disobeys. This argument also figures importantly in my later attempt (part 2) to meet the objections of philosophical anarchists.

My second major objection concerns the setting or conditions necessary to a system of rules that carry authority. The essentials of the argument can be introduced by reference to another familiar distinction fruitfully recalled for us by George Armstrong Kelly. The distinction is between, on the one hand, the view of Émile Durkheim and Talcott Parsons (and, I would add, Max Weber), according to which a society is "held together" primarily by values and beliefs widely shared among its members, and, on the other, the apparently conflicting understanding of Marx, Weber (according to Kelly), and Ralf Dahrendorf who hold that such social cohesion as we in fact find (at least in "modern" or "capitalist" societies) results largely if not exclusively from constraint and coercion imposed through power by a dominant class or stratum.[8]

As already noted in respect to Marx, theorists in Kelly's second category tend to deny the distinction between power and authority. They contend that what passes for authority is in reality power cloaked by an obfuscating and rationalizing ideology. But if this contention is meant to deny the reality of widely shared values and beliefs, or their importance in accounting for social cohesion, then it is untenable, as is the familiar distinction of which Kelly writes. Both are untenable because power itself—as distinct from episodic uses of raw force and violence—is impossible in the absence of values and beliefs shared between those who wield power and those subjected to it. (Such at least is one of my contentions in chapters 6 and 7, a contention grounded in part in the important arguments of Antonio Gramsci and Hannah Arendt.)

It does not follow (*pace* Parsons and what seems to be implied by some of Arendt's formulations) that power can or should be assimilated to authority. It does not even follow that we will always find the one where we find the other. But the distinction between the two explanations for social cohesion is more clearly untenable in societies and associations in which authority is in fact found. In order for there to be rules that carry and bestow *authority,* I will argue, there must be values and beliefs that have *authoritative* standing among the preponderance of those persons who subscribe to the authority of the rules. These values and beliefs do not take their standing as authoritative from adoption or promulgation by any agent or agency possessed of authority. Rather, the acceptance (however it came or comes about), by a preponderance of subscribers to authority, of the values and beliefs as authoritative is one of the conditions of authority. It is, for instance, in terms of authoritative values and beliefs that both authority as such and a practice of authority with a particular shape are acceptable (or not) as features of a society or association. And it is by reference to authoritative values and beliefs that the most basic of the rules that carry and that bestow authority are formulated, mutually understood by subscribers, and interpreted and acted upon in the ever-changing circumstances of social and political life. In trying, as it insistently does, to analyze and understand authority without reference to the setting of authoritative values and beliefs, F-P theory renders incomprehensible the distinctive feature of authority, that is rules and conduct guided by rules. It also excludes considerations vital to justifying or disjustifying any instance of the practice of authority.[9]

I will conclude these preliminary observations by returning to the suppositions to which I alluded after introducing Kelly's three theses about the ends of authority. Those theses, and the larger idea that they represent—namely that authority (as such) is susceptible of justification or disjustification as a feature of human arrangements—implicitly reject contentions about authority that continue to make their appearance in both systematic and more occasional discussions of authority. One of these contentions is that authority is a "natural," a "functional," or some other species of "necessity" of societies or associations and that therefore it has been, is now, and will of certainty remain a feature of all societies or associations—whatever the members thereof may think or do. On this view, of course, the question of justifying or disjustifying authority "arises not for deliberation." We may sensibly deliberate questions about the shape a practice of authority should take in this or that time and place, about the proper scope of its activities, about who should and should not be entrusted with it, and so forth. But the project of deliberating the merits of authority as such is fundamentally misconceived, and its yield will be confusion or worse.

Leaving aside numerous difficulties attending the various formulations of this contention (for example those concerning the notion of necessity), it is decisively refuted by the fact that societies and associations are known to us that are not only without authority but that have explicitly rejected it. An especially interesting example of such a society is that of the Fox Indians. I will discuss their arrangements and beliefs at various places in the chapters that follow.

A weaker contention, but one that nevertheless leads to the same conclusion about justificatory theorizing, is that the supreme value or importance of authority is so manifest, so undeniable, that those who question or defend it can hope to demonstrate nothing more than the deep deficiencies of their own intellects. Here again it is admitted that there are numerous genuine questions internal to practices of authority. But it is insisted that there are no such questions about the practice as such.

It is beyond dispute that special difficulties attend the project of justifying or disjustifying practices, institutions and arrangements as ubiquitous among and as central to social and political life as authority (or rights, or promising, or property, and so forth). In the case of authority, many of these difficulties arise from the fact that (according to my theory) authority presupposes and is deeply influenced by authoritative values and beliefs together with the further fact that the content of the values and beliefs that have had such standing has varied substantially through historical time and across social and political space. I address some of these difficulties at various junctures below, especially in chapter 4 and at the beginning of part 2. For the moment, however, I will rest with the following observations.

The contention being considered implies that no genuine argument for anarchism merits the slightest consideration. Now if it were proper to defend theorizing about authority by appeal to authority, I might say that the shallow character of this view is sufficiently indicated by the frequency with which the most profound thinkers about politics, although without exception rejecting anarchism, are to be observed paying the latter, at least *inter alia,* the high compliment of an extended refutation. What is more important, they were correct to do so. My own attempt to reassess authority has led me to the conclusion that the strongest objections to authority can in principle be met and a positive case of sorts made for accepting authority. But there are powerful objections to this conclusion, objections grounded in the most fundamental features of the practice of authority itself.

To subscribe to a practice of authority is to accord to each of the rules that recognizably partakes of its authority the standing of a good—indeed ordinarily a conclusive—reason for conforming to those rules. It is to accord those rules such standing despite what may be repugnant characteristics of the actions they require. As anarchists have always and rightly said, such an arrangement is objectionable in itself. Nor can it come as a surprise that, whatever may be its merits and however important may have been the advantages and benefits it has sometimes bestowed, the arrangement has been productive of great harms and sufferings.

A human arrangement or institution with such a characteristic and with a history of producing such consequences cannot be beyond justification and cannot be manifestly or obviously justified. Rather, such an institution *demands* justification; it demands a justification responsive to the formidable arguments against it. If the past is any guide to the present and the future, it is unlikely that any very large number among us will adopt an anarchist position. But if we cease to recognize the power of the arguments anarchism makes against authority we will almost certainly have lost the capacity to conduct a practice of authority that *is* justifiable. We will also have lost something of our humanity.

1.Analyzing the Practice of Political Authority

Alexis de Tocqueville

But obviously without . . . common belief no society can prosper; say, rather, no society can exist; for without ideas held in common there is no common action, and without common action there may still be men, but there is no social body.

1 Distinctions and Themes

Puzzles about Authority

"Who is the strongest man in the world?" "The policeman, because he can hold up a truck with one hand." This child's riddle conveys some of the puzzle, even the mystery, that surrounds authority. On the one hand, it calls attention to problems that inveterately arise when we attempt to say just what authority is, just how it is to be characterized and differentiated from a variety of closely related features of human affairs. On the other, it signals some of the difficulties we encounter in comprehending—and justifying or disjustifying—the recurrence of authority and authority relations, however their exact characterization should be formulated, in human history.

On the first point, consider the following well-rehearsed difficulties. The riddle suggests that the authority of the policeman has something to do with force or strength. But it also reminds us that the policeman is not himself able in any physical sense to stop the truck. Any success he may have in "holding it up" must be understood in terms of some other form of "force." Yet we all know that sheer physical force lurks more or less closely in the background of the activities of policemen. Thus many have been tempted to say that physical force is what "really" or "ultimately" explains any obedience policemen may win and hence that physical force is what authority finally amounts to. Truck drivers also stop for armed highwaymen, and perhaps there is after all no very significant difference between highwaymen and policemen. If authority is not purely and simply power or strength, it is at least a form thereof.

But truck drivers also stop for hitchhikers and persons in distress. The latter cannot physically compel truck drivers to stop, and unlike the policeman can rarely sanction truck drivers who refuse to do so. Moreover, truck drivers sometimes say things about stopping for hitchhikers and persons in distress—for example, that they ought to stop or that it would be wrong not to—that are more analogous to what they say about stopping for policemen than for highwaymen. If this line of thought is pursued, it is tempting to think that authority consists distinctively not in power or compulsion or sanctions but in some species of beliefs about what it is right or wrong to do.

Resolving the sorts of difficulties we have been discussing—difficulties about specifying just what authority is and is not—would not altogether eliminate the second sort of puzzlement that we mentioned at the outset. Truck drivers are well supplied with reasons for stopping as seldom as possible. More generally, if human beings are the prickly, prideful, idiosyncratically purposive creatures that they appear on the whole to be, how are we to comprehend that they often let the dictates of some authority determine their actions and even their thoughts? Despite our familiarity with it, on reflection there is about authority an aura of the surprising that is difficult to dispel. To take authority for granted, to find its recurrence in human affairs natural or to be expected, is to be in danger of misunderstanding it.

It is of course an aim of political philosophy to reduce the first sort of puzzlement and by this and other means to abate as far as possible the second. Political philosophers have made progress in these endeavors, and their achievements will facilitate the present effort. But it must be said that the first effect of reading the considerable philosophical and social scientific literature concerning authority will almost certainly be to compound confusion about what authority is and to deepen rather than diminish the aura of mystery that surrounds it. A preliminary look at some of the characteristic assertions of and disagreements within that literature will help identify issues and problems that must be considered in what follows.

Each of the following pairs of conflicting and even flatly contradictory propositions recurs in philosophical and social scientific discussions of our subject:

1 *a*) Authority yields (authorities issue) statements to be believed.

   b) Authority yields (authorities issue) commands to be obeyed or rules to be subscribed to, not statements to be believed.

2 *a*) Authority is an attribute of a person or persons.

   b) Authority is a creation of rules and is an attribute of offices and rules and commands issued by offices, never of persons.

3 *a*) It is impossible to understand authority or to participate in authority relations apart from an understanding and assessment of the substance and purpose of the rules or statements that constitute and express it.

   b) Authority has to do with form not function, procedure not purpose, antecedents and credentials not substantive content or consequences. Considerations of content or merit, of ends and purposes, are categorically irrelevant to understanding authority and to participating in authority relations.

4 *a*) Authority presupposes inequality and is destructive of equality in the spheres of its operation.

   b) Authority presupposes and contributes to the maintenance of equality in the spheres of its operation.

5 *a*) Authority is a form of force or power.

   b) Authority is altogether distinct from force or power.

6 *a*) The distinction between legitimate and illegitimate, *de jure* and *de facto,* authority is valid and vital to understanding authority.

   b) All authority is legitimate or *de jure.* The notion of illegitimate or merely *de facto* authority rests on a confusion.

7 *a*) Authority is incompatible with freedom, reason, and morality, and the latter are excluded from authority relations.

   b) Freedom, reason, and mortality are inconceivable apart from authority.

8 *a*) Authority is a functional necessity of human social life and is found in all human societies.

   b) Authority is an exceedingly rare phenomenon. It has been present in very few societies in human history and only for brief periods.

9 *a*) The distinctive characteristics of modern societies are incompatible with authority and the latter has (all but) vanished from them.

   b) The distinctive characteristics of modern societies foster authority and it is unprecedently ubiquitous in them.

10 *a*) The great evil of our time is the almost total lack of respect for authority and the erosion of all systems and structures thereof.

   b) The great evil of our time is the relentless growth of authority and the abject surrender thereto on the part of countless persons.

Leading theories of authority are constituted and differentiated one from another in large part by their allegiance to or rejection of various combinations of the propositions just listed. In particular, consistent acceptance of alternative *a* or alternative *b* in numbers 1–4 cluster to delineate two major accounts of authority that have competed for many centuries. As noted, we will call theories based on 1*a*–4*a* substantive-purposive theories (S-P theories) and those based on 1*b*–4*b* formal-procedural theories (F-P theories). The supreme instance of an S-P theory in political philosophy is Plato's argument concerning the philosopher king in the *Republic*. Versions of this type of theory are particularly common among writers (for example, Thomists) whose thinking about politics is substantially influenced by religious considerations, and they also recur in the work of social scientists of a functionalist bent. Plato's most celebrated competitor among F-P theories is in Hobbes' *Leviathan*. This latter type of theory of authority can fairly be said to be dominant at the present time.

In versus An Authority

Before pursuing this grand and recurrent division we should notice a further distinction, or rather set of overlapping distinctions, that appears to crosscut, and perhaps render nugatory, not only the sweeping division just referred to but also a number of the pairs that make up our original list of propositions. The distinction is between being *an* authority on some subject or activity and being *in* a position of authority in some sort of association or organization. The first is based on, is possessed by virtue of, demonstrated knowledge, skill, or expertise concerning a subject matter or activity. The notion of exercising this type of authority is, perhaps, somewhat odd. Those who have such authority issue statements or propositions about the subject matter, or perform the activity in question—statements and performances that allegedly have such qualities as truth, correctness, validity, profundity, exceptional grace or beauty, and so forth. And others interested in the subject matter will be inclined to accept the statements and performances as having these characteristics because of the authority of the person who issues them. (The notion of exercising such authority seems most at home where there has been a dispute and the person who is an authority concerning the subject matter settles it by issuing an authoritative statement or presenting an authoritative performance.) Sir Kenneth Clark is an authority on artistic treatments of the nude human figure. His authority is grounded in study and reflection that has led to books, articles, lectures, and television programs widely recognized as true, exceptionally enlightening, and so on. Persons interested in this subject matter turn to his works to learn about it, and disputes concerning the subject are commonly referred to his judgment. He will remain an authority until others interested in the subject matter no longer believe that his knowlege and understanding of it are superior to the knowledge and understanding of most other persons.

In equally schematic terms, *in* authority is a property of rules and offices created by rules. Individuals possess it by virtue of holding an office in an organization, such as a state, a corporation, a university, or a trade union, that is (partially) governed by more or less formalized or codified rules. Although we say that persons in such positions have authority, the authority they have is not their own in the sense of belonging to them as a piece of property or in the more plausible sense of being in virtue of their personal attributes. Rather, the authority belongs to the office that they occupy and does nothing to set them, as persons, above anyone else. Though their personal qualities may have been taken into account in selecting them for the office, their authority is inseparable from the office and may perfectly well remain constant over significant changes in the personal qualities of occupants. The notion of exercising such authority is altogether natural; doing so consists in making, interpreting, applying, and enforcing rules that are to be accepted and followed, as a matter of obligation following directly from their authority, by all persons under the jurisdiction of the office in question. *Qua* an exercise of authority, the only question relevant to deciding how to respond to such rules is whether they are *intra* or *ultra vires,* that is, whether they are consistent with the rules that establish and delineate the authority of the office. The only way for an individual to gain such authority is to accede to an office that confers authority; the individual loses the authority if the office is abolished or he ceases to hold it.

The *an* authority–*in* authority distinction will concern us at many junctures in what follows. For now we are interested in the possibility that it delineates not simply two types or forms of authority but two altogether distinct concepts of authority—only one of which commonly presents itself in distinctively political assocations. We can begin exploring this possibility by recurring to the distinction between S-P and F-P theories. Perhaps these are theories about two quite distinct phenomena, phenomena that have little more in common than the term that happens to designate their subject matters. F-P theories are theories of *in* authority and hence of authority in political and other associations, S-P theories are of *an* authority and have little if anything to do with politics and political associations. If these suggestions could be sustained, our task would be greatly simplified. Much commonly thought part of political authority could be set aside as irrelevant to it, and many recurring controversies revealed as instances of that bewitchment (as Wittgenstein called it) that ordinary language commonly works on the philosophical intelligence. (Parties to the controversies to which we allude are likely to be attracted to this manner of disposing of them. Few philosophical achievements are more satisfying than showing one's opponents to be categorially confused. But this possibility is no help at the outset of the inquiry because, of course, all parties will claim that it is their opponents who are talking about something other than they think. Certainly both Plato and Hobbes understood themselves to be theorizing about political authority.)

A number of considerations support these suggestions. Persons who hold offices in a political or other association are not thereby authorities on any subject. A person can be an authority on a subject matter and hold an office that carries *in* authority at the same time (as for example Thomas Masaryk was at once an authority on intellectual history and in authority as president of Czechoslovakia): the distinction between them is clear and important. Charles Goren is undoubtedly an authority on the game of bridge, but his standing as such is entirely irrelevant to political authority. Although standing as an authority on a subject matter might be treated as a condition of occupying an office that carries *in* authority, occupying the office presupposes the office, that is, the established rules that create it, its authority, and the qualifications for occupying it. In no case can standing as an authority on a subject matter be sufficient to bestow *in* authority.[1] Finally, whereas those in authority issue and apply rules and commands which themselves entail obligations to act, *an* authorities make statements, pronouncements, and performances. Persons who believe the statements or accept the pronouncements as of superior quality because of the authority of those who issue them may choose to act on the belief, imitate the performance, and so forth. But no action imperatives follow from *an* authority as such. "Doctor's orders" are at most "orders," not orders.

Owing to the ambiguity and outright disagreement that surround the concepts "politics" and "political," we cannot conclude from the discussion thus far that political authority is always *in* authority, never *an* authority. We can and should say that *an* and *in* authority cannot be assimilated. And the considerations we have reviewed strongly suggest that the most salient instances of political authority fall under the *in* rubric. But it does not follow that there are no significant relationships, conceptual as well as empirical, between *in* and *an* authority or that the theorist of the one can simply disregard the other. Both the conceptual and the empirical relationships between them concern us in what follows. For now we discuss three particularly important commonalities between the two.

First, both involve what has commonly (but, we argue in chapters 5 and 6, misleadingly) been called "surrender of judgment" by those for whom or over whom A is *an* or *in* authority.[2] Very baldly, in the case of *an* authority, B accepts A's statements as true, valid, etc. (or at least as deserving distinctively respectful consideration because especially likely to have these qualities), not because he himself has investigated the matter addressed by the statements but because A, whom B recognizes as an authority on that matter, has issued them. In the case of *in* authority, B accepts that he has an obligation to do what the order, rule, interpretation of a rule, or the like requires not because he has independently satisfied himself of the merits of the action in question but because he recognizes that (1) he falls within the jurisdiction of A's authority, and (2) the order, rule, or the like is within the scope of A's authority in that jurisdiction. By further exploring this notion of "surrender of judgment," which is one of the essential and intricate tasks in the theory of authority, we shall uncover more differences in the way it works in respect to *an* and *in* authority relations. But it is clear that no sense can be made of either type of authority apart from an account of this among their features.

Second, neither *an* nor *in* authority is comprehensible apart from the idea of criteria by which instances of it are identified. In the case of *in* authority the criteria of identification are commonly constitutions, charters, and other documents that authorize or otherwise establish the office in question. Moreover, that an office or officeholder satisfies the established criteria is often symbolized or abbreviated by insignia, or "marks" (as F-P theorists call them), such as crowns, thrones, seals, badges, uniforms, a distinctive letterhead, and the like. The point here has been made most insistently by F-P theorists, perhaps because of their general emphasis on credentials and antecedents and insistence that authority is created by and lodged in rules and offices and only administered or employed by particular persons. Those under the jurisdiction of such offices and rules, faced as we all are by a plethora of signs and signals, demands and directives, must be clearly shown which offices and rules actually carry the authority that they have an obligation to respect. *An* authorities do not typically possess such clearly established "marks" (robes and diplomas, titles and awards may be at least weak analogies of uniforms and badges); still, the notion of an authority would have no application apart from criteria by which to distinguish the pronouncements of authorities from those of all others. Neither Sir Kenneth Clark nor anyone else could be an authority on the history of art without agreed criteria by which to distinguish exceptionally reliable and informative statements, unusually insightful and illuminating interpretations, from those that are erroneous or misleading, commonplace or bizarre. As with the insignia of office, these criteria must be known to those who receive putatively authoritative statements.

Authority and Shared Values and Beliefs

Finally and most important, both *an* and *in* authority presuppose values and beliefs shared among those who participate in the practice. This requirement goes beyond the necessity of knowing what authority is and the necessity of criteria for identifying instances of it. It posits acceptance of some set of propositions according to which it is right or proper that there be authority at all and that such authority be established, lodged, distributed, exercised, and so on in this or that manner. Command of the *concept* of authority is necessary in order to know what kind of thing one is talking about in talking about authority. A *mark* of authority is necessary in order that the B's be able to pick out the A's and the X's from the welter of phenomena with which they (the B's) are presented. But without the values and beliefs we are now positing there would, and could, be nothing to talk about or to mark and pick out.

The issues here are difficult as well as important and they will occupy us for much of the remainder of this chapter and at numerous junctures further along. On the essentially Weberian argument we are advancing, both *an* and *in* authority depend on values and beliefs shared among those who participate in the relationships that surround and partly constitute any form of authority.[3] The A's have authority in part because some set of B's accepts values and holds beliefs according to which the A's do and should have authority.

We may think of these values and beliefs as distinguished one from the other by the extent to which they are directly, perhaps even exclusively, values and beliefs about attributions of authority on a particular subject matter or in a particular association. In the case of *an* authority, those most directly and exclusively related to authority in a particular subject matter consist in current fashions of what constitutes good work or performance in that subject or activity. In the 1950s and 1960s in England and America one could hardly be an authority in social science unless one's work had a discernible quantitative dimension, in philosophy unless one's work was "analytic," or in theater or criticism thereof unless one showed an appreciation of the differences between, say, Noel Coward, on the one hand, and Osborne, Pinter, and Wesker on the other (and preferred the latter!). For *in* authority similar fashions may influence the selection of individuals to fill various offices and positions. But here the values and beliefs most closely related to authority are the criteria determining formal eligibility for particular offices. For example the president of the United States must be more than thirty-five years of age and a natural-born citizen; the principal of the local school must have a B.A. or its equivalent and at least five years of teaching experience.

In respect to the *in* authority that is their primary concern, F-P theorists will object to calling these criteria values and beliefs; they make the valid and important point that rules are to be subscribed to, accepted, conformed with, perhaps acted upon, but not valued or believed. We nevertheless suggest that there can be no authority unless participants in a practice governed by rules believe that the putative rules are in fact the rules. It also seems to be the case, although this is a much more controversial point that will have to be discussed at length below, that there will not be any authority unless some substantial number of the participants believe that there ought to be rules of some sort and that *these* and not *those* putative or proposed rules ought in fact to be rules.

In respect to *an* authority, there is a further set or array of values and beliefs that are relevant to attributions of authority over a wider range of subject matters. Self-consciousness about assumptions and shadow implications, attention to evidence where it is relevant and available, concern to recognize and to meet plausible objections to one's arguments, the attempt to place one's investigations and conclusions in the context of previous work on the subject—these are canons of inquiry and argument that have survived many changes of "fashion." Commitment to these canons and some considerable success in satisfying them are all but necessary conditions of one's being an authority in a number of fields of inquiry.

For *in* authority, a candidate for a comparable set of beliefs is that larger set of rules that make up the constitutions or charters of organizations or associations under which a number of positions of authority are established. Some of these, although not specifying features distinctive to any particular position of authority, may nevertheless bear directly on a number of such positions. For example the equal protection clause of the United States Constitution sets a requirement that must be satisfied in filling all positions of authority. But the more important point here concerns the sense in which the constitution of an association is itself the recognized locus of *in* authority. If we ask how or why this is or can be the case, how or why the constitution can lend or transmit authority to its parts (which may change) and to arrangements set up under its provisions, at least part of the answer must be that it is *authoritative* because participants in the association believe that it is. The statement, "The Constitution is the locus of authority in this association," cannot be true unless participants in the association believe that it is true and believe that it should continue to be true.

Here again we encounter the nest of problems that surrounds the notion of *believing* statements that are, among other things, rules that carry authority. There would seem to be an impossibility here. If an alleged rule is not in fact a rule in the sense of actually carrying authority, then the belief that it is one should be given up. But for the belief to be correct or even plausible, it would seem that there must be some criterion, independent of the belief, by which it is established that the alleged rule is in fact a rule. Thus while the belief that X is a rule may be important from a number of standpoints, it would appear that it cannot be the criterion of whether X is in fact a rule that carries authority.

Some of the puzzlement here can be dispelled by attending to the distinction between proposed or putative rules on the one hand and established rules on the other, and by recognizing that the transition from one to the other takes place over time. A transition that culminates in a set of rules with authority must advance from a circumstance in which the belief that there are such rules would obviously be mistaken to a circumstance in which such a belief is not only plausible but widely held. Of course nothing is more commonplace than transitions from circumstances in which a proposition is believed by hardly anyone to a circumstance in which it is widely believed. This process can go forward in many ways, one of the most common being that someone becomes convinced that the proposition deserves to be believed, advocates belief in it, and over time convinces others to accept it. The advocate, of course, does not ordinarily recommend the proposition simply because he believes it. He himself believes it because he thinks that it satisfies some appropriate criterion, and he tries to convince others that the criterion is appropriate and that proposition satisfies it. But though the arguments he advances on these points may establish that the proposition is true, valid, profound, or in some other way meritorious, arguments cannot of themselves give the proposition authoritative standing. Propositions become authoritative only when they are believed or valued by those who form the group or association that the advocate addresses. Being true, valid, or otherwise meritorious is not the same as being authoritative.

In this perspective the distinctive feature of establishing authoritative *rules* is that the advocate believes and tries to convince his audience not merely that a proposition is true but that a proposed or putative rule ought to be a rule. Advocacy of such a belief presupposes criteria whose satisfaction will be viewed as providing good reasons for adopting the proposed belief. In familiar historical instances, two such criteria have been that the proposed rule must be consistent with previously established rules that delimit what can be rules, and that participants register their acceptance of the proposal through an established procedure. In these instances, to become a rule the proposal must be judged to accord with previously established rules both in its substance and in the manner of its adoption.

But proposed rules achieve *in* authority not merely because they and their manner of adoption accord with existing rules but because participants believe that they do so. If conformity with rules is the criterion by which genuine or established rules are to be distinguished from those merely proposed, alleged, or putative, this criterion must be satisfied not only in some objective sense but also in the sense that participants believe it satisfied. At least in this sense, the rules of a practice of *in* authority depend upon the belief that putative rules are in fact rules.

To say this much implies considerably more: it implies that authority depends upon belief in the further sense that participants must believe (1) that conformity with established rules is the criterion by which the authority of proposed rules is properly judged, (2) that *these* and not *those* alleged rules are truly the established rules, and (3) that *this* and not *that* interpretation of the established rules is the correct one. As we see below, these latter beliefs cannot be understood apart from a context given by a variety of other values and beliefs. Furthermore, though F-P theorists are correct that in an impressive number of the historical cases a "constitution" supplies the criterion of rules with this type of authority, a strict F-P account could accommodate all these cases only by conceptual fiat. Leaving aside (admittedly tempting) speculation about questions of origin and genesis for which no historical evidence is available, we are certainly familiar with instances in which rules have achieved *in* authority despite the absence of a constitution or system of antecedently established procedures by which they could have been adopted and legitimated. Owing to the less than overwhelming case for the *in* authority of the Constitutional Convention of 1787, the United States Constitution, ordinarily and quite properly regarded as a particularly clear case of a practice of *in* authority rules, can be viewed as a dramatic example of this phenomenon. Less spectacular examples abound in the form of conventions and norms that are found in every practice of *in* authority rules. That such conventions and norms have sometimes been (and could always in principle be) formally enacted does not alter the fact that many of them have acquired and have retained *in* authority by virtue of processes of value and belief formation that go forward without benefit of formal enactment or validation. If the F-P theorist denies that such rules have *in* authority, he saves his conception at the cost of greatly reducing its usefulness in analyzing authority as we encounter it in human affairs.

To proceed further in examining the beliefs and values that we are positing is to go beyond the clearly delineated and formally enacted rules that F-P theorists treat as the very stuff of authority. But there are further considerations that must be examined if the recurrence and importance of authority are to be understood and assessed. We will not explore these considerations in detail at this point. An example or two will indicate the line of thought that we develop in later chapters.

Particularly clear-cut instances of the sorts of values and beliefs we have in mind are provided by Christian religion for several centuries in the history of most of the countries of western Europe, by Mohammedanism in Moslem countries, by Marxism-Leninism in the Soviet Union, and by some of the belief and value systems of primitive societies. A commitment to Marxism-Leninism is a prerequisite for holding most positions of *in* authority in the Soviet Union and of achieving the status of an authority on most if not all subjects. Christianity and the Moslem faith have had a comparable standing during considerable stretches of European and Near Eastern history. Scientific theories, philosophical teachings, interpretations of historical events, rules proposed for adoption as law, and so forth are (were) rejected if judged at variance with these belief systems. Moreover, these doctrines inform, influence, and indeed constrain thought and action, including thought and action involving *in* and *an* authority, in a host of less direct and explicit ways. Each belief and value system may also contain propositions explicitly about *in* authority, propositions that explicitly validate authority. (A particularly clear example is the proposition that a ruler holds his position of authority by divine right or appointment.) But the larger setting that these beliefs provide is no less important for understanding (in a sense going beyond merely identifying) authority in society.

Of particular interest in the present context are the values and beliefs of the Fox Indians. The centerpiece of the beliefs of this people was the conviction that "since all men are made of the same clay, there should be no distinction or superiority among them."[4] This belief manifested itself in an uncompromising hostility to any arrangement that had the least appearance of or tendency toward hierarchy, command, or the expectation of "surrender of judgment" to assignable persons or officeholders. Children were taught (perhaps to counter the likely effects of sheer physical dependence) to think of their fathers as positively unworthy, hunting and fighting parties disintegrated at the first sign of disagreement, and village chieftanships were almost entirely symbolic offices with tribal decisions made unanimously or not at all. Religious ceremonies were conducted by designated leaders, but the latter were strictly forbidden to make the least departure from established ritual and were denied any special role outside the confines of the ceremonies themselves. There was no established pantheon in the usual sense, each person having his own God or "manitu" to whom he remained faithful only so long as he judged that doing so brought him success in worldly endeavors. Afterlife took place "over yonder," not "up there"; and, in general, in "death . . . as in life the greatest gift the Fox can ask of his Gods is the right to control his own behavior, and the greatest torture he can conceive is an eternity of being subject to orders."[5]

Here we have a set of values and beliefs that influence *in* authority and *an* authority in the sense of rendering both of them entirely unacceptable to the people in question. Whereas we cannot understand the working of authority in the Soviet Union without referring to the status of Marxism-Leninism in Soviet society, for the Fox we cannot understand the virtual absence of *in* authority and *an* authority without referring to the values and beliefs just listed. Moreover, as Miller points out, reflection on the case of the Fox alerts us to the fact that any society that sustains authority must reject (however self-consciously) the beliefs and values that rendered such arrangements unacceptable to the Fox. Presumably this also means that such societies accept some set of values and beliefs according to which authority is desirable or at least tolerable.

What we have said about the role of values and beliefs in respect to *an* and *in* authority suggests a distinction that we employ in much of what follows. The distinction is between *in* and *an* authority on the one hand and "the authoritative" on the other. The distinction can be explained by referring to the Fox. On Miller's account (which is substantiated in relevant respects by other studies),[6] there is very little evidence of *an* or *in* authority among this people. But there is an abundance of evidence of conventions, customs, practices, norms, and ways of thinking, speaking and acting that are widely accepted as distinguishing the proper from the improper, the right from the wrong, the appropriate from the inappropriate. So far as is known, few if any of these features of Fox life were adopted at a determinate time or through an established procedure; and those "offices" that developed to interpret and apply them carried little if any authority. Still, customs and conventions were regularly and sometimes quite self-consciously adhered to, knowingly taught or transmitted to younger generations, and even enforced in a variety of informal or decentralized ways when violated. For these reasons neither the conventions nor conduct conforming with them are to be understood as mere regularities detected by some observer and allegedly explainable by a notional set of causal factors involving no reference to human reflection and choice. But they do involve something like "surrender of judgment" because the Fox ordinarily respected and adhered to them as a matter of obligation arising from the distinctive standing of the conventions. That is, decisions to discharge the obligations were not grounded, or not grounded exclusively, in assessments, by the individual actors, of the advantages or disadvantages of the actions taken under descriptions making no reference to the custom or norm. When the Fox conformed to these arrangements they did so largely *because* they believed that the arrangements had a distinctive standing. When they did not conform to them they either thought their actions wrong *because* of the distinctive standing of the arrangements they had violated or thought their actions justified *despite* the distinctive standing of those arrangements.

We cannot analyze these values, beliefs and arrangements as instances of *an* authority because apparently there were no assignable A's whose authority the B's were respecting when they acted on the beliefs. We cannot think of them as instances of *in* authority on the F-P model because they lacked the formal credentials required by that model. There are important similarities between these arrangements and conventions that achieve standing in practices of *in* authority without benefit of formal adoption, legitimation and interpretation; but the arrangements were not in fact part of such a practice and did not cast up the positions of *in* authority characteristic of such practices. Yet, for the reasons we have canvassed, there is a case for thinking of them as having authority; or rather, for thinking of them, as we propose to do, as a part of "the authoritative," as among those features of a society or association that are authoritative for the members thereof.

On this conceptualization *in* and *an* authority—or their absence—are to be understood in relation to a wider phenomenon that we will call "the authoritative"—a phenomenon that in large measure consists in values and beliefs widely shared by the members of the social entity in which it is found. Thus an important part of the empirical study of authority in any society will be a study of the values and beliefs shared among its members; of their content at various times; of how they form and change; of the relations among various beliefs and between them and the institutions and patterns of action that are, among other things, reflections of those beliefs. And an important part of the philosophical study of authority will be clarification and critical scrutiny of the standing and role of such values and beliefs.

Let us return briefly to the starting point of this discussion. The thesis that led us to the topic of shared values and beliefs was that *in* authority and *an* authority mark two altogether distinct concepts that can and should be independently analyzed and assessed. There are substantial reasons for rejecting this thesis. We found that both imply some species (yet to be determined in its particulars) of "surrender of judgment" and both require identifying criteria. And we now see that both are grounded in shared values and beliefs to which we are referring as the authoritative. This set of shared characteristics does not establish that *in* and *an* authority are simply equivalent or interchangeable concepts, nor does it mean that the differences between them noted at the outset are apparent rather than real or real but theoretically insignificant. It does show that we will understand each of them better if we concern ourselves with both and with the relationships between them.[7]

Before summarizing this introductory discussion, we should note three related objections that might be made to the notion of the authoritative and to our emphasis on its place in the study of authority (a variety of other objections will be considered, *inter alia,* below): (1) these moves inflate the topic of authority beyond all recognition, rendering it indistinguishable from the much more encompassing subject of value and belief systems or even of "society" or "the social"; (2) these same moves, and particularly the emphasis on consensus concerning values and beliefs, distort authority by distracting attention from the disagreement that surrounds it and the conflict that is commonly engendered by its exercise; (3) our account turns authority into a purely subjective phenomenon in respect to which there cannot be rational or even interpersonally meaningful criteria for settling such disputes and disagreements as might arise.

Responding to the first objection, we cheerfully admit to the intention to widen the boundaries of the topic of authority—at least beyond those within which its study has been constrained by F-P theorists from Hobbes on. But it does not follow that theorists of authority must be concerned with the full range of values and beliefs that have authoritative standing in the societies or other associations that interest them. Let us distinguish among (1) values and beliefs that have intimate normative and conceptual links to authority; (2) those that have merely contingent, empirical relations with the latter concept; and (3) those that have no relation at all with authority. To illustrate, the values and beliefs of the Fox according to which authority is unacceptable provide a clear example of the first type. The Fox identified and understood both *in* and *an* authority as arrangements incompatible with their belief in equality and individual autonomy. An account of the absence of authority among them that made no reference to those beliefs would be so incomplete as to be useless. Reasoning from the case of the Fox has led us to hypothesize that members of societies in which authority is well established will be found to accept some set of values and beliefs that are integral to their identification and evaluation of authority—with the difference, as against the Fox, that the evaluation they yield is sufficiently favorable to sustain acceptance of authority. Later we will argue that the content of these authority-supporting beliefs and values varies importantly across time and place and hence that few useful generalizations can be made concerning it (that is concerning their content). But the difficulty of generalizing about content in no way diminishes the importance of the beliefs and values that have the standing we are positing.

No one would say, however, that an account of authority was incomplete because it made no mention of such widely shared values and beliefs, which are of the third type, as "regular physical exercise is conducive to good health" and "rose bushes yield more beautiful blossoms if pruned at appropriate intervals." These beliefs may have authoritative standing in a society, but they have nothing to do with *in* authority. An example of a belief with a merely contingent empirical relationship with authority might be the conviction that one's society is making ineffective use of its economic resources. Such a belief could well have effects with which a student of the practice of authority in question would be vitally concerned. For example, the belief might lead to an enlargement of the scope and activities of authority in the society in the hope of improving economic efficiency. But in such a case authority would have to have been conceptualized and identified without reference to the belief in question and then adjudged instrumentally valuable in respect to the problem of poor economic performance. One presumes, moreover, that authority would also have been judged to be an acceptable instrument by standards wider than economic efficiency. Thus an account of authority that neglected the belief about economic performance would be incomplete in the sense that it neglected one of the factors that influenced the workings of authority in the society. Unlike an account that neglected beliefs and values of the first type, it could nevertheless contribute importantly to the understanding and assessment of authority.

At this point we add only that it would be impossible to draw these distinctions in a definitive manner and neither a simple nor a very useful exercise to attempt to draw them with great rigor.

The second objection raises more intricate difficulties. A partial rejoinder to it draws on an understanding that finds its most emphatic expression in Hobbes' theory and that has become all but standard among F-P theorists of authority. The understanding is that it is exactly the acute awareness (among the members of a society) of conflict and disagreement, together with realization that at least some disputed issues must be resolved, that explains (and justifies) the general willingness to create and sustain authority. Authority is not merely compatible with conflict; it arises and is sustained in large part because of conflict. Authority does not suppose the elimination of conflict (and hence does not imply the absence of values and beliefs that produce conflict); it requires the belief that the decisions of authority concerning matters of conflict should be accepted as binding (until altered by authority) precisely in order to keep conflict within tolerable limits. Those who disagree with the substance of the decisions of authority are not expected to alter their views or to cease efforts to get their views adopted by authority. In short, at least some of the shared values and beliefs that make authority possible, so far from excluding or distracting attention from disagreement and conflict, presuppose the continuing presence of agreement and conflict.

The Hobbist understanding provides no more than a partial rejoinder to the second objection. This is because the assumptions on which the understanding rests do presume agreement on a number of vital and controversial propositions. Specifically, as formulated by Hobbes and his F-P successors, the understanding assumes agreement (1) that the society or association in question should continue; (2) that it cannot continue unless at least the more important disputes are resolved before disagreement about them disappears or becomes inconsequential without recourse to a decision by authority; (3) that decision by authority is the best way to resolve such disputes; (4) that *these* are the authorities in the association and *this* is the scope of their authority; and (5) that the decisions of authority should be binding regardless of their merits or the consequences of accepting them. Moreover, the views of some F-P theorists to the contrary notwithstanding, it seems unlikely that the foregoing propositions will be accepted and acted upon for long unless there is also agreement concerning the general purposes of the association, the advantages to members of remaining a part of it, the reasons that authority should be constituted in *this* rather than *that* manner, and so forth. Thus it appears that a viable practice of authority does exclude disagreement on a considerable inventory of questions.

But the previous paragraph almost certainly exaggerates the amount of consensus that is required for a viable practice of authority. Of course a theorist might make unanimity about basic values and beliefs a feature of an ideal-typical or limiting case conception of authority.[8] But while history presents us with a number of practices of authority that remained viable for substantial periods of time, we know of no such practices that eliminated disagreement, even widespread and intense disagreement, about propositions such as those iterated in the previous paragraph. Perhaps the most obvious evidence for this assertion is that every known practice of authority has maintained and regularly used an apparatus of coercion. Are we to think that coercion has in fact been unnecessary?; or that it has been necessary largely if not exclusively because of failure to act on beliefs and values that the members of these practices have in fact shared? Short of such assumptions, the recurrence of coercion would seem to betoken active disagreement about values and beliefs—including values and beliefs that were part of the authoritative in the societies in question.

At the same time, it is as important to remember as it is commonplace to observe that sustained coercion is impossible without substantial agreement among the members of the association about those very propositions whose rejection commonly brings coercion into play. Accordingly, we are not in fact presented with the dichotomy that Hobbes and other F-P theorists (and the social theorists mentioned in the Introduction) have cast up, that is between unanimous agreement excluding all conflict and unqualified dissensus excluding all shared values and beliefs. A measure of disagreement and conflict need not undermine *in* authority, but substantial agreement is necessary to it. One can, of course, identify and assess the consequences of the "mix" that obtains in particular times and places. For example, as of this writing (1978), in the Lebanon there is too little agreement, too much and too intense conflict to sustain a practice of authority or even any very effective use of power; in France there is an extraordinarily complex mix of agreement and disagreement and authority and power are generally sustained but frequently ineffective; and so forth. But it would be futile, or rather risible, to attempt to specify the mix necessary to sustain or to undermine *in* authority in any and all societies and associations.

The third objection noted above concerns important philosophical questions that are raised by these remarks about agreement and disagreement. It involves the criteria that must be satisfied in order to say that A is in fact in a position of *in* authority over a particular B. If A's *in* authority is by virtue of a set of values and beliefs Z, and if Smith rejects Z, does it follow that A's authority does not extend to Smith, that Smith is not a B vis-à-vis A? Does emphasizing the place of values and beliefs in practices of authority imply that each individual can cogently deny A's authority over him, can take himself out of A's jurisdiction, merely by rejecting certain values or beliefs? Does emphasizing shared values and beliefs reduce authority to a purely subjective matter?

Of course no theory of authority can itself compel Smith to believe that A has authority over him. And if Smith does not believe that A has authority over him, then *in Smith's view,* A does not have authority over him. Nor can any theory of authority itself prevent Smith's acting on such a view. But as important as these facts may be as a practical matter, theoretically they are trivial because in this sense all theories of authority must emphasize values and beliefs and must reduce authority to subjectivity. The significant theoretical question is this: Does emphasizing the sorts of shared values and beliefs we have been discussing itself give distinctive standing or cogency to Smith's denial of A's authority?

If Smith's denial takes the form of, or claims to be supported by, reasoned arguments, those arguments will be relevant to the denial only to the extent that they speak to the criteria by which authority is established in the association in question. Those criteria, we have argued, are given by, consist in, values and beliefs shared among the members of the association. Smith might try to show that A's claims to *in* authority do not meet the established criteria. If he convinces the requisite number or selection of associates on this point, A will presumably be denied authority; if he fails so to convince, other associates will presumably judge that, regardless of what Smith may believe, A has *in* authority and should be obeyed by associates—including Smith. Alternatively, Smith might try to show that the established criteria are inappropriate. In this case his arguments must speak not only to the criteria but also to the reasons for which the criteria are accepted by the members of the association. These criteria, we have suggested, must be given at least in part by, must consist at least in part in, shared values and beliefs that make up the authoritative in the association. These values and beliefs provide tests of the relevance and the cogency of Smith's arguments, tests by which other associates can accept or reject those arguments. If they reject them, they will presumably continue believing the criteria appropriate and A will continue to have authority despite Smith's belief that he does not. This situation will obtain even if Smith's belief is, by some criterion or criteria not established in the association, very well grounded. Outsiders may agree with Smith, may judge his arguments cogent and persuasive. They may say, as Smith himself is likely to do, that at best A has *de facto,* not *de jure,* authority. But that they make these judgments and statements will not alter the circumstance that others in the association believe, and perhaps cogently, that A has (*de jure*) authority.

We return to these matters in part 2. Here we stress that there can be no argumentation (as opposed to mere assertions or verbal ejaculations) without criteria by which to conduct it and by which to make judgments about relevance, cogency, and other desiderata. Indeed, in the absence of such criteria there can be no issues or questions over which disagreement can develop and to which argumentation can be addressed.

This requirement, of course, applies to all forms of argumentation (in a yet more general formulation it applies to the entire realm of human thought and communication). In later chapters (especially chapter 4) we look at some of the very general formulations developed in the philosophy of language to see whether it is plausible to view rules of language as part of the authoritative or whether they can help us in other ways to understand authority. Thus far we have suggested that criteria necessary to (but not sufficient for) meaningful argumentation about authority are provided by shared values and beliefs of the sort discussed above. Each person's values and beliefs are his own in the trivial sense that it is he who values and believes them and in the anything but trivial sense that he values and believes them on grounds that he chooses. Thus as a logical matter (we leave aside psycho-logical and socio-logical points concerning the formation of values and beliefs and the ways it may be influenced by the values and beliefs of others) it appears that Smith can reject A's authority for reasons that others in the association regard as totally irrelevant.

Neither Smith nor anyone else can reject A's authority without knowing what it is and hence cannot reject it without knowing the criteria that distinguish it from other things. Although Smith's values and beliefs are his own, the authority that he accepts or rejects is not "his" in this sense. Rather, authority is a feature of an association made up of a number of persons; it is a feature that is what it is (in part) by virtue of values and beliefs shared among the associates. If Smith rejects authority for no reason at all, or out of purely idiosyncratic considerations having nothing to do with the values and beliefs in which its acceptance is grounded, other associates will be correct in viewing Smith's rejection as irrelevant to whether there is authority or whether they should accept it. This requirement no more guarantees agreement (or excludes well-grounded disagreement) about authority than analogous requirements guarantee agreement about any other subject of knowledge or belief. But they do allow meaningful exchange and argumentation concerning authority. So far from distinctively infecting discourse and judgment about *in* authority with "mere subjectivity," shared values and beliefs and the criteria they supply contribute to allowing participants in authority relations to transcend such subjectivity.

Let us now summarize the discussion of these three related objections. Emphasizing the place of shared values and beliefs in practices of *in* authority (1) enlarges but need not distort the topic; (2) permits recognition of both agreement and disagreement in authority relations; and (3) helps to account for the possibility of meaningful exchange. If these contentions are correct, an examination of values and beliefs relating to authority must be a major concern of the student of authority relations.[9]

Concluding Remarks

In this introductory chapter we have tried to delineate some major distinctions, to identify significant issues, and to introduce some of the more general assumptions at work in the discussions that follow. Clearly more attention should be given to the issues and controversies listed on pages 14 and 15; to the topic of values and beliefs and the roles they play in practices of authority; to the idea of rules, and to relationships among such statements as "X is a rule that has authority," "It is good that X is a rule that has authority," "X is a good rule"; to the delicate and conceptually vital issues of "surrender of judgment"; and to the distinction between authority and related notions such as power and coercion. In approaching these questions we will continue to use the overlapping sets of distinctions that we have developed thus far, namely those among *in* authority, *an* authority, and the authoritative, and between S-P and F-P theories of authority. We reject both the view that the *in–an* distinction is categorial and the related position that F-P theories are exclusively about *in* authority, S-P theories about *an* authority. Broadly speaking, we will appeal to "the authoritative" in order to identify and analyze commonalities between *in* and *an* authority and in order appropriately to integrate F-P and S-P theories.

We do not contend that *in* and *an* authority can be assimilated or that there are no genuine disagreements between F-P and S-P theories. To argue that a distinction is less than categorial is not to imply that it is useless. The point will be to put both the similarities and the differences in proper perspective. Moreover, and despite our criticisms of F-P theories, the F-P position is and deserves to be the leading account of authority as the latter presents itself in the state and in formal organizations generally. Therefore, in chapter 2 we attempt a sympathetic account of the F-P theory, first summarizing its major contentions as they have been put by leading proponents, then assessing it as a theory, and finally noticing some of the questions that it unsatisfactorily addresses. The third and fourth chapters explore the limitations of F-P theory as an account of *in* authority and begin enlarging the theory to accommodate *an* authority and other aspects of authority that F-P theory denies, omits, or distorts. These same chapters also begin integrating the most persuasive aspects of F-P and S-P theory. The remaining chapters in part 1 develop the emerging argument by bringing it to bear on the "surrender judgment" and the relationship between authority and power. Part 2 is addressed to traditional questions concerning the justification of the practice of political authority as a feature of human associations. Primarily at issue will be the question whether—and, if so, when and how—a practice with the generic characteristics identified in part 1 can properly be accepted by persons who value their standing as free, rational, and moral agents.

2 Authority as an Attribute of Rules and Offices The Formal-Procedural Theory of Authority

By all accounts *in* authority is "practical" in the sense that it bears upon actions that should or should not, ought or ought not, be taken. Put another way, authority is one of the considerable array of devices by which one person or set of persons, one agent or agency, attempts to determine, control, or at least to influence the thought and action of some other person or set of persons, some other agent or agency. From the perspective of determining what authority is and is not, the question is just what distinguishes authority from the various other devices that make up this array.

In our judgment the most plausible general answer to this question has been advanced by writers in the tradition of formal-procedural theory. According to this tradition, at bottom authority is an attribute of certain kinds of rules, of offices created by such rules, and of subscription to those rules by those for whom the rules carry authority. Theorists in this tradition elaborate their account of authority by explicating "rule," "office," and related notions and by working out the implications of subscribing to practices constituted by them.

Finding this analysis to be the most plausible of those available, our procedure in this chapter is as follows: we begin with an account of the analysis of *in* authority by leading F-P theorists, we then examine the primary considerations that support acceptance of this analysis, and we conclude by noting both metatheoretical and substantive issues that remain to be dealt with after the insights of the theory have been recognized. Our primary purpose is to advance the present analysis of authority, not to do an exegesis of other theories. But close attention to the arguments of certain theorists is an efficient way to pursue this objective because they have arrived at a good deal of the truth about what authority is and is not.[1]

Inclusions and Exclusions

In its narrowest essentials F-P theory consists in a two-part thesis concerning the criteria that must be satisfied in order to predicate authority of a rule, office, agency or agent and about the implications that follow from such predication. There are also versions of the theory that include theses, like those discussed in the Introduction, concerning the distinctive place or point of *in* authority relations. We do not deal with these broader versions in the present chapter.

The first part of the criteriological thesis can be formulated as follows: (1) "Authority can be correctly predicated of A only if there are established rules by virtue of which A has authority." The second part of the thesis draws an implication from the meaning of "authority"; (2) "If A has authority X, those persons (B's) who are in A's jurisdiction therefore have an obligation or obligations Y." Part 1 purports to state only a necessary condition of, not a sufficient condition for, predication of authority. Part 2 does not state all of the implications of such a predication. But 1 and 2 together are put forward as such central, such prominent characteristics of authority as to justify treating them as its distinguishing features.[2]

The meaning of the thesis emerges more clearly when we examine what each of its parts is intended to exclude. The F-P account of what *in* authority is, in other words, becomes clearer when we examine its account of what authority is not (but has persistently and mistakenly been thought to be). Part 1 is intended to exclude, as categorially irrelevant to A's authority, any considerations concerning the merits, purposes, or consequences of the rules or offices, the agencies or agents, that are alleged to have authority. Part 2 is intended categorially to exclude these same types of considerations from deliberation whether B has an obligation or obligations in respect to A's authority (albeit not necessarily to exclude them from deliberation whether particular B's ought to discharge their obligations in this or that specific circumstance).

These contentions have been given an especially accessible formulation by Richard B. Friedman. When B concedes A's *in* authority to act, Friedman writes, he passes a judgment "on the source of...[A's] claim..., not on the *content* of his action. Thus to concede or to deny that some particular person has the authority to perform some action is not precisely to approve or to disapprove of that action itself, but rather to affirm or reject his warrant (his 'authorization') to be the one entitled to do such a thing."[3] The claim of A to be obeyed, Friedman goes on to say, "is simply that he has been put 'in authority' according to established procedure, rather than that his decisions are, on independent grounds, sound, meritorious, or superior decisions. What makes an act obligatory is that it has been declared obligatory by the person invested with authority over that class of actions. . . . The merits and demerits of the actual decisions are strictly irrelevant to the 'obligation' to obey, and therefore the claim to obedience is not compromised by showing that it is inferior to some other decision that might have been taken." "Indeed," Friedman continues, "the whole point of setting up this sort of authority is to dissociate the claim to obedience from the question of the merits of the particular decisions one is being asked to accept."[4]

The last sentence exemplifies that second thesis of F-P theory to which we alluded above, the thesis about the "place" or "point" of *in* authority among the institutions and arrangements of an association. But before we examine the second thesis we must look at refinements of the distinction between form and substance, procedure and purpose.

Friedman concedes that the rules which establish A's authority and the X's that A promulgates *have* a substantive character that allows of judgments concerning their merits. His point is not that such judgments are impossible but that they are irrelevant to whether the decisions are within A's authority and to whether B has an obligation to obey them.[5] Michael Oakeshott goes further and contends for a deeper sense in which questions of substance and purpose are excluded from relationships considered in terms of authority and obligation. His discussion is the most elaborate version of F-P theory available and we consider it in some detail.

Practices and Rules

Relationships in terms of authority and obligation form part of what Oakeshott calls "practices." "A practice may be identified as a set of considerations, manners, uses, observances, customs, standards, canons, maxims, principles, rules and offices specifying useful procedures or denoting obligations or duties which relate to human actions and utterances. It is . . . an adverbial qualification of choices and performances, more or less complicated in which conduct is understood in terms of a procedure. Words such as punctually, considerately, civilly, scientifically, legally, candidly, judicially, poetically, morally, etc., do not specify performances; they postulate performances and specify procedural conditions to be taken into account when choosing and acting."[6] All actions involve both substance and procedure. The former enter through the agent's choice of an "imagined and wished-for" outcome or satisfaction, the latter are given by practices which specify conditions in which the choice is made and acted upon. A "practice is an instrument to be played upon, not a tune to be played." Procedures do not "prescribe choices or substantive actions. A rule (and *a fortiori* something less exacting, like a maxim) can never tell a performer what choice he shall make; it announces only conditions to be subscribed to in making choices." "The appearance procedures and rules may have of excluding (forbidding), or more rarely enjoining, substantive choices and actions is illusive. Practices identify actions adverbially; they exclude (forbid) or enjoin them in terms of prescribed conditions. A criminal law . . . does not forbid killing or lighting a fire, it forbids killing 'murderously' or lighting a fire 'arsonically.' "[7]

When conjoined to the basic F-P thesis that authority and obligation are attributes of rules and offices, this analysis puts considerations of substance and purpose at a further remove from deliberation about authority and obligation than does Friedman's account. Such considerations are irrelevant to authority and obligation because the rules that constitute authority and that yield obligations are themselves indifferent to matters of substance and purpose. One cannot act on or question the purpose or merits of the rules for the deep-going reason that rules as such *have* neither purposes nor merits to question. Such questioning is not merely irrelevant, it is impossible.

Types of Association and Their Authority

To follow Oakeshott's elaboration of this argument we must attend to his distinction between two types or modes of human association, a distinction that he presents as categorical and that structures his discussion of authority. The modes of association are labeled, respectively, "civil" and "enterprise." The fundamental difference between them is that the former "begins and ends in the recognition [of the authority of] rules" that are "totally indifferent to all substantive purposes and objectives," while the latter is defined and constituted by its devotion to substantive purposes and objectives shared among associates. Enterprise associations are nevertheless species of the genus "practices" and hence involve rules that are said to carry a kind of authority. As in any practice, these rules set conditions under which the purposes of the association are to be pursued. But such rules "are instrumental to the purpose" of the association, and the purpose provides "the ready and appropriate criterion for judging their propriety." "A rule which hindered its pursuit would be recognized as undesirable and one manifestly unnecessary on this account would soon fall into neglect or be repealed." Associates will ordinarily be expected to observe the rules, but because rejecting them might in fact contribute to the purposes that define the association, observing them need not be a condition of membership. In civil association, by contrast, "the terms of association . . . [are] the rules themselves," and hence refusal to subscribe to them is, *à la* Hobbes, "itself an act of disassociation."[8]

Oakeshott's argument about enterprise association qualifies not only the deep form of F-P theory that is part of his notion of a practice but also the less radical version of that theory argued by Friedman.[9] Friedman's version allows that A's decisions have substantive and purposive characteristics; its only insistence is that considering those characteristics takes B out of the authority relationship. Oakeshott's account of authority in enterprise associations makes substantive and purposive characteristics internal to authority relations and permits B *qua* B to deliberate concerning their merits.

Civil association and its authority are understood in part by seeing that they do not have the characteristics of enterprise association and its authority. Because civil association has commonly been (mis)understood as having the latter characteristics, this is, Oakeshott claims, a significant advance in our thinking about authority. But this is by no means the only misunderstanding that must be dispelled. Here is a catalogue of prevalent misunderstandings of authority in civil association: "on account of its prescriptions being subscribed to on most occasions" by associates; because of "the efficacy of the sanctions attached to . . . rules"; by identification with a " 'will' of any sort, that of a ruler, a majority of *cives* [that is, associates], or a so-called 'general' will"; derived from "purported access [of A's] to 'scientific' information about the tendencies of human actions to promote the general happiness or about so-called 'laws of historical development' "; as "deference to a trusted few" or the "charismatic authority of a leader"—"charisma being 'wisdom' and therefore not authority" and "civil rulers are not leaders, their subjects . . . not followers"; in terms of a postulated " 'higher' law . . . such that . . . authority . . . is conditional upon a correspondence with it."[10]

What then *are* civil association and its authority? In terms equal in brevity to the foregoing statement of what they are not, they are "nothing other than the acknowledgement of *respublica* [that is, the comprehensive conditions of civil association][11] as a system of moral (not instrumental or prudential) rules, specifying its own jurisdiction, and recognized solely as rules: that is, as conditions to be subscribed to in conduct and binding to consideration independently of their origin or likely or actual outcome in use and of approval of what they prescribe."[12] Civil association and its authority are found where there is such a system of rules and those rules are "acknowledged" or "subscribed to" in this manner. Understanding authority (in this its most distinctive mode) consists in grasping the idea of such a system of rules and of subscription to them.

The expression "nothing more than," and the entire discussion in which it occurs, is forcefully reminiscent of the key phrase G. E. Moore borrowed from Bishop Butler, "Everything is what it is and not another thing." Indeed Oakeshott's discussion must remind us of the indefatigable manner in which Moore contended that good is not the many things it had been mistakenly thought to be. Although Oakeshott cannot be accused of thinking that authority in civil association is an undefinable, nonnatural property that we know by some sort of intuition, he has about it the confidence that Moore had about good, namely that we know it when we encounter it. "The recognition of rules is one of our most familiar experiences. We do not always have clearly before us the features in terms of which we distinguish and identify rules, but for the most part we deal confidently with the puzzles this experience throws up."[13] Presumably, then, these features can be stated more fully.

The rules that constitute authority in civil associations prescribe norms of conduct such as that contracts ought not to be violated, elections ought not to be rigged, and so forth. These rules call for subscription or assent to their status as rules, that is as conditions to be satisfied in such activities as commercial exchange, working for a political party, and the like. They do not specify, require or forbid particular business transactions or party strategies and hence they do not solicit (much less require) approval or disapproval of particular actions or policies. They are commonly but not necessarily enacted by agents with designated credentials employing a specified procedure (the credentials and procedures themselves given by rules), and where this is the case they can have "no jurisdiction before that enactment" and its publication. Because they and they alone constitute the association, they must be self-authenticating,[14] and must specify their own jurisdiction,[15] the assent, recognition or subscription of associates being no more than (but equally no less than!) a condition (as opposed to a criterion) of their standing and validity. Whatever their origins, they form a "language of understanding and intercourse continuously used in conduct and enacted and re-enacted in being used."[16]

The rules of a civil association form a *persona civica* which composes "a self-sufficient (although not a self-explanatory) system."[17] Because the association is exclusively in terms of this system of rules, all questions that arise concerning relationships among associates as such must be resolved out of the resources of the system itself.

Thus far, then, Oakeshott presents an exceedingly lean, a most narrowly circumscribed, conception of the sort of association that would, were it instantiated empirically, manifest authority in its most distinctive and important form. The association as such appears to be severely impersonal, to be devoid of purposes of its own and of the influence of the sort of idiosyncracy that enters relationships as individuals pursue personal objectives and desires. The authority of the association consists exclusively in the rigorously formal conditions established by rules that have nothing whatever to do with such objectives and desires.

(It must be stressed, however, that it would be an entire misunderstanding to interpret Oakeshott as hostile to individual or group interests and desires, objectives and purposes, or the vigorous assertion and pursuit of them. In the tradition of Hobbes, Hegel and English pluralists such as Maitland and Figgis, he clearly favors a society in which individual and group interests proliferate. His insistence, again familiar to students of the theorists just mentioned, is that civil association and its authority are lost if they are identified with individual, group, or any other interests and purposes. Civil association and its authority are the setting within which individuals and groups form, adopt and pursue their interests and purposes.)

However we may finally assess the idea of a civil association, it is undeniable that Oakeshott's discussion of it captures familiar and vital aspects of the experience of participants in more or less well-established practices of political authority. There are important similarities among the communications I receive from the Internal Revenue Service, appeals from charitable organizations and, say, blackmailing letters. For example all intend that I send a check in return, all hold out the prospect of ill consequences to me if I do not do so, and I may heartily disapprove the persons and purposes who send all three. Nevertheless, I readily distinguish the communications of the Internal Revenue Service from the other two. And if I attempt to explain the differences—that is, that the first carries authority—my account will undoubtedly make important reference to the credentials, procedures, laws, constitutions and so forth that are stressed in all versions of the F-P theory of authority.

Thus the considerable plausibility of the theory we have been tracing results partly from its congruence with our experience as participants in authority relations. But its plausibility also depends heavily on its presentation in abstract, static terms, that is in terms of what rules, authority and obligation *are* and *are not* in what deserves to be characterized as an essentialist conception. When Oakeshott begins to describe rules *in use,* considerations enter that would seem to be excluded by its abstract formulation. To follow the account far enough to assess it, we must examine the conditions said to be requisite to civil association.

Postulates of Civil Association

Properly, the rules that constitute such an association are to be cast in the form of "general abstract conditions." But in practice questions arise among associates in terms of individuals taking specific actions in particular circumstances. Primarily for this reason, civil association "postulates" three types of authoritative procedure and an associated mode or focus of interaction—which Oakeshott calls "politics"—all of which, although inseparable from the system of rules, go beyond the rules themselves and their strictly formal characteristics. First, because the system of rules is only self-sufficient, not self-explanatory, an authoritative procedure is required to determine whether particular actions comport with the conditions prescribed by the rules.[18] Did taking the election official to dinner constitute an attempt to rig the election? Did I commit arson when the pile of leaves I left smoldering set my neighbor's picket fence on fire? Questions such as these require a procedure of adjudication. Second, because substantial changes occur in the conditions that present themselves to the association, a legislative procedure is required through which new rules can be deliberately enacted and existing rules deliberately changed. This procedure, and the interactions ("politics") for which it is the focus, involve deliberation of the system of rules "in terms of its desirability."[19] Has the urbanization of life rendered obsolete the existing rules about the ownership of firearms? Do excessive accumulations warrant alterations in the rules governing possession of property? Finally, civil association is not merely relationship in terms of rules but also "in terms of the assurance, or at least the expectation, that the conditions will be generally and adequately subscribed to."[20] For this reason, and because a system of rules "is unable to interpret, to administer, or to enforce itself,"[21] civil association postulates procedures and office of "ruling," that is ways of requiring "substantive responses from assignable persons in particular contingent situations."[22] A summary of Oakeshott's comments about these procedures and modes of interaction will help us to identify the merits of the overall construct as an understanding of authority in what he at least clearly regards as its most important formulation.

Adjudication

Adjudication is exclusively concerned with settling disputes about actions or utterances of agents alleged to have "failed adequately to subscribe to the norms" of the civil association.[23] The court is to settle such disputes by ascertaining what was said or done by whom and to reach a conclusion about the relation of that performance to the rules. It does not arbitrate or umpire between competing interests, interpret the intentions of legislators, make "social policy," or invoke general moral considerations except insofar as they are explicitly part of the law. Interestingly, however, a judge's having jurisdiction over a case is not itself sufficient to allow the decision he reaches to "pretend to the authority" of the association. Although such a decision cannot be said to be correct or incorrect in any useful sense, neither can it properly be made in an arbitrary, intuitive or subjective manner. It must be shown to be a conclusion that existing rules will "tolerate," a conclusion that "shelters under the authority of the system."[24] This is not a process of "finding" a conclusion in the rules or previous interpretations thereof, it is not a process of "deducing" a conclusion from those materials, and it is not a matter of arguing from precedent in the sense of discovering similarities and differences between the case at hand and previous cases. The meaning of the rules (including previous interpretations thereof) for the contingent circumstances of the case at hand is necessarily indeterminate and hence must be given by the judge. The reasoning by which the judge arrives at that meaning is "analogical"; it seeks the "propensities" that are lodged in the "more general and least fluctuating concepts" of the system and it attempts to "amplify" (pursue the intimations of?) those meanings in respect to the issue before it. "If a hole in a fence large enough for a child to squeeze through has been declared a circumstance which may transform an infant intruder from a trespasser into an invitee, what is to be said about a gate without a latch in respect of an adult?"[25] This process of interpretation and application is subject to a variety of abuses. But the integrity of the system of rules requires that remedies for abuses be found within that system itself.[26]

The discussion of adjudication provides a first glimpse of the rules of civil association in use—as opposed to the severely abstract account of what they are and are not. Seeing them in this way blurs the edges of categories Oakeshott uses to distinguish rules from other features of associations and in terms of which he distinguishes civil association from all other modes. The very human figure of the judge enters in a vital role and his entry is accompanied by criteria of judgment which, though tied to the rules, cannot be mere reiterations of or deductions from the latter.[27] Whatever else we might say about these comments (for example, that they pass lightly over many of the hardest questions in jurisprudence), they diminish the impression that civil association as such is entirely formal and impersonal, that its rules can be understood and followed without reference to objectives, purposes and reasoning concerning them.

Ruling

With the topic of "ruling" (we postpone to last the larger questions of legislation and "politics") we make our way back to that policeman with whom (in part because he is the prototypical figure of legal authority for so many) this exploration began. And we find the policeman of civil association doing those things that garden-variety policemen do. He enforces the orders of courts and "administers" rules by requiring that "*lex* itself is incapable of demanding," namely, "the performance of substantive actions by identified persons."[28] In Oakeshott's distinctive prose, ruling "will be concerned (somewhat cautiously) with preventing conduct in breach of... prescriptions, more confidently with seeking, apprehending and holding putative delinquents pending their accusation in a court of law, with imposing temporary order upon a confused situation likely to compromise the civil condition if it is left unregulated, and with similar administrative engagements."[29] Although these actions will often have to be taken in the absence of any judicial conclusion, they involve authority bound by procedures and they "refer to *lex* and are eligible to be judged in terms of the norms prescribed by *lex*."[30]

Oakeshott insists that rulers as such are not managers, arbitrators, patrons of interests, or persons with substantive wants, and that ruling is indifferent to the objectives of individuals or groups.[31] In the light of the passages we have been considering, this insistence makes it increasingly difficult to dispel the impression that terms such as "objectives," "substantive" and the like are used in some special way and that the distinctions they are used to make are artifacts of their special uses. However this may turn out, it is clear that law and ruling in a going civil association will have consequences difficult to distinguish from those they have in associations significantly at variance with Oakeshott's model.

Legislation and "Politics"

Adjudication is necessary to civil association in order that associates may know the meaning of established rules in particular circumstances and ruling is necessary to insure as far as possible that associates act consonant with that meaning. These two procedures concern what already established rules require. Legislative procedure and "politics" concern which rules should be established or repealed. Although such procedure should be used sparingly, it is necessary in order that a civil association be able to adapt, in a deliberate manner, to "notable" changes of belief or sentiment about the desirable conditions of civil conduct. Judges and rulers must justify their decisions and actions in terms of established rules; but legislators, although they must act in accordance with the procedures that give them the authority to act at all, not only may but must justify the rules they enact in terms of their desirability. Nevertheless, authority itself is said to have nothing to do with desirability of any sort. Hence politics and the legislative procedure stand in a complicated, not to say a peculiar, relationship to authority. Legislation *presupposes* authority because the office of legislator must have authority and because all associates, even while participating in the "politics" in which the desirability of legislative proposals is deliberated, must accept that the authority of enactments is independent of their desirability. Owing to its concern with desirabilities, the deliberations and interactions that take place in respect to the legislative procedure are not strictly a part of civil association or a part of the activities of associates as such. But they are necessary to civil association for the reason given and they are unique to it in that they must be conducted on the understanding that they relate "to that which distinguishes civil from all other modes of association," namely that it is "association exclusively in terms of rules that are indifferent to all substantive outcomes."[32]

It would be understandable if participants in politics confused the question of the desirability of the proposals they are deliberating with the question of the authority they have once adopted. But if they do so, enterprise association—or no association at all—has replaced civil association. Nor is this the only restriction on the understandings with which participants may properly enter the deliberative process. The process is exclusively about the desirability of changes in rules that themselves must be indifferent to the purposes of actors and the outcomes of actions. Proposed changes in the rules are to be judged according to the alterations they would make in the conditions under which associates act, not according to any effects they may be expected to have on the outcomes of actions. True, such proposals commonly take their genesis or inspiration from the purposes or objectives of participants ("there is, indeed, no want which may not set going a project to change *respublica*") and if adopted they commonly yield "benefits or advantages . . . to assignable interests" (for example, "every piece of legislation has an outcome of advantage to a legal profession").[33] But these facts about proposals are irrelevant to their merits as changes in the rules. In the course of deliberation they must lose whatever character they have taken from their genesis and acquire another, namely the character of "being understood, advanced and considered as a proposal for the amendment of the *respublica* of a civil association."[34] Further, these amendments must be just that, proposed changes in particular items that make up the system of rules. Legislation and politics are concerned neither "with the worth of civil association itself (this relates to the authority of *respublica* and is not called in question)" nor "with the desirability or otherwise of an entire system of civil conditions, for there are no criteria in terms of which this might be deliberated."[35]

It is therefore something of an understatement that engagement in this "politics" entails a disciplined imagination.[36] If participants confuse questions about desirability with the question of authority, authority and civil association are gone and there can be no "politics." If they confuse questions about the desirability of rules with questions about the advantages or disadvantages of the outcomes of particular actions taken under rules, civil association is transmuted into enterprise association. This severe self-discipline, moreover, must be maintained in the course of an activity that takes participants away from pursuits in which they seek to satisfy the interests and desires, objectives and purposes that give each of their lives its distinctive character and, no doubt, much of its savor.[37] And the discipline must be maintained despite the certainty that "there must always be more than one opinion" about the desirability of a proposal and hence that the engagement to deliberate it is likely to be "vexatious." Oakeshott does not warn us off of participation in politics in the manner of his great predecessor Hobbes, but no reader can be surprised by his concluding judgment that participation "calls for so exact a focus of attention and so uncommon a self-restraint that one is not astonished to find this mode of human relationship to be as rare as it is excellent."[38]

Answers and Questions

The fundamental insight of F-P theory is captured in a characteristically pithy formulation of Thomas Hobbes: "This device therefore of them that will make civil laws first, and then a civil body afterwards (as if policy make a body politic, and not a body politic made policy), is of no effect."[39] In Oakeshott's words, it is that "authority cannot be attributed to *respublica* in virtue of what can exist or be achieved only in the recognition of its authority."[40] Identifying, assessing, and reasoning about the purpose, the consequences, the merits, or any other attributes of a rule alleged to have authority *presupposes* recognizing its authority such that these other questions can be raised about something with authority. This insight is the basis of the two-part thesis with which we began the present summary of F-P theory and it informs much of the elaboration of that thesis we have been tracing. The only way to delineate authority consistent with its distinctive standing is in terms of the recognition of rules on the basis of their formal properties—on the basis of their credentials.

The precise formulation of this insight remains to be determined below. But the insight is fundamental to the theory of authority. The concept of authority loses its distinctive identity if authority is identified with, is reduced to, the substantive characteristics or consequences of actions or policies, agents or agencies.

When this much has been agreed, however, hard questions remain as to just how we should formulate the definitional thesis and conceptualize the relationships between authority and those many things that the thesis says authority is not. Those examples of F-P theorizing that we have looked at give their emphasis to sharpening the distinction between authority and various other phenomena with which it has commonly been identified, to elaborating categories that parse the items distinguished, and in general to erecting high and strongly defended conceptual barriers between authority and other features of human affairs.

Manifestly, however, the fact that an M is not an N does not exhaust the questions that might usefully be asked about M and N and the relationship between them. Although not reducible to or identifiable with one another, there might be significant conceptual relationships between them. A husband is not the same thing as a wife, but we do not understand much about these concepts if this is the extent of our knowledge concerning them. Or perhaps there are no conceptual relationships whatever, but very important empirical relationships such as the one being a condition of the other. To put the point somewhat differently, F-P theorists are not engaged in the ridiculous enterprise of arguing that authority is not that indefinite but very large number of things that no one has ever thought it to be. It has seemed plausible to treat authority as a species of power, of knowledge, of shared opinion or will, because all of these are commonly found in the same circumstances as authority, because the consequences of any one of them are difficult to disentangle from the consequences of the others, because they influence one another, and so forth. Authority and authority relations have presumably been thought to involve judgments about the merits and consequences of actions and policies, about the intentions and purposes of legislators and judges, about the consent of citizens, because of the ways in which these several factors, even though or even because they have been inexactly identified, are perceived to be intertwined in human affairs. A specification of what each of them is not is a useful (albeit a risky) step toward understanding them and their interrelationships, but it itself cannot yield such an understanding.

These very general remarks have no simple application to the version of F-P theory that has occupied us at greatest length. In at least one perspective Oakeshott's theory recognizes an exceptionally wide array of variables and relationships. Authority in enterprise associations is conceptually related to shared purposes and objectives. Hence a species of authority relationship is not only open to but positively invites judgments about substantive merits. This in turn permits, among other things, the possibility that a kind of expert knowledge, namely knowledge of which rules or decisions would best serve the purposes of the association, could play a significant role in authority relations. (It might well be objected, or perhaps suspected, that Oakeshott's discussion of authority in enterprise associations is not in fact a discussion of authority because it gives so little weight to the basic F-P insight, makes so little effort to identify the distinctive, the defining features of authority.) More important, though civil association is initially defined very narrowly, by the end of the account of what it postulates and presupposes a large and diverse array of additional considerations have been treated as essential to it. Finally, there is the question of Oakeshott's conception of the relationship between these "ideal characters" and historical instances of associations that have involved authority. Ideal characters are neither descriptions of empirical instances of human associations nor generalizations over prominent features of a number of such associations.[41] "Civil association" is particularly distant from empirical instances, being at best "glimpsed here or there in the features of human goings-on."[42] Actual associations, and particularly the many examples of the "modern European state," have all been ambiguous compounds consisting in the elements (among others) that make up the two ideal characters. Thus an analysis of (what has passed for) authority as it has in fact presented itself in the thought and action of members of those states would look very different from, would include much more than, the theory of authority in civil association that we have summarized.

The difficulty here is that Oakeshott recognizes this wider array of variables and relationships primarily for the purpose of setting them aside as irrelevant to his theory of authority in what he clearly regards as its genuine form, that is as it is displayed in the ideal character "civil association." On metatheoretical and epistemological grounds (and indeed, certain protestations to the contrary notwithstanding, on normative grounds as well), Oakeshott contends that authority *is* what a suitably elaborated theory of authority shows it to be. Empirical instances are to be characterized and assessed in terms of the theory rather than the theory being tested by its correspondence with the instances. This idealist position underlies Oakeshott's judgment that few if any modern European states have achieved authority and that most of their claims (or rather pretensions) to it have been supported "by the most implausible and gimcrack beliefs," beliefs "which few could find convincing for more than five minutes together." This "conspicuous failure" has in turn "provoked the belief that authority is of no account." As a result, the constitutional histories of European states have been "for the most part, and not unexpectedly," much less a history of authority than the story of "somewhat confused and sordid expedients for accommodating the modern disposition to judge everything from the point of view of the desirability of its outcome in policies and performances and to discount legitimacy."[43]

These epistemological and metatheoretical views pose serious difficulties for the critic (however sympathetic) of Oakeshott's theory. Evidence that the theory ignores or is at variance with recurrent features of thought, speech and action is not so much denied as dismissed as irrelevant. Despite his acceptance of the position that languages are "made by speakers" and are not "the creation of grammarians,"[44] he contends that most of the uses which speakers of modern languages have made of "authority" have been so muddled as to be irrelevant to the analysis of the concept which that term marks. Although numerous citizens, politicians, statesmen, revolutionaries, civil disobedients and philosophers have understood themselves to be building, attacking, defending, exercising, respecting, challenging or theorizing about authority, so few of them have in fact been doing so that their thought and action are neither here nor there as regards what authority is or is not.

It does not follow that we must set aside either the theory or those large stretches of experience that are at variance with it. Critics are not, to begin with, obliged to accept the epistemological and metatheoretical views to which we have been referring. They are at liberty to reject or simply to ignore them and to judge (as opposed to explicate and understand) the account of authority by whatever canons of analysis and theory construction they find defensible. Moreover, in addition to his claim that we know authority when we encounter it, Oakeshott himself contends that use of his ideal characters will allow us to make "a considerable advance" upon the understanding of particular "goings-on" that we could otherwise achieve.[45] Although not simply descriptive, the ideal characters do purport to illuminate such goings-on. This claim presupposes knowledge of the goings-on sufficiently independent of the theory to allow the claim to be tested by comparing the theory and the goings-on. Finally, other theories of authority, perhaps most importantly Max Weber's, accept the insight that authority cannot be reduced to those many things from which F-P theory distinguishes it but argue for that insight out of quite different views about epistemology and the theory of inquiry.

Our brief excursus into metatheory suggests a rough distinction that may facilitate assessment of F-P theory generally and Oakeshott's version in particular. The distinction is between what we will call internal and external questions about the theory. The former focuses on the cogency of the notion of authority as a property of an association constituted exclusively by the recognition of rules and offices that are, *qua* rules and offices, indifferent to the purposes of subscribers and to the substantive outcomes of actions taken in subscription. Are the distinctions on which this notion depends defensible? Are there rules that are no more than adverbial? Is it possible for an associate to know what would count as adequate subscription to a rule without considering objectives that the rule serves or affects? Can we make sense out of the action of subscribing to rules and offices without reference to objectives and purposes that the actor hopes to achieve by that action? Does the theory itself remain consistent with its basic distinctions, or do the concessions we have noted undermine those distinctions? There is an understanding of the relationships, or at least one possible kind of relationship, between thought and action implicit in the theory. Can that understanding be generalized and defended? The theory purports to tell us what authority is and is not. Assessing it internally largely consists in asking whether authority could be what it is said by the theory to be given that it is none of the various things that the theory insists it is not.

Very roughly, external questions concern the relationship between the theory of authority and authority as it has presented itself in the arrangements of various political associations and in the thought and action of the members of such associations. Granting that no theory is a mere description of events or circumstances, does the F-P theory increase our understanding of the range of events and circumstances in which "authority" has been salient? Does it, moreover, contribute to understanding if the criteria of "contributes" require a closer relationship between theory and practice than Oakeshott's?[46] Does F-P theory deny the significance of, exclude, or perhaps simply fail to recognize conceptual or empirical relationships that are in fact vital to understanding authority? Do authority and authority relations presuppose beliefs or values concerning this or that mode of equality and inequality, this or that relationship between the human and the divine, between material conditions and thought and action, and so forth? Do they presuppose the availability of some set or range of concepts that F-P theory treats as irrelevant or simply disregards?

The distinction between internal and external questions parallels at least two of the other distinctions that have made an appearance above. Noticing these parallels will draw the discussion to this point to a close and put us in a position to specify instances of both types of questions and to begin to try to answer them.

The internal-external distinction parallels our original distinction between two types of puzzlement in respect to authority and also the distinction between authority and the authoritative. The first type of puzzlement, it will be recalled, concerns what authority is and is not; the second concerns how we can comprehend—and justify or disjustify—the recurrence of authority in human affairs. The distinction between authority and the authoritative sets out formal placeholders for what we hope will be solutions to the two forms of puzzlement. "Authority" in this distinction stands primarily for what authority is and is not. "The authoritative" stands for a wider set of values, beliefs, arrangements, and practices attention to which will help us to comprehend and assess the recurrence of authority among us. F-P theory aims to tell us what authority is and is not. Thus internal questions about it concern the extent to which it abates the first form of puzzlement, fills in the first of the placeholders. External questions ask whether or to what extent the F-P answers to internal questions need to be amended or supplemented in order to comprehend and to assess the place of authority in our arrangements and practices. At this juncture we emphasize what should in any case be tolerably clear, namely that these distinctions must be understood as analytic conveniences. Clearly we cannot understand the place of authority in human affairs if we know nothing of what it is and is not. Equally, knowing what something is and is not, at least if that something is as complex and as salient in human affairs as authority, cannot be altogether distinct from understanding and assessing its place among us.

3 Rules and Rule Following An Internal Critique of the Formal-Procedural Theory of Authority

The F-P theory of authority is a theory of rule-governed association: a theory of rules, of offices created and defined by rules, and of conduct guided by rules adopted by such offices. Internal questions about the theory are therefore primarily questions about the cogency of its account, both explicit and implicit, of the concept of "rule" and of such related notions as recognizing a rule, subscribing to a rule, following a rule, being guided by a rule. In the terms toward which our discussion will now gradually progress, internal questions concern the theory's (largely implicit) account of the notion that rules invested with authority provide subscribers with a distinctive species of reason for action.[1]

Rules and Rule Following

It is a presupposition of an association governed by rules that its members know what a rule is and have some more or less definite idea of what X's being a rule implies for them. In addition, rules form a large and diverse family and associates must be able to distinguish among the various types of rules and the rather different implications that attach to the several types. At one level of analysis this knowledge consists in little more than knowing how to use the several ordinary language concepts usually marked by the term "a rule." The task of characterizing and accounting for this knowledge is in principle no different from the task of characterizing and accounting for knowledge of any concept whatever. It is part of theorizing about language, not theorizing about authority and obligation as such. Thus in its most general dimensions it is relevant to a theory of authority mainly insofar as such a theory seeks to locate its subject matter in a wider setting or context, perhaps by locating it as part of the authoritative. In this perspective the question of how associates know what rules are and what they imply is external to F-P theory and we take it up in the following chapter.[2]

Command of the concept of "rule" is in any case only a necessary condition of, not a sufficient condition for, picking out various types of rules from the welter of phenomena and of knowing how to respond to them. More particularly, such command is not more than a necessary condition of picking out instances of those rules that carry *in* authority and of determining which actions would adequately discharge the obligations that those rules entail for associates. These further judgments require not only command of the concept "rule" but knowledge of the criteria and mark of rules invested with *in* authority and understanding of the distinctive implications carried by rules that are so invested.

As F-P theorists emphasize, in many societies associates quite readily identify rules that have *in* authority simply by noting the procedure from which they have emerged and the credentials they have acquired by passing through that procedure. As participants in an established, institutionalized practice, large numbers of associates become "fluent" in the constitutional-legal-political "language game" in which authority largely consists. This is a rather remarkable achievement and should not be taken for granted by the theorist. But even if we simply assume the language game and fluent participants in it, there are complications here to which F-P theorists have given too little attention, complications that require attention to the intentions, and through them to the objectives and purposes, of the officeholders who use the procedures in promulgating rules.

The minimal point is that some officeholders must intend, and nonofficeholding associates must know that they intend, this and that particular enactment to be a rule that carries *in* authority. Most pieces of legislation include a variety of sentences, only some of which are intended to be rules of any sort and only a yet smaller selection of which are intended to be rules that entail obligations. There are prefaces that explain the objectives of the legislation; there are definitions of terms, specifications of jurisdictions and administrative arrangements, provisions for funding, and, not uncommonly, expressions of sentiments and wishes. The same must be said yet more emphatically of judicial opinions and their curious and often all but unparsable mixtures of *obiter dicta* and holdings. Yet these entire assortments pass through one procedure, are printed on the same paper, bound in the same distinctive sort of books, and registered, deposited and distributed in the same ways and places. Although in some systems it is in principle true that nothing that lacks these "marks," these insignia, can have *in* authority, it is by no means the case that everything that bears them does so. One cannot sort the matter out without attending to what was intended by those human beings who put the procedure to work. The well-rehearsed and very real difficulties of identifying the intentions of what are often collective actors make this a complicated and indeed an uncertain business, but those difficulties cannot relieve associates of the task.

Nor are intentions and purposes relevant only to distinguishing rules from other statements that may be issued by those in authority. Associates must know not only that a statement is a rule, but also *what* rule the statement states. They must know what the statement, *qua* rule, means, what it enjoins, forbids, permits. If such knowledge were altogether unavailable to associates, either because the rule had no meaning or because they were unable to discern it, the idea that X was a rule for them, a rule to which they subscribed, would be utterly empty.

Oakeshott in particular minimizes this point, sometimes seems to deny it entirely. On the one hand he insists that rules are "indeterminate" in the sense that it is impossible to deduce, to infer, or otherwise to extract specific directives or prohibitions from a rule as such. Meaning cannot be extracted from a rule. It must be *assigned* by a judge, ordinarily operating after the fact of an action by one or more associates and with respect to that action. On the other hand Oakeshott argues that even these determinations speak only to "adverbial" conditions that must be maintained in acting, not to the actions associates take in the garden-variety sense of a form of conduct deliberately chosen to achieve an outcome. There are several points of importance here and they all bring intentions, objectives and purposes, interests and desires into the theory of *in* authority rules in ways that go beyond the intention of officeholders that X be invested with authority.

The first of these points concerns Oakeshott's distinction between the adverbial conditions of an action and the action itself in the sense of the deliberate pursuit of a "substantive" objective or outcome. This is undoubtedly a valid distinction, one vital to the theory of authority. If we abandoned it entirely we would thereby have given up the distinction between doing X because it is required by authority and doing X because we think X will have, perhaps altogether apart from its being so required, desirable consequences. But the distinction is not between actions that are done intentionally and to achieve a desired outcome and those that are done out of no intention or for no substantive purpose whatever. Doing X because it is required by authority itself involves an intention and a substantive purpose. And if we say with Oakeshott that A does X in order to maintain a condition, whether the condition of authority being subscribed to in the association or the more specific conditions that the particular rule establishes, there is as it were a further intention, even a further purpose, involved. This point does not itself invalidate the distinction between conditions and substantive outcomes, between "adverbial" and "substantive" rules; it does indicate that the distinction we need is not between intentional or purposive actions on the one hand and some other species of the genus "action" (assuming there is or are such) on the other.

The adverbial condition–substantive outcome distinction is in fact a distinction concerning the perspective from which we choose to characterize a rule and the actions taken in response to it. Smith, let us say, is a merchant. He buys and sells goods and the usual "imagined and wished-for" substantive outcome of his actions is making a profit. But Smith is a decent man who aims to be polite to his customers and trading partners, who keeps his promises, honors his contracts, represents his merchandise accurately, and values the circumstance that he and others live by these principles and rules. Of the ordinary run of his actions it will be not only plausible but simply correct to say that his purpose is to make a profit; it will also be correct to say that he aims to do so honestly, fairly, politely, and so forth. The purpose-procedure, substantive-adverbial distinctions are easily drawn.

But perhaps Smith notices that he and many of his customers and competitors have become careless of the adverbial considerations, have taken to a variety of sharp practices that violate both the letter and the spirit of the norms and rules in question. Unhappy about this state of affairs, Smith goes out of his way to initiate a series of transactions with the primary if not the exclusive purpose of demonstrating to all concerned that their suspicions about him will henceforth be without foundation— and that everyone would benefit from more explicit and vigorous attention to the conditions of their interactions. He may or may not hope that these transactions also prove to be profitable in the usual commercial sense. But his chief purpose in initiating them is not monetary gain but reestablishing a certain quality of relationship between himself and his associates.

The type of conduct we have attributed to Smith is not notably rare. There are many people who assign great value to, who place great emphasis upon, doing what they do "in a proper way," who would rather forego an activity or an objective than pursue it in a careless, shady, gauche or inelegant manner. Classicism in many of its manifestations is an expression of this outlook. It involves making matters of form, style or procedure into (what they are always eligible to be) the primary, the overweening consideration in an action or set of actions. (It is said—with what truth I do not know—that Ted Williams refused, perhaps at some cost to his batting average, the fortunes of his team, and hence his pocketbook, to spoil the classical elegance of his swing in order to hit to left field.) Nor is the F-P theorist well placed to object to this outlook. Surely there could be no civil association if participants were not committed to maintaining certain adverbial conditions—were not prepared to sacrifice other purposes to the objective of maintaining such conditions.

By way of transition to the second of the points referred to above, let us consider one of the specifics of Oakeshott's discussion of legal rules. He contends that the criminal law enjoins not particular substantive actions but particular ways of performing certain classes of actions. It does not prohibit killing and setting fires, it forbids killing "murderously" and setting fires "arsonically." Granting that much fire setting is not arson and much killing not murder, in this application the distinction amounts to little more than verbal play. The person who can be said to have killed "murderously" can usually be said to have committed murder. "To murder" is a verb that identifies a type of act prohibited by the criminal law.

Oakeshott's discussion of "arsonically" is an expression both of his argument that rules are purely adverbial and of his contention, which is the object of the second point to be made here, that rules are "indeterminate" in meaning. This second contention is something of a commonplace in jurisprudence. Legal rules are general and prospective. Consequently they involve a considerable element of "open texture"; their meanings in this or that circumstance are indeterminate and they require interpretation before they will yield guidance to associates, rulers or judges.

It must first be emphasized that the notion of "indeterminate meaning" in this context is comparative, not absolute. An absolutely indeterminate rule would presumably be meaningless and hence no rule at all. The meaning of the class of statements called rules could be less determinate than other classes of statements (for example commands), and some species of rules (say legal rules) could be less determinate than other species (say the rules of games). But no rule is a string of nonsense syllables.

Second, the proposition that rules are indeterminate commonly involves an equivocation between two senses of the term "general." All rules are general in the sense that they apply to or hold for classes of instances, not single, named instances. They are general as opposed to *particular*. A directive that was particular in the sense that it applied only to a single, named instance could at most be an order or command, not a rule. (Thus bills of attainder are not rules.)[3] Here are two familiar legal rules, both of which are general as opposed to particular: (1) "No citizen may be deprived of due process of law." (2) "Bus Lane: Buses and Taxis Only, 8:00 A.M.–10:00 A.M., 4:00 P.M.–7:00 P.M., Monday to Friday." Manifestly, however, in respect to their "indeterminateness" these two legal rules are as different as night and day. The bus lane rule is *specific* as well as general. The language of the rule itself identifies with some precision both the boundaries of the class of cases to which it applies and the permitted and prohibited modes of action within that class. It is, comparatively speaking, determinate in its meaning. By contrast, the due process rule is general as opposed to particular as well as general in the sense of unspecific. It is unspecific in that the language of the rule does comparatively little to identify the boundaries of the class to which it applies or to specify permissible or impermissible conduct. For this reason it is comparatively indeterminate in its meaning. If we attend to the distinction between general and particular on the one hand and general and specific on the other (and remember that "indeterminate" is always comparative), we will surely see that, although all legal rules are general as opposed to particular, some are determinate, some highly indeterminate in their meaning. The unqualified generalization that legal rules are indeterminate is not very helpful.

It does not follow that specific, comparatively determinate rules leave associates no choices or that they can be followed in a mechanical, unreflective manner. The bus lane rule does not tell the automobilist whether he may enter the proscribed lane to make way for an ambulance or fire truck. And if it is amended to cover this point it still does not tell him whether he may enter the lane in order to relieve unusually heavy congestion, to stop his car to aid someone who has had a heart attack on the sidewalk, to block the passage of a drunken taxi driver, or to chase out a wasp that has flown in his window. And if all of these issues were settled by further additions to the language of the rule, nature, society and the ingenuity of associates would soon enough cast new issues up.

On the other hand, rules that are unspecific and even vague do not leave associates at liberty to do whatever they list. "No person shall be deprived of due process of law" is not a string of nonsense syllables that is literally without meaning. Most moderately informed speakers of the English language know the areas of activity to which it applies and the kinds or classes of actions that bring it into play. Any person who does not have this sort of command can easily acquire it by asking a question or two or by having recourse to a dictionary (just as the speaker of some other language can get a translation of the rule). Thus even associates with no specialized training, having no day-to-day involvement in the detailed workings of the legal system, garner some instruction from the formulation of the rule. These points are yet less contestable in regard to that considerable array of legal rules that stand somewhere between the due process rule and the bus lane rule in respect to their specificity. Although there are hard cases in the law of homicide, pretty much anyone who commands the concept "murder" knows that the law against it forbids retaliating against an insult by intentionally plunging a knife into the breast of one's antagonist.

The foregoing discussion of this topic, however, suffers from a characteristic that severely limits the value of it, of F-P accounts of *in* authority rules, and indeed of many treatments of legal rules in the literature of jurisprudence. The characteristic is a tendency to discuss rules and rule following as a phenomenon apart, as something that takes place in its own environment or context, an environment largely isolated from other dimensions of the activities of participants. Rules and rule following are treated as things-in-themselves rather than as integral parts of a pattern of actions and interactions.

When so viewed, it is indeed difficult to see how associates could garner more than minimal guidance from rules.[4] Or rather, it is easy for theorists, who may have their own reasons for wanting to emphasize the indeterminateness of rules, to argue (with an apparent cogency) that associates cannot garner much guidance from them. Consisting as they do in words, rule formulations put at the theorist's disposal an unspecifiable but very considerable possibility of constructing new applications for the combinations of words in which the rules consist. As linguists emphasize, speakers of a language routinely construct, employ, and understand statements that have never been previously formulated. They do so, typically, not by inventing new words but by putting established words and expressions to new uses. The theorist with even modest powers of imagination will almost always be able to do this with the words of which legal or other rules consist.

But the fact that the set of words in which a rule consists can be given a range of meanings does not show that *the rule* lacks a more or less definite meaning in the practice or pattern of activities in which it is a rule. A rule is not just a collection of words. It is a statement intentionally made in the course of a more or less distinctly recognizable and recognized activity or practice, a practice that involves the setting of particular arrangements and institutions, participants who have shared certain experiences, accept certain beliefs and values, and so forth.[5] Consider the bus lane rule. It is readily understandable to persons who live in modern cities with heavy traffic, multilaned streets, elaborate systems of traffic regulation, and a familiar distinction between public and private transport. In these circumstances it applies in a quite unproblematic manner to a veritable host of cases. And when questions arise about how it ought to be applied to novel cases, those familiar with its uses are not at sea. The range of considerations relevant to interpreting the rule are ready to hand in their day-to-day experience. Disagreement is indeed likely. But as with all disagreement—as opposed to mutual incomprehension—this is possible because the issues arise in a more or less familiar setting that yields criteria for identifying and thinking about them. If we imagine away the familiar setting, the idea of the rule or of someone trying to follow it loses all its sense. What sense would be made of the bus lane rule by persons whose experience, vicarious and direct, was limited to the conditions that obtain in the Australian outback?

The same must be said of the due process rule, although here an additional complication enters the picture. As indicated by various attempts to export legal systems and instantly implant them in the lives of peoples with substantially alien practices and traditions, this and related legal rules are all but unusable, at least for considerable periods of time, outside the settings in which they developed and became familiar. The problem is not that the rules are vague and indeterminate, it is that, *qua* rules (as opposed to *qua* a collection of words in which the rule formulation consists—each of which may be perfectly familiar), they have virtually no meaning. They acquire meanings, very likely substantially different ones from those they had in their place of origin, only as they come to have uses in the lives of the people in question.

The complication concerns the fact that the due process rule is a part of a specialized practice, a practice regularly participated in by, and hence familiar in its details to, a limited segment of the population for whom it is a rule. Of course this rule is part of the legal arrangements of entire societies and as such is in some degree familiar to a large proportion of the populations of those societies. It connects with the whole notion of limited government, the rule of law, established procedures and criteria for resolving disputes, and beyond these ideas to yet wider norms such as justice, fairness, and equality. But at this level due process is perhaps less a source of directives and prohibitions to be applied to this or that particular action, more a principle or an ideal by which to judge the overall workings of the legal system. It is by no means meaningless. A number of instances in which associates are punished for crimes which it is widely believed they did not commit, incarcerated for long periods without indictment and trial, prevented from acting in ways that have not been prohibited by law, or deprived of their property without compensation will bring the ideal into public discussions in a forceful as well as intelligible manner. There is nothing meaningless or even notably indeterminate about the charge that the governments of the Soviet Union and South Africa regularly fail to accord due process to their subjects. Disputes about the conduct of these governments would be significantly different if this notion were not available to large numbers of people.

But the notion, now in the form of something more properly thought of as a rule than an ideal, also operates in more specialized contexts. Governments make decisions to do or to refrain from doing X because they believe that due process of law requires that decision, citizens (or more commonly their lawyers) advance claims that due process was denied when X was or was not done, judges find for or against such claims, compensation is awarded or denied, convictions overturned or not, prisoners released or kept in jail, and even, in some jurisdictions, legislation struck down on the ground that it violates due process and hence in fact lacks the authority with which the legislature had sought to invest it. All of these events recur, on a day-to-day basis, in a considerable number of countries.

The tendency of philosophers, whether F-P theorists, Legal Realists, or some other variety, to dismiss this feature of legal systems as ceremonialism or worse admittedly has a counterpart in the suspicion and even hostility the the rule sometimes evokes in associates who neither participate in nor regularly attend to the detailed processes through which decisions about due process are reached. To the latter, the decisions of prosecutors and judges about due process often appear to be a kind of legerdemain whose particulars stand to the materials from which they are alleged to derive about as the rabbit stands to the movements of the prestidigitator—frequently an altogether well founded assessment of them. But the thesis that this skeptical assessment *must* be justified, that detailed conclusions *cannot* be arrived at by reasoning from the rules (which is of course what the F-P theorist is contending), rests largely on that lack of attention to context that we have been discussing. In the context of the continuing activity of legal interpretation the due process rule is more than a bare formula and more than a highly abstract ideal. It is part of a practice or tradition; a set of past decisions and the reasoning presented in support of them; a range of more or less consciously held assumptions and presuppositions as to what is and is not relevant to such decisions; a pattern of expectations about how participants will and will not go about reaching decisions; a set of understandings about the relationships between the due process rule and a variety of other rules at a comparable level of abstraction; a melange of beliefs concerning the proper purposes and objectives of the association in which the rule has standing. And in a more-than-metaphorical sense it is a number of persons who, by virtue of training and continuing involvement in an activity, have become skilled practitioners of that activity.

As will be evident to readers who are familiar with the writings of Ludwig Wittgenstein, the foregoing remarks owe much to the latter's analyses of such concepts as "rule," "following a rule," "being guided by a rule," "being able to go on," and so forth. A passage or two from his work may help to bring the main contentions of the last paragraphs together and carry us forward to the distinction between authority and desirability.

Characteristically, most of Wittgenstein's discussions of rules and rule following focus on examples drawn from familiar, everyday activities and involve directives that rarely cause us practical difficulties when we encounter them in the course of those activities. One of these examples is the instruction "Stand roughly there" (given, say, by someone taking a photograph). Despite the ease with which we ordinarily deal with such a directive, the theorist of rules is apt to treat it as problematic; he is likely to object that it is inexact and to call attention to the many interpretations that can be given to it. "But," Wittgenstein responds, "let us understand what 'inexact' means. For it does not mean 'unusable.' And let us consider what we call an 'exact' explanation in contrast to this one. Perhaps something like drawing a chalk line around an area? Here it strikes us at once that the line has breadth. So a colour-edge would be more exact. But has the exactness still got a function here: isn't the engine idling?" The "engine is idling" in that the theorist's concern about exactness has no place in, does not connect up with, the activity to which it appears to be addressed.

"Inexact" is really a reproach, and "exact" is praise. And that is to say that what is inexact attains its goal less perfectly than what is more exact. Thus the point here is what we call "the goal." Am I inexact when I do not give our distance to the sun to the nearest foot, or tell a joiner the width of a table to the nearest thousandth of an inch?

No *single* ideal of exactness has been laid down; we do not know what we should be supposed to imagine under this head—unless you yourself lay down what is to be so called. But you will find it difficult to hit upon such a convention; at least any that satisfies you.[6]

Wittgenstein knows that theorists have in fact tried to "hit" not merely upon a convention but on whole theories of meaning intended to specify such an ideal of exactness (he himself made such an attempt in his *Tractatus*). The following passage is one of his many responses to such attempts, this time in respect to general rules as opposed to a particular instruction.

I said that the application of a word is not everywhere bounded by rules. But what does [for example] a game look like that is everywhere bounded by rules? whose rules never let a doubt creep in, but stop up all the cracks where it might?—Can't we imagine a rule determining the application of a rule, and a doubt which it removes—and so on?

But that is not to say that we are in doubt because it is possible for us to *imagine* a doubt. I can easily imagine someone always doubting before he opened his front door whether an abyss did not yawn behind it; and making sure about it before he went through the door (and he might on some occasion prove to be right)—but that does not make me doubt in the same case.

A rule stands there like a sign-post.—Does the sign-post leave no doubt open about the way I have to go? Does it show which direction I am to take when I have passed it; whether along the road or the footpath or cross-country? But where is it said which way I am to follow it; whether in the direction of its finger or (e.g.) in the opposite one?—And if there were, not a single sign-post, but a chain of adjacent ones or of chalk marks on the ground—is there only *one* way of interpreting them?—So I can say, the sign-post does after all leave no room for doubt. Or rather: it sometimes leaves room for doubt and sometimes not. And this is no longer a philosophical proposition, but an empirical one.[7]

A "person goes by a sign-post," he adds later, "only in so far as there exists a regular use of sign-posts, a custom."[8]

Where such a custom or practice exists there is in fact sometimes real—that is to say, practical—doubt about what a rule requires, sometimes no doubt whatever, sometimes mixtures of doubt on this point, complete certainty on that. But too often the doubts of theorists and the ideal certainty or exactness they have tried to imagine (both as a way of making the doubts seem genuine and as a way of banishing them) have had little or nothing to do with the practical, the day-to-day doubts and certainties of participants. The doubts present themselves not as a "result of investigations" into rules and rule following but as "requirements" of such investigations.[9] Unless we have thoroughly misconstrued the F-P discussions of rules that we have considered, these remarks of Wittgenstein have an uncanny bearing upon them.

Issuing and following *in* authority rules presuppose the possibility of distinguishing rules that carry authority and of identifying the meaning of those rules. These activities are incomprehensible apart from patterns of belief and action, activities and practices, that give the rules their sense and that provide the criteria of judgment that are essential to participation in the association. Insofar as F-P theorists have attempted to account for authority without reference to these considerations, insofar as their favored distinctions between conditions and objectives, between procedures and purposes, between determinate and indeterminate directives, ignore these considerations, their theory is not a coherent account of the very feature—namely rules—that it itself (quite rightly) makes central to authority. To this extent it is not a coherent account of authority.

Authority and Desirability

The centerpiece of the F-P account of *in* authority is undoubtedly its distinction between authority and desirability—between the authority of a rule and the merits of the content of that rule. The points we have been considering will not settle the question of how this distinction should be drawn. (*That* it should be drawn, that it is an important distinction, is not at issue.) Indeed this question cannot be entirely settled on the basis of internal features of authority or internal questions about F-P theory. But the foregoing discussions do carry implications for that distinction. The remainder of this chapter seeks to draw those implications out.

In order for B to know that X is a rule that has *in* authority he must know at least three things about it: first, that it was or is some A's intention that X be such a rule; second, that X has successfully been invested with the necessary credentials; and third, how to make informed and defensible judgments as to what acting in conformity with the rule would consist of in circumstances that fall under it. Each of these kinds of knowledge, we have suggested, is impossible apart from some understanding of the practice in which the putative rule has been promulgated. This generalization, however, as well as other points discussed above, applies to the three kinds of knowledge, and through that application to the authority-desirability distinction, in slightly different ways.

In the case of the first two types of knowledge the most important connection with the authority-desirability distinction results from the fact that rules are directives that must have a meaning for associates. An associate can know that A intends that X be a rule with *in* authority only if he commands the concepts "intention" and "rule" as they are used in the practice in question.[10] It is part of the notion of having an intention that there is an object thereof—that there is some action or state of affairs that A intends. Moreover, A must have what is sometimes called a pro-attitude toward that object; he must want, desire, wish to take that action, to bring about that state of affairs.[11] He "must" have such a pro-attitude toward X because the pro-attitude is part of the intention; the intention cannot be formed without the pro-attitude.

It follows that other associates cannot know that A intends X without knowing that A has a pro-attitude toward it. Because pro-attitudes have to do with desirabilities, considerations of desirability enter the process of promulgating, and recognizing the promulgation of, *in* authority rules in a necessary way: they enter that process through the conceptual fact that recognizing these processes entails recognizing intentions. (Because the features of "intention" in question are features of the practices in which "intention" has a use, we can also say that recognizing *in* authority rules is dependent upon familiarity with features of those practices.)

In the case we are considering, to move on to the second point, one of A's intentions (one of the objectives he has a pro-attitude toward) is to promulgate X as a rule with *in* authority. F-P theorists emphasize that in most cases this intention can be realized only if the proposed rule is adopted in a manner that accords with other established rules and procedures. But they also argue that such adoption itself realizes the intention. This argument is specifically intended to establish the terminal point of the relevance of A's pro-attitudes to the question of the authority of the rules that he promulgates. They concede, in short, that intentions, and hence pro-attitudes or desirabilities, have a necessary part in the genesis of proposals. But they insist that the only consideration relevant to whether X has acquired authority is the procedure by which it was adopted.

It is true that proposals ordinarily acquire authority by being adopted in an established manner. But how is it known *what* the X is that has been proposed or adopted? Let us distinguish between maximal and minimal knowledge of the content of a rule. Maximal knowledge enables one to reach informed and defensible judgments concerning the requirements a rule places on associates. Minimal knowledge is no more than the ability to give paraphrases of the rule, to provide dictionary-like explanations of the phrases in which it consists, and so forth. Minimal knowledge of the meaning of an X is a necessary condition of adopting and of recognizing a rule.[12] And such knowledge, we want to argue, is impossible apart from knowledge of the intentions (and hence the pro-attitudes) of those who propose it, promulgate it, interpret it, and so forth.

Mention might be made at this point of controversies in the philosophy of language that have been just beneath the surface of the discussions in this chapter. There is a school of thought in linguistics and the philosophy of language according to which sentences in a language have meaning by virtue of syntactic, semantic and other rules that make up the grammar of the language; that is they have meaning altogether apart from the intentions of any speaker or auditor. Some version of this theory of meaning may be implicit in F-P accounts of rules and rule following, a speculation suggested by the tendency of those accounts to ignore or positively to deny the relevance of intentions and pro-attitudes to the understanding of rules. We are skeptical of this theory. We find much more persuasive the position that P. F. Strawson has described as its generic opposite.[13] According to this second view there is no such thing as a meaningful statement or sentence apart from the communication that some speaker intends to convey by it. Fortunately, we do not need to decide between these theories in order to deal with the question presently before us. The theories agree that the meaning of *speech* (as opposed to language), the meaning of statements made and interpreted by these or those speakers or writers, auditors or readers (as opposed to *sentences* that are allowed by the language, that are grammatical), is inseparable from the communication intentions of those speakers and auditors. F-P theory overlooks the fact that it is part of the notion of an *in* authority rule that it is *speech* in this sense, that it is intended to communicate a particular meaning or delimited range of meanings to an audience. We noted earlier that rules are not promulgated merely for the sake of exercising the authority to do so. Similarly, rules are not promulgated in order to display instances of grammatically correct sentences or the speakers' capacity to formulate such sentences. Rather, they are promulgated to give authoritative direction to associates.[14] Thus quite apart from the "maximal" knowledge necessary to conform to them, rules cannot be recognized or identified as such without "minimal" knowledge of their meaning. The procedures by which *in* authority rules are adopted are certainly necessary to their having that status, and knowledge of the procedures is certainly necessary to recognizing that they have acquired it. But without "minimal" knowledge of the meaning of X, there would be nothing to which to apply the procedures and no question of recognizing the results of their application. If both this and our earlier argument about intention are correct, it follows that pro-attitudes—that is desirabilities—enter necessarily into both the formulation and the identification of rules that have *in* authority.[15]

We come finally to the point that the B's must know the meaning of rules in the stronger or "maximal" sense of knowing how to make informed and defensible judgments as to what the rules require of them, judgments about what would count as adequate subscription to the rules in this or that case. Of course our discussion of "minimal" knowledge and its implications for the authority-desirability distinction is relevant to this matter. It is less than clear what could be meant by saying that B knew the meaning of a rule if he did not have moderately definite information about what that rule required of him. The person who has minimal knowledge of the meaning of the bus lane rule *thereby* knows what the rule requires of him in a large number of cases. But even if we made the absurd supposition that A could anticipate all of the cases that might arise under a rule that he is promulgating, it would be impossible to formulate X so as conclusively to settle what B must do in each of those cases. We might even say that the impossibility is conceptual, that such a formulation would be not a rule but a list of commands. Thus minimal knowledge cannot be a sufficient basis for rule-governed interaction or association. (This is one of the reasons we are using the cumbersome phraseology "knowledge of how to make informed and justifiable judgments about the meaning of X" rather than simply "knowledge of the meaning of X.")

But this feature of rules and rule following serves to complicate the process of drawing the distinction between authority and desirability. It also enhances the importance of knowledge of the wider features of the practice in which the rule-governed interactions take place.

A passage from Wittgenstein that we quoted above is a good starting point here. The notions of exactness and inexactness in relation to rules, he remarks, are connected with the notion of a goal. "Am I inexact when I do not give our distance to the sun to the nearest foot, or tell a joiner the width of a table to the nearest thousandth of an inch?"[16] How does one know what will count as inexact in such a context? Well, one knows the goals, the purposes involved in the activities in question. One knows what the astronomer or the joiner is trying to do, and this knowledge permits an informed and defensible judgment about whether a particular set of measurements will be exact or inexact. The astronomer or joiner might disagree with the judgment and request "more exact" or "better" figures. "More exact" and "better" will make sense in terms of the way the information will be used in pursuing the goals or purposes of the activity. The disagreement might or might not get resolved, but it could be conducted in a mutually intelligible manner.[17]

To what extent can Wittgenstein's reasoning be generalized to apply to the activity of following *in* authority rules? There is a wide range of cases here and it would be surprising if a single pattern of reasoning applied in the same way across the whole of that range. In respect to comparatively specific regulations such as the bus lane rule, the analogy with the measurement examples is both close and apparent. Just as anyone familiar with making tables thereby understands the relationships between the measurements employed and the goals and purposes of the tablemaker, so people familiar with traffic regulation in large modern cities thereby understand in at least a general way the relationship between the bus lane rule and goals and purposes of traffic regulation. Legislators can be seen to have those purposes in view in framing rules, and traffic wardens, policemen, judges and indeed ordinary citizens call upon their understanding of the purposes in applying the rules to unforeseen cases. No such understanding will itself yield a decision about the wasp in the car, but it will allow participants to discuss such questions and to reason their way to informed and defensible decisions concerning them. Most important here, it is difficult to see how such questions could meaningfully arise if participants had no understanding of the goals or purposes that the rules are intended to serve. The goals and purposes—that is, desirabilities—are not extrinsic to, are not dispensable accompaniments of action and interaction governed by *in* authority rules, they are among the necessary features of the latter. B cannot be guided by *in* authority rules apart from considerations of desirability in at least this sense.[18]

As one moves to less specific rules, particularly those that express basic norms of the legal system or constitution, it becomes more difficult to identify goals that are at once clearly delineated and characteristically involved in all or even most applications of particular rules. This is partly because the basic and usually less specific rules (for example, the due process rule) apply not just to a large number of cases but to an extraordinarily wide range of types of cases. In Wittgenstein's terms, they figure in a wide range of activities each of which has characteristic goals and purposes. The circumstances that make the purposes of the bus lane rule understandable—hundreds of bus passengers stalled in traffic con-

sisting primarily in motor cars with one passenger each—repeat themselves at least twice daily on thousands of streets in most large cities. By
contrast, the due process rule can come into play in a variety of ways in
any one of a vast range of activities in which governments use their
authority to regulate the conduct of citizens.

The differences, however, are of degree not of kind. Generalization
about the goals or purposes of all applications of the due process law will
of necessity be very abstract and hence will be more useful in discussions
of the ideals to which the association is devoted than in deciding what the
rule requires or forbids in particular cases. Such ideals are hardly insignificant to the workings of authority. They give the content of some of
the deeper layers or strata of the authoritative, which in turn set the
context for *in* authority rules and relationships. Nor are these the only
statements that can be made about the goals and purposes of the due
process rule. Participants in a legal system that includes this rule can
readily enough identify subclasses or types of activities to which the rule
recurrently applies. These subclasses consist in part in their characteristic
goals and purposes. The rule retains attributes it has by virtue of its
standing as a very general ideal or norm of the entire legal system, but it
also acquires characteristics distinctive to the several particular activities
in which it figures. In the United States constitutional system, for example, the due process rule has worked differently in the context of the
regulation of commercial and property relations than in the context of the
rights of defendants in criminal cases. A person capable of an informed
and defensible judgment whether the minimum wage legislation passed by
Massachusetts in the 1920s denied due process of law to factory owners
would not thereby have been able to reach such a judgment about whether
the Scottsboro Boys were denied due process of law when they were
arrested by the Alabama authorities in the same period. Neither judgment
could be made without reference to goals and purposes of the due process
rule, but the goals and purposes in question would vary significantly between the two cases. We should add that they would also vary
significantly within each type of case at different periods of time. The
widely shared understandings of the goals and purposes of the due process rule at the time of *Adkins* v. *Children's Hospital*[19] had changed
significantly by the time of *West Coast Hotel* v. *Parrish*[20]—and they have
hardly remained static since. Recognizing the place of goals and purposes
in a system of *in* authority rules does not entail acceptance of a fixed,
substantive teleology on the Aristotelian model.

Where do these considerations leave the distinction between the authority of a rule and its desirability? As noted at the outset, our objective
has not been to deny the validity or the importance of this distinction but
to improve on the manner in which it is drawn in F-P theory. In summary

formulation, our contention is that F-P theory overlooks or underestimates the several respects in which considerations of desirability are internal to framing, promulgating, identifying, and being guided by rules.

How then should the distinction be drawn? As the very formulation of this question may suggest, the question cannot be fully answered apart from normative questions concerning the place of authority in human affairs, questions that are "external" in the sense in which we introduced that term in the previous chapter. For this reason identification of the possibilities cannot be complete until we have examined the latter type of questions. We conclude the present chapter with some remarks that seem to be justified by our discussions to this juncture.

A cannot formulate or promulgate and B cannot identify, recognize, or follow *in* authority rules apart from considerations of desirability. But neither can A or B do any of these things simply or exclusively in terms of considerations of desirability. There are no *in* authority rules apart from desirabilities, but desirabilities are not sufficient to yield an *in* authority rule. However much A or B likes or dislikes, approves or disapproves of X, X can be an *in* authority rule only if it acquires the requisite formal credentials. In most practices of authority such credentials can be acquired only if X is adopted and promulgated through certain established procedures.

Once invested with authority, a rule becomes a distinctive whole or amalgam consisting in interwoven features and carrying implications and consequences not present if X is a rule without authority (say a rule of thumb), an ideal, a request, or merely a statement of A's interests or objectives. Intelligent thought and action concerning X's or proposed X's will take their distinctive characteristics into account. For example, although neither A nor B can identify or be guided by an *in* authority rule apart from considerations of desirability, it is, to say the least of the matter, open to them to give special weight to its formal credentials. Someone might strongly favor a moral, religious or prudential rule such as "Do not manufacture, sell, or consume alcoholic beverages," but altogether oppose the idea of investing such a rule with *in* authority. They could not promulgate, recognize or be guided by (including guided negatively in the sense of refusing to obey because X is an *in* authority rule) such a rule apart from considerations of desirability, because apart from such considerations they could not know *what* rule was being promulgated, recognized or followed. But given an understanding of such considerations, they could decide to promote or oppose its adoption, and to obey or disobey it if it were adopted, on grounds of its formal standing.

Let us emphasize that if one focused exclusively on the element of desirability, that is left out of account the formal-procedural elements, the idea that the rule had *in* authority would be gone. Thus the present account does not destroy the distinction between "X is a rule with *in* authority" and "X is a good rule." B must understand that considerations of desirability are internal to X, but he can recognize its authority and know what it requires of him without himself thinking it desirable or good, undesirable or evil. So far as internal considerations are concerned, B need neither agree nor disagree with the judgment that X is a good rule, he need only understand it. (This topic, however, will require further discussion below.)

These possibilities, moreover, are open to associates as the basis of general rules (albeit not *in* authority rules) of conduct. Examples of such general rules would be: "All *in* authority rules should be obeyed"; "no *in* authority rules should be obeyed"; "all *in* authority rules that are also ...should be obeyed." Such rules of conduct are commonly encountered in both practical and theoretical discussions of political authority.[21] To frame one, a person need do no more than abstract out one of the elements of the amalgam that is an *in* authority rule and make that element the basis of a decision procedure for dealing with instances of the whole. And this point brings out what (from an internal standpoint) is correct and what is misleading in the F-P distinction between authority and desirability. The F-P theory is correct in arguing that an *in* authority rule is more than an affirmation of the desirability of *X,* and largely correct both in its identification of that something more and in arguing that the latter can be isolated for purposes of certain important forms of thought and action. But the theory is seriously misleading in its contention that the formal-procedural elements are all there is to *in* authority rules as such and that it is possible to identify and subscribe to such rules in terms of such elements alone. Properly speaking, the distinction we seek is not between authority and desirability but between the formal-procedural and the substantive-purposive elements which (from an internal perspective) together make up *in* authority rules.

It may be useful to restate this conclusion in the terms in which we identified the main features of F-P theory in the previous chapter. We attributed to F-P theory a criteriological thesis about *in* authority according to (the first part of) which "*in* authority can be correctly predicated of an A or an X only if there are established rules in virtue of which A or X has authority." We further said that this thesis is "intended to exclude, as categorically irrelevant to whether A or X has authority, any and all considerations concerning the purposes, consequences, or substantive merits of the rule or arrangement, the agency or agent, that is alleged to have authority." The criteriological thesis itself is not damaged by the results of our investigations. As a capsule account of the single most distinctive characteristic of *in* authority offices and rules it is essentially correct. But the implications of the statement as intended and interpreted by leading F-P theorists are unacceptable. Considerations of purpose, consequence and substantive merit are internal to *in* authority rules and cannot be excluded from an account thereof. It follows that what we called the basic insight of F-P theory, namely (in Oakeshott's formulation), that "authority cannot be attributed to *respublica* in virtue of what can exist or be achieved only in the recognition of its authority," is true but misleading. It is true because the (first part of the) criteriological thesis is true, and it is misleading because that thesis is interpreted to exclude considerations necessary to recognition of the authority of *respublica*.[22]

One final point. Inasmuch as the foregoing considerations qualify the F-P account of rules and rule following, they also require amendment of Oakeshott's distinction between civil and enterprise association. If intentions, purposes and desirabilities are internal to *in* authority rules, no form of rule-governed association *could* exclude or be without these considerations. This conclusion follows, not from historical evidence about modern European (or any other) states, but from the logic of "rule." An "ideal character" that excluded such considerations could be formed only if it operated with a concept of "rule" (and everything that is conceptually dependent on it) altogether unrelated to the concept that we in fact have. Such a construction may or may not be conceivable, but it manifestly would not be Oakeshott's construction.

Oakeshott's distinction is nevertheless a valuable one. A word about how it might be reconstructed will form a convenient transition to the next issues on our agenda. Recall our reconstruction of the closely related distinction between rules that establish adverbial conditions and those intended directly to serve a particular substantive purpose or set of purposes. We argued that this distinction is in fact between alternative ways of characterizing a state of affairs logically eligible to be regarded as either a condition or a substantive purpose. If this construction is accepted, it follows that there is no way of knowing *a priori* how a particular formulation will in fact or should properly be viewed. There is no inventory of rules that must be exclusively viewed in one of these two ways. An X viewed by Jones as a condition at $T1$ may be viewed by him as serving a distinct substantive purpose at $T2$ and one viewed as a condition by Jones may be viewed as serving a distinct substantive purpose by Smith. A concept of civil association that is going to have roughly the role of Oakeshott's, then, must be formed in a manner consistent with at least the following considerations: (1) all rules and rule following involve considerations of purpose and desirability; (2) any rule is eligible to be regarded either as stating a condition to be maintained across the pursuit of a range of purposes or as serving a definite purpose or delimited subclass of purposes; (3) the manner in which a particular rule is regarded may change over time and circumstances and may vary from person to person.

These considerations could be accommodated by a conception of association, not implausibly called "civil," with the following features: most associates accept as particularly important certain values or ideals, possible examples of which might be respect for justice and individual rights, life under authority rather than mere power, the rule of law, and an element of stability and predictability in their relationships. Although formulated at a comparatively high level of abstraction, these ideals will not be regarded as high-flown but essentially useless phrases. Associates are able to distinguish more or less clearly between conditions that accord with them and those that do not. And they make it one of their chief purposes, a purpose to which other objectives will be sacrificed in cases of conflict, to maintain conditions that accord with these ideals.

Some at least of the ideals will be formulated as rules and the latter will be collected into a constitution of a more or less formalized sort. The rules that form the constitution are not only abstract but (comparatively speaking) general. Hence they can be applied to broad or encompassing classes of actions, to actions taken under the guidance of a number of more specific rules and in pursuit of a wide range of more limited purposes. When viewed in this perspective, the ideals-*cum*-rules of the constitution will be understood as establishing conditions to be subscribed to in making and following more specific rules and in pursuing more specific purposes. But it will always be possible to view them as describing desirable states of affairs and to urge action to maintain or renew those states of affairs. Over time or changes in person and circumstance the understanding of the ideals may change, the agreement about their importance may increase or diminish in scope or intensity, and controversy concerning them will ebb and flow.

On this construction of the concepts, the distinction between civil and enterprise association is, of course, less sharply drawn, less likely to be treated as categorial than in Oakeshott's intention. Once again, the most compelling reasons for the adjustments that we have entered stem from the fact that both types of association involve rules. In our view a further advantage of the present version of the distinction is that it renders the concept of a civil association a more useful instrument for analyzing and assessing actual human associations and their authority. One of the ways in which the amendments we have made contribute to this objective is by directing our attention to the authoritative, to beliefs and values that form part of the context in which *in* authority rules play their distinctive role.

4 The Setting of Rules and Rule Following
An External Critique of the Formal-Procedural Theory of Authority

Introduction

There are several mutually complementary ways to identify and characterize the issues taken up in this chapter. Because understanding the character of the issues is itself a considerable part of the task of a philosophical treatment of them (as opposed to a social scientific or historical analysis of them as they arise in particular times and places), we begin by noting some alternative perspectives and the relationships among them.

One of the more arresting of recent contentions about *in* authority is Hannah Arendt's argument that it has all but disappeared from the modern world. Firmly established in ancient Rome and lingering on in a weakened form in medieval Europe, in her view authority was then grounded in a set of beliefs about tradition and religion, beliefs that were not themselves questioned and that therefore provided a basis for recognition and largely unquestioning acceptance of authority. Later, however, acceptance of these beliefs eroded away. Because *in* authority depended on them, their decline left Western societies with no more than the appearance of authority. Of course there were and are constitutions, rules, procedures, insignia and credentials aplenty. But having lost their grounding in a deeply held and widely shared system of values and beliefs, with few exceptions these artifacts could only float cloudlike above the surface of politics and society, scudding hither and yon before the passing breezes of opinion and fancy.[1]

Arendt's argument amounts to the assertion of an exceedingly strong connection between the practice of *in* authority and a specific set of values and beliefs. Indeed, her argument seems to be that there is a necessary connection between *in* authority and a quite definite and complex constellation of values and beliefs about tradition and religion. This constellation is not merely one possible set of conditions in which *in* authority might take root and flourish, it is necessary to *in* authority. If and when this particular constellation of values and beliefs has disappeared, *in* authority has *thereby* disappeared as well.[2]

We permit ourselves one further characterization of Arendt's argument. On her view, an analysis of beliefs, on the ancient Roman model, about religion and tradition would not be "external" to the F-P theory of authority. There might be other beliefs or conditions that are external (in our sense) to *in* authority and theories thereof, but in Arendt's view this particular set of beliefs cannot be understood in this way. This characterization of her position invites a comparison with arguments of Oakeshott and of Friedman.

We have seen that Oakeshott is inclined to agree with Arendt's judgment that *in* authority is a less than conspicuous feature of modern European states. His explanation for this (in his view unhappy) fact, however, is radically at variance with Arendt's. Authority has been feeble and evanescent primarily because a persistent misunderstanding of what it is and is not has stood in the way of action to establish and maintain it. Indeed the explanation that Arendt has given for its health and vigor in Rome and its subsequent decline constitutes a striking instance of that very misunderstanding. So far from a necessary condition of *in* authority, shared beliefs about religion and tradition (or about anything else) are wholly irrelevant to it. Authority is what it is and not another thing. The "*only* understanding of *respublica capable* of evoking the acceptance of all of the *cives* without exception, and thus *eligible* to be recognized as the terms of civil association, is *respublica* understood in respect of its authority."[3] Search for putative foundations for authority is a distracting exercise in the irrelevant. On this view, an inquiry into the "external" conditions of authority could yield one and only one conclusion, namely that there are not and could not be any such things.

On the historical question, Richard B. Friedman offers an interpretation that suggests that both Arendt and Oakeshott could be correct; that the apparent conflict between them disappears if account is taken of changes that have taken place in the concept and practice of authority.[4] There may have been (perhaps there still are) times and places in which authority has been inseparable from certain beliefs about tradition and religion. When so understood, a breakdown of those beliefs weakened or destroyed authority as it had existed. But the occurrence of such a breakdown did not (and does not) leave those who had valued authority altogether without recourse. Seeing (perhaps welcoming) the breakup of a once stable system of beliefs, philosophers and statesmen self-consciously set about to rethink authority, to refashion it by breaking the connections between it and beliefs about tradition and religion. Realizing that those beliefs had become divisive to a destructive degree (and perhaps not holding them in any very high esteem on other grounds), they sought a conception of political association and its authority that would be viable despite diversity and conflict in respect to religion, tradition, and related matters.

And they succeeded in this endeavor: they succeeded in formulating a conception of authority that left it independent of any particular beliefs and in getting that conception accepted and established in a number of societies and associations.

Of course if we accepted Arendt's essentialist analysis of what authority was, we would have to agree with her judgment that authority, or perhaps genuine or true or real authority, had disappeared. Similarly, if we accepted Oakeshott's equally essentialist analysis of what (genuine, true, or real) authority is and is not (and also accepted Arendt's account of Roman history), we would be forced to say that no authority had existed prior to the development that Friedman describes. On Oakeshott's view, it was only when systems of rules and offices achieved independence from beliefs and values that genuine authority developed. The merits of talking in either of these two ways will concern us momentarily. But describing the situation as we have just done has at least one salutary effect, namely making it clear that the issue between Arendt and Oakeshott is an issue about how to use the concept of authority.

The reconstructed conception of authority that Friedman describes is of course formal-procedural in character. But Friedman's version of F-P theory differs from Oakeshott's in a respect material to our present concerns. The difference centers on what we earlier called the second thesis of F-P theory, the thesis about the "point" or the "that for which" of a practice of *in* authority. The "point" of such a practice, Friedman argues, is to be understood in terms of the "predicament" it was (is) designed to remedy. That predicament consists exactly in the recurrence of intractable and conflictogenic disagreement over "substantive" questions, over questions concerning religion, tradition, justice, economic distributions, and so forth. The predicament is remedied by turning such issues over to the persons who occupy offices invested with *in* authority and agreeing to accept their resolutions—agreeing to accept those resolutions regardless of one's judgment of their merits.

If successful, this maneuver might indeed reduce the dependence of *in* authority on the shared beliefs which, on Arendt's analysis, had once sustained it. But it manifestly cannot altogether eliminate such dependence. To mention only the points closest to the surface of Friedman's argument, such a practice of *in* authority certainly depends on there being a widely shared belief that the condition of being without *in* authority constitutes a predicament. If associates or potential associates relish the disagreement, conflict, danger and so forth that breakdown of the "Roman," "medieval" or any other belief system had set loose, no authority could develop or be sustained. Or if they think, as the Fox Indians apparently did and as anarchists claim to do, that establishing *in* authority would produce a worse predicament than the one they are in, authority will be impossible. In short, the notion of authority having a "point" brings along with it the necessity of some set of values and beliefs in terms of which that point is defined and can be acted upon.

Oakeshott's position is clearly untenable—untenable not only as a possible analysis of historical systems of *in* authority but also as an ideal character. We have already seen ways in which use of *in* authority rules necessarily brings into play factors such as intentions, purposes, and desirabilities. And we have seen that in any given system of *in* authority some intentions, some purposes, some desired objectives will be internal to thought and action concerning *in* authority (for example, those that go into the choice, promulgation, and recognition of *in* authority rules). But the concepts "intention" and "purpose" as such are manifestly not internal to authority in this sense. They are concepts that operate throughout the ordinary language of a society, not merely in particular practices or activities. And this is only one of a host of ways in which civil association—as with any form of human association—presupposes a language and a variety of beliefs shared among associates.

Much of this language and many of these beliefs, of course, will be so distant from *in* authority that calling attention to them will do little if anything to add to our understanding of it. The general question that arises here, the question of the light that the philosophy of language and the sociology of belief might shed on the theory of authority, must be considered below. But there is a rather more specific point about language that bears directly on Oakeshott's attempt to treat civil association as *sui generis* and autonomous. "Civil" association is comprehensible only as a species of the genus "human association." Its features are distinctive by comparison with other species of that genus. (Recall that Oakeshott's own exposition of civil association is consistently by contrast with "enterprise" association.) Thus any person who understands the concept of a civil association also understands the concept of at least some other species of human association. It might be argued that thus far such an understanding need presuppose nothing more by way of beliefs than those that go along with knowing the language of which these concepts of association are a part. But notice that the conceptions in question are put forward as objects of choice, as forms of association among which associates could in principle choose as modes of organizing their lives. Certainly no reader of Oakeshott's book can fail to see that he believes civil association to be vastly preferable to enterprise association as a mode of organization for the state (albeit not for the many activities that take place under conditions established by virtue of the existence of the state). A form of association can be an object of choice only if there are grounds on which such a choice could be made, grounds on which to make the judgment that it is preferable to other modes of association.

Despite his animadversions against the very idea of such a ground, Oakeshott himself proffers one when he observes that rule-governed association on the civil model is distinctively valuable because it "abates contingency."[5] If one believed this (and it is a proposition that is logically a proper subject of belief or disbelief), and if one also believed that abating contingency is one of the things that an association should do, then one would be in a position to prefer civil association over other modes that lack this virtue.

At least two related points should be emphasized about the proposition that civil association abates contingency. First, neither the proposition nor belief in it has any necessary connection with the concept of a civil association. Abating contingency is something that civil association is said to do; it is a result that such association is said to bring about. The concept of a civil association (and, no doubt, numerous of the virtues manifested by adequate subscription to it) is perfectly intelligible without reference to this among its alleged consequences. (If one is thinking of causality in Humean terms, it is a condition of saying that civil association abates contingency that this be so.) Second, any one of a large number of other propositions could serve just as well as a ground for preferring (or rejecting) civil association. There must be some values and beliefs that provide grounds for preferring civil association, but no particular set of values and beliefs is necessary for this purpose.

The last two considerations also point to the difficulty with Arendt's argument. She is correct that *in* authority requires values and beliefs that provide grounds for preferring forms of association that include *in* authority over those that do not and for preferring some particular version of those forms that include it. She may also be correct in her historical thesis that certain beliefs about tradition and religion in fact played such a role in ancient Rome. But it is implausible in the extreme that those particular beliefs are a necessary condition of any and all systems of *in* authority. The experience of one society (or the writings of one theorist) does not legislate to all future practice. The writ of no *in* or *an* authority runs so far.

There is a good deal to be said for Friedman's position in this regard. Whatever may have been the case in ancient Rome, *in* authority as we now experience it in numerous societies and associations has a salient formal-procedural dimension. The rules that constitute this "dimension" are not simply beliefs or expressions of values. Thus there is room for and a point to the distinctions between *in* authority and the authoritative and between internal and external elements in theories concerning authority. At the same time, practices of *in* authority do require values and beliefs in terms of which authority can be preferred over alternative arrangements. It may be that certain specific sets of values and beliefs have in fact frequently played this role or have in fact proved to be particularly effective in playing it. Comparative historical and social scientific inquiry might support empirical generalizations of this sort. Such generalizations might also form part of a prescriptive theory as to how *in* authority should be structured, limited, and so forth. But these could only (!) be theories of what authority has been, is, or should be, not theories of what it must be or could not be.

Taken in its formal character, something like Arendt's view has been at least implicit in a considerable number of theories of authority. This is hardly surprising. According to the present analysis, at any given time and place *in* authority is connected in various important ways to values and beliefs that have a standing and play a role analogous to beliefs about tradition and religion among the ancient Romans. Thus when someone sets out to theorize about authority, the substantive values and beliefs with which it has been connected in the theorist's experience are likely to enter into the theory he or she constructs. This process will be visibly at work in our own justificatory theory of authority in part 2. In this perspective Arendt's argument is distinctive mainly in its explicit insistence that there is genuine authority *only* where there is the *particular* constellation of substantive beliefs that she found to have been characteristic of a society far removed from her direct (as opposed to vicarious) experience. These features of her argument are largely responsible for its arresting and paradoxical appearance. But they do not alter the fact that hers is an account of authority at a particular time and place and could be accorded a more general standing only on the basis of studies showing that authority was tied to the same substantive beliefs at other times and places.

If correct, these contentions are important because they rule out an entirely general, all-encompassing theory of authority as opposed to an analysis of this or that, these or those, instances of practices of authority. A practice of authority cannot be fully understood apart from its connections with substantive values and beliefs, but the values and beliefs with which practices have been connected have in fact varied over time and place, and there is nothing to prevent them from continuing to do so. If a theory of what authority is and is not must be entirely general, such a theory is impossible. Attempts to escape this difficulty—for example, Oakeshott's—achieve such appearance of success as they may enjoy by a combination of conceptual fiat and refusal to give attention to the range of values and beliefs that their own stipulations about "authority" presuppose.

(In addition to excluding essentialist theories, this conclusion also implies the implausibility [though not the impossibility] of constructing a perfectly general normative theory of authority, a theory that states in general but substantive terms the conditions under which *in* authority would best be established. Such a project—including versions aiming to show that all forms of *in* authority are unjustifiable—is implausible because it involves prescribing a value and belief system without any reference to the conditions under which the values and beliefs are to be held.)

In more prosaic terms, our reasoning thus far about the authoritative implies that there is an inescapable historical or empirical—and hence limiting—dimension to theorizing about it and its relationships to *in* authority. Given the "craving for generality" evident in the literature on the topic, this is not an insignificant conclusion.[6]

Our reasoning does not imply, however, that the study of authority and the authoritative must or even could be entirely restricted to analyzing particular cases. Picking out cases for study, to begin with, requires criteria of selection—criteria that distinguish instances of authority and the authoritative from other things. These criteria, these conceptualizations, are not given by timeless platonic forms that we know independent of our familiarity with concepts having or having had an established use in historical languages and societies. What has counted as an instance of (what in English is termed) authority has undoubtedly changed over time and place and—as some of the continuing controversies in the theory of authority suggest—is by no means entirely agreed at the present time. Thus, in addition to eschewing the sort of grandiose essentialism of Arendt and Oakeshott, caution is appropriate in positing—as for example Joseph Raz does—a "non-relativized" notion of authority that is a presupposition of the "relativized" notions we in fact find among this or that historical people.[7]

We are not, however, making the first known inquiries into societies that have little knowledge of one another and that have exercised little or no influence on one another's conceptualizations and practices. There is an abundance of evidence, provided and interpreted by actors and theorists with an understanding of more than one conceptual scheme, that something very much like the contemporary English language notion of authority has been or is now part of the conceptual schemas of a great many societies and peoples. In addition, historians and other students of human experience have taught us a good deal about the processes of mutual influence through which the considerable commonalities among instances of that concept have been produced and sustained. If we are sensitive to interesting variations and alert to the possibility of counterexamples (which is what the "caution" urged above properly consists in), we have the wherewithal for a conceptual analysis that lays a reasonable claim to generality.

Are we in a comparable position in respect to the content of the authoritative? Can we generalize responsibly about the beliefs and values that provide the setting we contend is necessary to a practice of authority? Although we have rejected the substance of Arendt's generalizations, reflection on her argument in this regard suggests that we may be able to identify kinds or families of beliefs and values which, in varying formulations and combinations, have in fact been widely shared in most societies that have included a practice of authority. It is wrong to say that the ancient Roman beliefs about religion and tradition are a necessary condition of a practice of authority. But perhaps beliefs of this *kind*, beliefs of some sort about religion and tradition, about the sacred versus the profane, the traditional versus the merely historical, have been and are regularly and importantly connected with *in* authority. (We may note, by way of giving initial plausibility to this speculation, that theorists such as Hobbes and Locke, who were important in effecting the transition Friedman has analyzed, felt obliged to deal explicitly and at length with issues about religion and tradition.) We explore some possibilties of this sort in the remainder of this chapter. Even if these explorations do not yield defensible generalizations about the content of the authoritative, they may help to clarify the standing of that notion in analyzing rule-governed practices such as the practice of authority.

Authority and Shared Language

The first possibility we explore is that shared language is itself a part of the authoritative as we are using that concept. It is clear that the participants in a practice of authority must share a language.[8] A shared language consists in, among other things, semantic and syntactic rules that are known to and on the whole followed by those who speak it. Few if any of these rules are or ever were promulgated by anything like *in* authority, but it might be said that they have authoritative standing for the speakers, and it can certainly be said that there are *an* authorities concerning them. If it is useful to use the concepts "authority" and "authoritative" in respect to language, the most plausible applications would be in contexts of language learning. Children learn the correct and incorrect uses of the language they are acquiring from persons who already have a command of them and whose performances and explicit instructions are only rarely questioned or subject to question. This process, moreover, may be one of the important ways in which children become familiar with and accept the idea of rules and other norms that are authoritative and the idea that there are persons who are *in* and *an* authorities. Because learning a language is an integral part of learning other things, the process is also part of the child's introduction to and acceptance of other dimensions of authority and the authoritative in his society.

A number of social theorists, particularly those who make up the school of thought sometimes called symbolic interactionism, have elaborated upon and generalized from these ideas.[9] They have hypothesized that beliefs about language are a necessary (or at least an invariable) part of the authoritative in all societies that sustain a practice of *in* authority. Whatever may be the case with beliefs about religion and tradition on the Roman model, authoritative beliefs about language are a necessary condition of a practice of *in* authority. Although not without foundation or interest, two substantial reservations must immediately be entered concerning these reflections. First, acceptance of the beliefs about language discussed above is a condition not only of *in* authority but of virtually every feature of social life. Any enlightenment to be gained from studying these beliefs will not be specific to questions about *in* authority. Moreover, even if necessary to *in* authority, wide acceptance of these beliefs does not guarantee the viability or even the existence of such authority. Many persons—indeed, whole peoples—have accepted such beliefs and yet firmly rejected the further idea of *in* authority.

The second reservation is conceptually more complex and important. It concerns the criteria that distinguish "belief" and "knowledge" from various related phenomena and hence (assuming "belief," "knowledge," and "authority" to be connected) the criteria of the proper use of "authority." At least since Plato, thinkers in the Western philosophical tradition have distinguished belief from knowledge in terms of the quality of the evidence or reasoning that is necessary to support each. "Belief," as with the epistemologically yet weaker term "opinion," is used to denote less certain grounding than "knowledge." In this usage, however, "belief" and "knowledge" share an active psychological component. Holders of a belief and possessors of knowledge must be more or less conscious of, even self-conscious about, their acceptance of the propositions of which the belief or knowledge consists. Also, both concepts imply that acceptance of the propositions is grounded, albeity differently so, in evidence or reason and can and should be given up if the latter are shown to be inadequate.

In this respect belief and knowledge should be distinguished from psychological states of which the agent has little or no active, critical awareness or self-consciousness and to which the notion of supporting evidence or reasoning is in fact rarely if ever applied. Do I know or believe that sugar has a sweet taste? That the conjunction "and" is spelled *a-n-d*? That I have two hands? These propositions are eligible subjects of knowledge and belief because there are criteria by which their correctness or incorrectness, plausibility or implausibility, could be tested and established or disestablished. But though we can imagine unusual circumstances in which such testing would in fact be performed, in the ordinary course of events our "acceptance" of the propositions (if even that term is not misleading) is indicated primarily if not exclusively by the ways we behave. We reach for the sugar bowl to sweeten coffee, purchase gloves by the pair, and spell the conjunction in the usual way without, as we sometimes say, "giving so much as a thought" to doing so. In this respect the standing of these propositions can be contrasted with such assertions as "Abortion is murder," "The United States ought to withdraw from the United Nations," and "The evidence obtained from the experiments of the Viking project show that there is life on Mars."

The first question, then, is whether propositions about shared language should be regarded as the subjects of knowledge or belief. Several considerations support this view of them. First, they may be shown to be correct or incorrect, plausible or implausible. Second, they are taught, sometimes in explicit ways, to children and to adults learning languages other than those native to them. Third, individual speakers do sometimes question and seek to alter them, and such efforts prompt controversies that cannot be settled without self-conscious, reflective attention to them and their standing. Fourth, they are the subjects of critical study and theorizing by linguists and philosophers of language and meaning. These several considerations show that the propositions are not innate or the results of conditioning on a Pavlovian model. It is possible for them to become objects of active concern such that it is no longer misleading to say of them that they are known or believed.

Against the view that they make up knowledge and beliefs, however, is the consideration that these propositions ordinarily play their role in human behavior in a largely unselfconscious, unreflective manner. Although taught and learned, not simply insinuated and ingested, mastering them typically leads to a degree of what might be called internalization that takes the propositions out of the realm of continuing, active acceptance, belief or knowledge. Their standing might be likened to what Wittgenstein called "general facts of nature"; though important, they are "hardly ever mentioned because of their great generality."[10]

If or insofar as this latter view of most rules of language is correct, there are serious difficulties about treating such rules as part of *in* authority or the authoritative. These latter notions, we suggest, presuppose a degree of self-conscious and reflective acceptance or rejection on the part of those who participate in the practices of which they are part. To say that X has authority or is authoritative for B ordinarily implies that B is aware of the claim and consciously accepts or rejects it. A person's circumstances and behavior can be affected by force or some set of conditions without his being aware of them or their influence upon him. This cannot be true of authority or the authoritative. Authority is not a species of force that causes people to behave in a certain way. It is, rather, a *reason for* thinking or acting in a certain way. If the X in question is presented as a law or command, this claim about it—that is the claim that it has authority for B—is a reason for B doing or refusing to do what X requires. If the X is a proposition to be accepted as true or plausible, the claim that it stems from an *an* authority or that it is authoritative in B's association is a reason for B to accept it or at least to accord it respectful consideration (or for refusing to do these things). B cannot do these things without being aware of X and giving more or less reflective attention to it, and hence an X cannot be authoritative or have authority for B if B is unaware of it.[11] Thus if it is true that shared language, its rules, and the beliefs about them are "hardly ever mentioned," it is at least misleading to treat them as part of *in* authority or the authoritative. They are better regarded as a background condition of the latter, a condition that may sometimes become a matter of explicit concern and hence rise to the level of the authoritative or of authority.

There is, however, a further point to be considered about shared language and its relation to authority. It is wrong to say unqualifiedly that beliefs about shared language as such are part of authority and the authoritative (and hence wrong to say that there is authority or the authoritative wherever there are beliefs about shared language). But there is a better case for thinking that certain elements or aspects of shared language are (1) necessary to *in* authority and (2) deserving of designation as part of the authoritative. From the standpoint of the former, among the most obvious candidates are the concept "authority" itself and such intimately connected concepts as "legitimate" and "legitimacy," "obligation" and "rule." It would be difficult to give sense to the claim that a society or association included authority if its members lacked the concept (the concept, not the word) "authority," and it would be equally difficult to give sense to the claim that they had "authority" if they lacked "rule," "obligation," a distinction between "legitimate" and "nonlegitimate," and other concepts in terms of which the notion of authority is ordinarily understood. If there is a problem about this thesis, it is that it is rather a truism (which is not to say that all languages include or must include these concepts or that all societies and associations include or must include authority).

It would be more controversial, however, to argue that even these concepts deserve to be treated as part of the authoritative; it is not obvious that they escape the difficulty involved in treating shared language as part of the authoritative. A number of theorists have in effect contended that "authority," "obligation," "rule" and so forth are paradigm cases of elements of ordinary language that are ingested and responded to in an unselfconscious, unreflective, and certainly uncritical manner. Some have celebrated this (alleged) circumstance, arguing that it is only when the mere appearance of authority triggers unquestioning, matter-of-course behaviors on the part of most participants that a society or association can be tolerably stable. If this is the way participants respond to authority, it is unlikely in the extreme that they respond critically to "authority" and the rules governing its use. Other theorists have conceded that authority often stimulates such responses but have deplored the fact. They have contended that it is this very feature of "authority" and the concepts connected with it that renders them incompatible with free, rational, and moral conduct.[12]

We have suggested a reason for thinking that *authority* cannot stimulate unreflective responses. If it is true that "authority," "obligation," "rule," and "legitimate" give reasons for or against actions, then it is implausible to think that these concepts are used or responded to in an unselfconscious, habitual manner. But it might be argued that this line of reasoning overlooks the distinction just alluded to, namely, between the manner in which agents accept the linguistic rules governing the concepts and the manner in which those agents act when presented with rules and commands cast in those concepts. Perhaps such applications of "authority" as "X has the authority of law and you ought to respect it" always involve an element of awareness and reflection, whereas semantic rules such as " 'X has authority for A' implies that A has obligations in respect to X" and " 'X has authority' presupposes an established rule by virtue of which X acquired authority" have been completely internalized and are followed with no more reflection than goes into spelling the conjunction "and." If (or insofar as) this is the case, it would be misleading to treat the presence of the concepts we are discussing in a shared language as making up part of the authoritative. They would have to be treated as a "background condition" of authority and the authoritative.

As noted above, we can imagine circumstances in which just about any linguistic rule might become a subject of conscious attention and perhaps controversy. Even apparently innocuous rules of orthography have become objects of contention where alternative languages or dialects are points of competition and conflict. For the most part, however, linguistic rules remain " a matter of course." And if they do attract attention, it is likely to be as counters in or symbols of some political, cultural, or perhaps religious dispute, not in their own right.

But "authority" seems to be an example of a perhaps small but important class of concepts in which the linguistic rules themselves have controversial implications and (when followed) consequences of a more than linguistic character. The linguistic rules governing the concept of "a right," to take an example related to "authority," themselves carry substantial and controversial implications concerning interactions that take place in terms of this concept, so much so that a number of political actors and theorists have felt that the very concept should be expunged from our political vocabularies.[13] "Authority" has generated similar reactions. For some anarchist theorists the idea that language and other social arrangements should include an attribute that itself entails obligations is altogether unacceptable. Because this idea is part of the rules governing the concept itself, these theorists have felt that the concept must be scrapped.

Owing, then, to the implications they carry for both speaker and auditor, in the case of concepts such as "a right" and "authority" there is reason to expect a more widespread and more intense awareness of linguistic rules. If this expectation is realized, and the concepts are part of the shared language of a society, then the concepts and the rules that govern them form part of the authoritative in that society or association. Given that these two conditions are in fact widely satisfied, this is an element of the authoritative which, if not invariably connected with *in* authority, is regularly and importantly associated with it. This is perhaps as close as we can come to an unqualified generalization about the content of the authoritative.

Authority and Rules

The second possibility that we explore concerns the notion of a rule and the belief that rules are a desirable or at least an acceptable feature of the life of a society. If *in* authority always involves rules, it follows that it always involves values and beliefs according to which rules are an acceptable device for arranging and conducting at least some dimensions of social life. Thus values and beliefs about rules would appear to be a promising source of generalizations about the substance of the authoritative. Here again, however, we meet with a number of complications, some of which are analogous to those we encountered in discussing shared language.

There are a number of different types of rules; we ignore the distinctions among them at the risk of confusion or worse. For present purposes we restrict our attention to four common types that we will label, respectively, (1) instructions, (2) precepts, (3) regulations, and (4) authorizations. Instructions offer nonobligatory guidance or advice as to how best to achieve an objective that is adopted or not at the discretion of the agent to whom the advice is given. "*If* you want to strengthen you triceps, do thirty push-ups every day" would be an example of a rule of this type. Precepts are typically in the imperative rather than the conditional mood. They require or forbid actions that are thought right or wrong, good or bad, and they do not leave the agent at liberty to reject the rule by disavowing the objectives the rule serves. "Respect the rights of others!" and "Promises should be kept!" are representative examples. Regulations are like precepts in that they carry obligations, but differ from them in that they issue from some established *in* authority and are commonly enforced by that authority. Authorizations also presuppose *in* authority; but rather than require or forbid this or that class of actions, they authorize or permit an action on the part of a designated agent or class of agents.[14]

Merely listing these distinctions is enough to show why assertions about rules in general are not likely to be terribly enlightening. The distinctions are clear enough—and the differences they mark important enough—to show that favorable beliefs about one type of rule need not carry over to the others and indeed that beliefs and attitudes are likely to reflect the important differences among the types. Someone might be quite comfortable with instruction or precept-type rules that have evolved out of experience and yet emphatically reject authorizations and regulations that are adopted and enforced by designated agents with *in* authority. Accounts of a number of "primitive" societies suggest that such a pattern of beliefs has been common in them, and it certainly has been the view of anarchist thinkers such as Kropotkin, Thoreau, and Proudhon. Again, a person might be prepared to accept regulations and authorizations in his church, corporation, or civil defense brigade but strenuously resist them in his political party, neighborhood improvement association or fraternal organization.

If we are correct that reactions to rules are differentiated in these ways, it seems probable that there will be consciously and critically held beliefs about them. It is implausible to think that these differences result from or are sustained by an unreflective and undifferentiated disposition to accept or to reject rules "as such." Rather, one would expect the differences to reflect the ways in which substantial numbers of people think and act in respect to rules; their decision to have recourse to this rather than that type of rule in various kinds of situations in which rules seem appropriate to them, their choice of the content of the rules they adopt, their interpretation and application of the rules they have adopted, and so forth. Some generalized disposition to accept rules may lie in the background of these more differentiated choices and actions, but focusing on it will not teach us much about rules and rule-governed conduct.[15]

So far as the presence of active, consciously held values and beliefs is a criterion of the authoritative, then, there is reason to include prominent aspects of thought and action concerning rules in this category. But the considerations that support this conclusion also suggest definite limitations on the possibility of generalizing about the content of this aspect of the authoritative. Preferences for this rather than that type of rule are likely to form a part of a larger set of beliefs that develop out of and must be understood in the context of particular historical circumstances.

Of course we can say that *in* authority presupposes authorizations and almost certainly involves regulations. Hence we can also say that practices involving this type of authority presuppose reasonably wide acceptance of the belief that rules of these types are desirable or at least acceptable. But this generalization is nothing more than an elaboration on what is involved in the concepts that distinguish authority. It is so obvious that such beliefs are presupposed by *in* authority that, while the fact itself is by no means insignificant, drawing attention to it takes such theoretical significance as it has from the circumstance that theorists of authority sometimes overlook or deny it.

Much more significant are the reasons these beliefs are accepted or not and the ways they have connected with a variety of other beliefs that have made up the authoritative in societies and associations that have included *in* authority. A number of theorists of authority claim to have identified recurrent patterns in this regard. Oakeshott and other F-P theorists, for example, although eschewing the notion of shared beliefs, have argued that acceptance of authorizations and regulations has been associated with the distinction between form and substance, between substantive purposes and the formally defined conditions under which those purposes are pursued. Belief in the importance of such conditions of action, they argue, is essential if associates are to be prepared to respect authorizations and obey regulations despite disagreeing with their content. This argument is persuasive because authority does depend on some degree of willingness to subordinate transient and idiosyncratic purposes to continuing and general procedures and forms. But the willingness to do so can rest on quite diverse considerations and support radically different systems of *in* authority. Members of the Roman Catholic church and the Communist party of the Soviet Union, the Quakers and the French Radical Socialists, have displayed such willingness to a degree sufficient to support some measure of *in* authority in their associations. But members of the former pair of associations seem to do so because they believe that procedural devices such as hierarchy, centralization and a quite sharply defined division of labor accord with their religious and political dogmas and best serve their religious and political purposes; members of the latter pair take virtually the opposite view and employ these devices minimally or not at all. There is *in* authority in both pairs of associations, but its scope and significance varies importantly between them. Similarly, any number of parliaments, legislatures, councils and assemblies accord the standing of authority to procedural devices such as rules of order and to offices such as speaker, chairman, and parliamentarian and it is part of the authoritative among them that these devices be respected. But no knowledgeable person would argue that these devices work in the same way in all such bodies or would deny that the differences in the way they work are largely a result of values and beliefs that have achieved authoritative standing concerning the devices and offices.

Concluding Remarks

Acceptance of certain features of shared language and of authorization-type rules is necessary to any practice of *in* authority, and it is a plausible generalization that acceptance of regulation-, instruction-, and precept-type rules commonly accompanies such practices. Acceptance of these features of language and of these types of rules, moreover, is likely to be active, self-conscious, and critical. Hence we can treat it as reflecting values and beliefs that are part of the authoritative.

In denying the relevance of these beliefs to *in* authority, F-P theory blinds us to salient features of known systems of *in* authority and renders its account of the concept of *in* authority seriously incomplete. It would appear that there is no such thing as a practice of *in* authority apart from values and beliefs of these kinds.

Putting the matter this way, however, requires that we give further attention to the distinctions between "internal" and "external" questions about F-P theory and between authority and the authoritative. If the beliefs (not the background conditions) we have been discussing are invariable features of a practice of *in* authority, it would seem to follow that they must be internal to any theory of such authority. If so, it would also follow that the distinction between authority and the authoritative would have no application to these beliefs. Both of these contentions are true of such values and beliefs in what we might call their formal character, that is as *kinds* or *types* of values and beliefs—as values and beliefs that support the acceptance of certain concepts and certain types of rules. But the contentions are not true about the substantive character of such values and beliefs in any of their instantiations. That is, the contentions are not true concerning the specifics of the grounds on which associates accept the concepts and the types of rules in question.

It may be that in certain known practices of authority a cohesive and consciously held set of values and beliefs about these concepts and types of rules has been so closely and importantly connected with *in* authority as to justify treating it as a constitutive feature of authority as it presents itself to us at given moments or stretches of time. This is Arendt's contention about the Roman case. Even where such a situation exists, however, the content of the values and beliefs is liable to change. And such change, although certainly altering the practice of authority, would not necessarily betoken its disappearance.

Let us assume for purposes of argument that there is a practice of *in* authority in the Soviet Union and that the values and beliefs which make up Marxism-Leninism are now among the constitutive features of that practice. If so, a widespread rejection of Marxism-Leninism by Soviet officials and subjects would surely work important changes in the practice of authority among them. Is there any reason to think that it would necessarily destroy the practice of authority among them? The answer depends on what takes the place of Marxism-Leninism. If the result is a kind of axiological void—say an extreme form of anomie or widespread skepticism or nihilism—then according to our argument the practice of authority would indeed disappear. It would disappear because there would be no set of authoritative values and beliefs to sustain it. Equally, of course, authority would disappear if Marxism-Leninism were supplanted by widespread acceptance of some species of anarchism. In this case authority would disappear because it would be judged incompatible with authoritative values and beliefs.

Imagine, however, that the erosion and final rejection of Marxism-Leninism were accompanied by acceptance of, say, the doctrines of Sun Myung Moon of Korea. Historians of the Soviet Union would presumably treat the change as a transformation of revolutionary proportions. But given that the values and beliefs that make up Sun Myung Moon's doctrines are hospitable to concepts such as authority and legitimacy, and to regulation and other types of rules, historians would not treat the change as ending the practice of authority in the Soviet Union. Or rather, they would do so only if they had made the essentialist's error of confusing the necessity of some set of authoritative values and beliefs that support authority with the necessity of a particular, substantive set of authoritative values and beliefs.

Of course, most societies and associations, including many that have established any operative practices of *in* authority, do not display anything approaching a monolithic belief and value system. Most of the citizens of the United Kingdom, the Netherlands, the United States and Canada, most members of the British Medical Association, the Social Credit Party, the Netherlands Trade Association, and so on, share a good deal more than the view that authorization-type rules have a proper place in their affairs. Knowledgeable students of the values and beliefs—and indeed the broader traditions, political cultures, national characters, shared ideologies or what have you of these societies and associations—are able to defend certain generalizations concerning them. So much would be implied by, would be a condition of, the claim that there is something that can be called the authoritative among them. As we argued in chapter 1, however, and as most students who employ the broader but related concepts just mentioned would agree about their favored conceptualizations, the concept "the authoritative" does not imply unanimity or entire homogeneity, does not require the complete absence of disagreement and conflict concerning the values and beliefs prominent in the authoritative. Regional, ethnic, class, occupational, age, party, interest group, religious, elite and nonelite, and other familiar divisions (to say nothing of just plain individual differences) may extend to the substantive aspects of the values and beliefs that make up the authoritative. They may do so without so weakening its acceptance as to make *in* authority unworkable. No doubt F-P theorists are correct in arguing that there is very little likelihood of a single set of consciously held, cohesive values and beliefs that are accepted by all of the members of modern states (or even by all of the members of the larger and more prominent substate associations). For this and other reasons these same theorists are correct in arguing that *in* authority cannot be defined in terms of the presence of a particular set of such values and beliefs. But they err in ignoring (at least for the purpose of analyzing what *in* authority is and is not) the possibility—or rather the reality—of a web of overlapping, sometimes conflicting, sometimes complementary and mutually reinforcing values and beliefs that inform, influence, and, to varying degrees in various situations, support *in* authority.[16]

One further point deserves emphasis by way both of summation of what we have been arguing and by way of anticipating the significance of that argument for questions about individual freedom, rationality and morality in a practice of authority. Crucial to these normative issues are the questions whether, to what extent and under what conditions assessment of the substantive merits of A's and X's is possible and appropriate. Such assessments will be possible (we take up the matter of their appropriateness in the next two chapters and in part 2) only if associates have available the criteria and the other sorts of materials for reflection that are necessary to making an assessment. In contending that the authoritative is a part of every practice of *in* authority, we are in effect arguing that such materials are available to the B's in every practice of authority. In addition to conditions that have the standing of "general facts of nature," A's authority depends upon a set of rules that cannot be called into question without thereby denying that authority. Acceptance of those rules, in turn, is supported by a wider set of actively held values and beliefs that are more or less widely shared among the B's. If all or even the most important of those values and beliefs are rejected (and not replaced) by the B's, *in* authority will disappear—an event by no means unknown in the troubled history of *in* authority. But the event has not been restricted to cases in which all of the B's entirely reject the idea of *in* authority (become philosophical anarchists). More common have been instances in which a significant proportion of the B's have become convinced that *in* authority had ceased to work consonant with the broader set of values and beliefs on which its acceptance was based—and hence, acting on those values and beliefs, put a partly or even a largely new practice of *in* authority in its place. Most common, perhaps, are cases in which the B's generally support a practice of *in* authority because that practice accords with values and beliefs that are authoritative among them—while at the same time referring to those values and beliefs in assessing the performances of the A's and the merits of the X's. However badly such thought and action accords with essentialist definitions of authority or ideal-typical models of human association, it is commonplace in the societies and associations that include *in* authority. The notion of the authoritative, referring to a body of widely shared values and beliefs standing (as it were) between "general facts of nature" and more transient interests and desires, objectives and purposes, is intended to contribute to the theory of authority by helping to make this commonplace comprehensible. It is intended to accommodate the fact that such conduct presupposes criteria of relevance and judgment which connect with but are not reducible to the rules that establish and define *in* authority, and also accommodate the historical fact that these criteria have varied significantly from one practice of *in* authority to the next and from time to time in any given practice of *in* authority.

5 Authority and the "Surrender" of Individual Judgment

There has been a remarkable coalescence of opinion around the proposition that authority and authority relations involve some species of "surrender of judgment" on the part of those who accept, submit or subscribe to the authority of persons or a set of rules and offices. From anarchist opponents of authority such as William Godwin and Robert Paul Wolff through moderate supporters such as John Rawls and Joseph Raz and on to enthusiasts such as Hobbes, Hannah Arendt, and Michael Oakeshott, a considerable chorus of students have echoed the refrain that the directives that are standard and salient features of practices of authority are to be obeyed by B irrespective of B's judgments of their merits. As Richard B. Friedman puts the matter, B does not and cannot "make his obedience conditional on his . . . personal examination of the thing he is being asked to do. Rather, he accepts as a sufficient condition for following a prescription the fact that it is prescribed by someone acknowledged by him as entitled to rule. The man who accepts authority . . . surrender[s] his . . . individual judgment . . . [in that] he does not insist that reasons be given that he can grasp and that satisfy him, as a condition of his obedience."[1] Joseph Raz presents a more complex analysis that treats rules with authority as themselves giving B reasons for action that he can grasp and that (should) satisfy him. But Raz nevertheless accepts a notion of surrender of judgment in that he contends that the reasons given by X itself ordinarily exclude consideration of possible competing reasons for action. Indeed he makes this notion of "exclusionary reasons" the defining feature of *in* authority.[2]

Those comparatively few writers who have dissented from this proposition, for example, neo-Thomists such as Yves Simon and rationalists such as Carl Friedrich,[3] have been dismissed as not understanding the difference between authority and authority relations on the one hand, and advice, counsel and reasoned exchange and argumentation on the other.

Because they are so central to the notion of A or X having authority for or over B, the questions that come together under the rubric of "surrender of judgment" are crucial to the analysis of what authority is and is not. They are also at the heart of the normative theory of authority. Numerous writers contend that this feature of *in* authority should be crucial to our judgments concerning its merits as a feature of political life. From Hobbes to Oakeshott, F-P theorists have insisted that "surrender of judgment" allows political societies to order and regulate social life in the face of disagreement over substantive issues and the merits of actions and policies. In respect to *an* authority, it has of course frequently been argued that "surrendering" judgment to the wiser, the better informed and the more skillful is good or right (Plato went so far as to make doing so a part of justice) because it leads to true beliefs and correct decisions and actions. Even deeply antiplatonic thinkers, for example utilitarians such as J. S. Mill and especially George Cornewall Lewis, have contended that such "surrender" to *an* authorities is rational because of the great increase in efficiency that it introduces into human affairs.[4] On the other hand, opponents of authority have always argued that this very feature of it necessarily destroys the moral integrity of the B's, thereby rendering all forms of authority intolerable.

In our judgment the normative views just referred to are exaggerations if not outright errors; the salient issues about justifying authority cannot be resolved, positively or negatively, in terms of this alone among its alleged characteristics. But our judgment in this respect depends upon rejecting interpretations of "surrender of judgment" that have been shared among most opponents and proponents of authority; defending the judgment requires an alternative analysis of the place of B's judgments and action on his judgments in the practice of authority. In at least this sense normative questions will be very much before us in this and the following chapter.

Authority and the Notions "By Right" and "Rightfully"
In Authority

The thesis that *in* authority always involves some species of "surrender of judgment" on the part of the B's is perhaps most difficult to dispute in situations in which there is some person (A) who occupies an office and promulgates, interprets or applies a rule (X) to, for, or against B's who are in the jurisdiction of that office. In this type of case some form of "surrender" of or at least limitation on judgment on B's part seems to be indicated by one of the basic dictionary meanings of the term "authority." "Done by authority" means "rightful" or "done by right." Anyone who accepts the proposition that A has authority in doing X thereby concedes a sense in which X was done rightfully or by right. B cannot cogently concede the authority of X and yet continue to reserve judgment whether it is done rightfully or by right. Exactly what this concession amounts to, exactly how we are to construe the implications of "rightfully" in such contexts, is a matter of some complexity. But even the more latitudinarian constructions of these concepts leave B with fewer options than he would have if he did not concede their applicability to A's actions. It is clear, in short, that there is a genuine issue here. Acceptance of authority does itself place limitations on B's judgments and action on his judgments. The question is just what those limitations consist in and whether it is appropriate to think of them as involving some sort of "surrender" on B's part.

Much the same reasoning holds for cases in which the A or the X is a rule or norm (for example, a part of the constitution or a feature of the authoritative) that does not present itself, immediately as it were, as a decision of some assignable person or persons. In conceding that the rule or norm has authority or authoritative standing the B's do not, or do not appear to, turn over their judgment to other assignable persons—a point that is emphasized by some F-P theorists (though certainly not by Hobbes) and that serves to reduce the appearance of an unacceptable "surrender of judgment" in their accounts of *in* authority. But the B's do concede that the rule governs rightfully, or by right. Thus if a B conceded the authority of a rule and nevertheless claimed that he would be right not to conform to it, at the very least he would take on the burden of showing that, and why, he had not contradicted his concession that X has authority. On the face of the situation, moreover, it would appear that in acting on the apparently contradictory statement he does an action that is at least legally and perhaps in some other way wrong.

An Authority

The case of *an* authorities is more complicated in this regard; the complications are interesting in themselves as well as useful in providing a comparative perspective in which to clarify the relationship between *an* authority, *in* authority, and the authoritative. Accordingly, we turn to B's relationship to *an* authorities and return to *in* authority below.

Would we say that Sir Kenneth Clark issues statements on art history "rightfully" or "by right"? To simplify, let us set aside cases that involve a mixture of *an* and *in* authority—for example, when Sir Kenneth's standing as an authority concerning art history is accompanied by an office or other position such as a lecturer on the subject or as B's agent in buying and selling paintings. The minimally institutionalized relationship between B and A, and hence the relationship that presents the question of "surrender of judgment" to someone who is an authority in its purest form, is where B is simply interested in the subject matter, for whatever reason, in or on which he accepts that A is an authority. A has a field of competence or expertise, not jurisdiction over or any type of authorized or representational relationship with B, and B has a range of interests and concerns and a belief about A's competence, not a membership, subscription or contract. In such cases the relationship between A and B varies across a range delineated by the degrees of expertise possessed by each. If B is a beginning student in the history of art and A is Sir Kenneth Clark, or if B knows little about the human heart and A is Michael De-Bakey, A has all the authority there is in that part of the relationship between them that concerns these subject matters. But if B undertakes a program of disciplined studies in art history or on the heart and heart disease, the differences between A and B (in respect to the attributes that warrant A's standing as an authority) will diminish and perhaps disappear. If the improvements in B's knowledge are not widely known among people interested in the subject matters, A may continue to have a general standing as an authority that B does not enjoy, but the basis of the relationship between A and B, particularly the basis of any "surrender of judgment" on B's part, will have changed, and the relationship itself will properly—whether or not it does in fact—change as well.

There may be, then, some cases in which it is appropriate to say that *an* authorities make their pronouncements rightly or by right, but the justification for and the implications of saying this vary according to a number of considerations. To explore this matter further, let us recur to the argument that whereas *in* authorities issue rules or commands to be subscribed to or obeyed, not statements to be believed, *an* authorities issue statements to be believed. If we connect this distinction with the thesis that authority entails "surrender of judgment," the strongest interpretation of the thesis in respect to *in* authority is that the appearance of an X establishes conclusively and indefeasibly that B has an obligation to obey X. The corresponding interpretation of the thesis in respect to *an* authority would be that a statement issued by an authority is a conclusive reason for B to believe that statement, perhaps even a conclusive reason for B having an obligation to believe the statement. "Rightful" or "by right," as they attach to the statements of A, mean that A has a right that B believe his statements and that B has a duty or obligation to believe them.

This interpretation cannot be correct. The only conclusive reason for believing a statement is that the statement is known to be true; but knowing that A has said X cannot be equivalent to knowing that X is true.[5] The argument for this conclusion can be made in several ways, one of which is as follows: A becomes an authority by recurrently making statements that prove to be true (or profound, insightful, and so forth), and this process presupposes that those who regard him as an authority have tests and procedures, independent of A's statements, for determining their truth. Because the tests of the truth of any X are independent of the fact that A has said X, any statement by A can, logically, prove to be other than true. Thus, to say that B has an obligation to believe A's statements is equivalent to saying that B can have an obligation to believe what is false. Although it has not been unknown for A's to adopt this view and to urge it on B's, the view is pernicious nonsense.

This contention requires that we pause to consider a recurrent confusion concerning authority, autonomy and the "surrender of judgment." The foregoing argument is not meant to deny that there are plenty of situations in which it will be rational for B to accept what A says. Totally ignorant of the workings of automobiles, Smith's car breaks down in a small and isolated village. The one mechanic in the village diagnoses the difficulty and prescribes a remedy. Although the mechanic is totally devoid of *in* authority over Smith, and might very well be mistaken in his judgment about Smith's car, it will be rational for Smith to accept that judgment. The rationality of accepting it results directly from such evidence as Smith has that the mechanic is, by comparison with Smith, an authority about cars. (The evidence might consist of nothing more than that the putative mechanic is surrounded by the usual appurtenances of automobile mechanics, but it is likely to be supplemented by the testimony of those who have availed themselves of the mechanic's services and found them of good quality.) The judgments of the village grocer will neither deserve nor receive such a response.

Situations such as the one just described are more common than one might wish. The combination of a moderately technical body of knowledge that has some general applications and a division of labor that yields specialists concerning it is likely to put laymen in just such predicaments. This combination is of course commonplace—perhaps especially so in modern, technologically developed societies. So much so that no less vigorous an opponent of "surrender of judgment" to authority than Robert Paul Wolff has not only conceded that "there are at least some situations in which it is reasonable to give up one's autonomy" but wondered aloud "whether, in a complex world of technical expertise, it is ever reasonable *not* to do so."[6]

Now the notion that B's judgment or action can be characterized as reasonably made or done and also said to forfeit his personal autonomy is puzzling on its face. "Reasonably done" ordinarily suggests that some analysis and reflection have occurred and these notions form at least a part of the idea of autonomy and autonomous judgment and action. We return to the most general aspects of this question in part 2. What is immediately clear is that "surrender of judgment" to (and because)

someone who is an authority can never, as such, entail logically unqualified acceptance of A's statements as true. As already noted, the idea
that A is an authority presupposes tests and standards of truth (or wisdom, or whatever) by which it can be determined that A qualifies for that
designation. There may nevertheless be circumstances in which, as a
practical matter, B will not be in a position to bring those tests and
standards to bear on A's statements. This is the predicament of Smith in
the example above. But at least three points need to be emphasized about
the kind of situation which that example represents.

First, when B seeks out the garage mechanic rather than the grocer, he
is almost certainly acting on beliefs that are established in his society.
Second, such beliefs can be used and commonly do get used not just to
pick out *an* authorities but to assess the continuing performances of persons who have been so established. Although Smith himself might never
be in a position to make critical assessments of automobile mechanics,
there will be other B's who, without having achieved the status of *an*
authorities on automobile repair, know enough about the subject to do so.
(Even Smith will know whether his car has been rendered operative by
the ministrations of the mechanic.) Garage mechanics have been known
to go out of business for lack of trade and to be fired for incompetence. It
is part of the notion of "an authority" that they are liable to this fate.

It follows, and this is the third point, that the sense in which the *only*
reasonable action open to Smith is to accept the mechanic's judgments is
a consequence not of the A-B relationship as such but of Smith's mis-
fortune in finding himself in a circumstance in which only a part of that
relationship is, as a practical matter, available to him. As trivial as this
observation is in respect to the particulars of the example, the observation
points to at least part of the confusion in the passage quoted from Wolff.
The paucity of options available to Smith is less a consequence of the fact
that he is a participant in a species of authority relations than that he lives
in a world over which he has a good deal less than entire control. If we are
to say that he has forfeited his autonomy by accepting the mechanic's
judgments, we might as well say that he gave it up when he took the
journey because his mother became seriously ill, took the journey by car
because there was no reasonable alternative mode of transportation available, took the route in question because it was the only one open to him,
and so forth. If we are to talk about personal autonomy in the stipulated
circumstances, it would be better to emphasize the respect in which
Smith's participation in the *an* authority relationship creates at least one
more or less acceptable option. This gives the notion of autonomy at least
a limited foothold, indicated by the fact that we can say that it is reasonable for Smith to accept the mechanic's judgments. Imagine Smith in a
society in which there are no authorities concerning motor cars, or

imagine him in a society with such authorities but personally unaware of them or even unfamiliar with the whole notion of *an* authority. On these scenarios Smith would be altogether without options and hence entirely devoid of the possibility of an exercise of autonomous judgment or choice.

The point, of course, is that judgment is not "surrendered" because circumstances evolve in ways that leave a person with no choice but to do this or that less than desirable act. If it were surrendered in this way, we could retain our judgment only by circumscribing the range of our activities so as to avoid or to reduce to an absolute minimum the likelihood of becoming involved in situations in which we have few if any attractive options.[7] If authority is equated with brute, alien and ineluctable forces, no questions about judgment or autonomy can arise concerning our relationships with it.

This confusion aside,[8] how are we to construe "rightful" and "by right" as they attach to A by virtue of B's acceptance of A as an authority? A possibility is that A's possession of authority yields not a right to be believed but a right to distinctively respectful attention to all that he says about the subject matter on which he is an authority. "Distinctively" and "all" in this formulation are necessary in order to distinguish the A-B relationship from the kind of civil or polite responses that we ordinarily owe to one another's statements regardless of any special credentials that may attach to us or to them. A polite response is owed quite apart from any assumption that the statements are especially likely to be true, are particularly weighty or profound, and so forth. And there are many circumstances in which one can be civil or polite merely by not interrupting, not treating with disdain or contempt, not ridiculing the statement or performance. The distinctively respectful attention of the A-B relationship, by contrast, involves not only attending to what A says or does (or explaining why one is not doing so) but going out of one's way to do so and adopting what might be called an expectant, a receptive posture as part of doing so. It involves an assumption, based on the evidence that warrants A's standing as an authority, that A's statements or performances will be especially instructive, enlightening, useful, or whatever and hence especially deserving of attention.

On this view, the A-B relationship varies (according to variables discussed above such as degree of competence on the subject matter) within a range which itself can be thought of as somewhere between the merely polite responses appropriate where there is no authority of any kind and the definite and substantial obligations (whatever their exact content or rationale) characteristic of *in* authority relations. Persons with *an* authority do not have a right to have their statements believed, and those who recognize them as *an* authorities do not have an obligation to believe their statements. But *an* authorities are entitled to distinctively respectful attention, and those who recognize them as such thereby leave themselves subject to criticism if they do not accord such attention to them.

This view of the matter is at least a part of the truth concerning it. If the point about distinctively respectful attention is denied, the notion that *an* authority is a species of *authority* seems to evaporate completely; at the same time, the assertion of a right to be believed or an obligation to believe is clearly unacceptable. But perhaps more can be said about distinctively respectful attention, about what it does and does not involve.

We explore the matter further by considering an argument of Professor Elizabeth Anscombe according to which B is "liable" to believe those who are *an* authorities. To learn, Anscombe observes, "is necessarily to accept, i.e., to believe, a good deal of what one is taught. If a child were liable not to believe his teacher, how could it happen that he selected only those things to disbelieve that were in fact untrue? So he needs to be liable to believe his teacher. If he is, he will learn at any rate some truth; by its aid he will eventually be able to reject what he is taught that is false so far as it is important that he should; or so it is to be hoped."[9]

What is it exactly to be "liable" to believe someone? While clearly including distinctively respectful attention to what A says, the notion appears to go beyond that requirement in the direction of some stronger presumption that B ought to accept what A says in most cases. "The right that a fallible teacher has, in that he has [standing as an] authority, then, is the right that those he has to teach should be generally prepared to believe their teachers."[10]

The Oxford English Dictionary has "liable to" ranging from "legally bound or obliged" through definitely "exposed or subject to" and on to at least one further stage involving a probabilistic sense that it renders by "subject to the possibility of." One is legally liable to jury duty, exposed or subject to being made the beneficiary of a bequest, and subject to the possibility that one's car will break down at inopportune moments. The first of these formulae is excluded as an account of Anscombe's meaning because it presupposes *in* authority and the applicability of legal sanctions for unexcused failure to perform. The third, on the other hand, is too weak because it makes the occurrence of the event a matter of chance rather than a feature of a rule-governed relationship. One could regret the event, but one would not be guilty of anything because of the mere fact that it occurred. By elimination, then, Anscombe's use of "liable" would appear to fall in the second category—understood to include the idea that B is subject to the application of some kind of blame or criticism analogous to but not the same as legally imposed sanctions. Her argument takes the A-B relationship beyond what we might call the procedural requirement of distinctively respectful attention to the more substantive requirement that the B's are positively expected to accept what A says and are properly subject to criticism if they do not ordinarily do so. The B's "surrender" their judgment in the sense that they accept as a feature of their relationship with A that A's pronouncements are not only especially deserving of attention but ordinarily to be believed.

Consideration of two further features of Anscombe's argument will help us to assess its merits. The first of these—unsettling but instructive—is that much of Anscombe's reasoning proceeds from consideration of the case of children. Depending somewhat on the range of ages one has in mind (which, unfortunately, she does not specify), children present, at best, a very special instance of authority relations. Children do not pick out authorities or choose to enter into authority relations with this or that selection of them. Their authorities are the array of parents, teachers, older siblings, and so forth with whom the brief span of the lives they have thus far lived has happened to confront them. It is only with the accumulation of experience that they are able to accord the kind of variable weight to the judgments of the members of this array that the notion of an authority entails. The notion of *surrender* of judgment is difficult to apply to them because they have comparatively little judgment to surrender or to retain. (Perhaps this consideration explains why Anscombe writes of the "need" of the child to be liable to believe his teacher.)

This feature of Anscombe's argument is instructive because it calls attention to a general point that has (to our knowledge) received too little consideration in the literature concerning authority and authority relations. A good deal has been written about the characteristics that do or are likely to bestow authority on A, and quite a lot of attention has been given to the personality and other attributes that predict acceptance, compliance and submission on the part of B (for example studies of the so-called authoritarian personality). But these latter questions can arise about an agent only if he has those characteristics necessary in order to be eligible to stand as a B vis-à-vis one or more *an* authorities. A cannot be an authority for (and cannot be in authority over) a putative B unless there is some sense in which, some level at which, B is capable of judging the merits of A's pronouncements and performances. There are no *an* authorities for rocks and stones, trees and flowers, and none for subhuman animals. For the same reason, there can be *an* authorities for young children only in that special, even analogical, sense in which we also speak of their rights, duties, responsibilities, and so forth, (perhaps) because of our recognition of their potential for the kinds of exercise of judgment that the concept presupposes in its usual range of uses.

This consideration is of general importance because it calls attention to the fact that, as P. H. Nowell-Smith has recently emphasized, authority cannot be analyzed exclusively in terms of attributes of A or of A's actions or statements.[11] We cannot analyze authority without examining the role or status of B and B's responses to A's actions and statements. The consideration is important in the present context because it goes some way to indicate what the "liability" of which Anscombe writes— and hence any "surrender" of judgment—is not and cannot be. B cannot be liable to believe or otherwise to accept A's pronouncements or performances entirely apart from, altogether regardless of, B's judgment of the merits of those pronouncements or performances. Construing "liable" in this way would have the effect of taking the A-B relationship out of the ken of authority relations. A condition of saying that B recognizes A's standing as an authority would have been removed and we would have to conceptualize the relationship between them in some other manner, for example, as A dominating or manipulating B or perhaps—in the case of young children—of B's not yet having the capacity for judgment in respect to the subject matters in question.

As party to a relationship with someone he recognizes as an authority, B has reason to give distinctively respectful attention to A's statements and performances and is liable to believe them in a sense that does not hold for persons who are not *an* authorities for him. This liability, however, must be understood in terms of the reasons that justify distinguishing it from relationships such as sheer dominance and submission, namely B's recognition that A has, by comparison with himself and others, generally superior knowledge, understanding, skill, etc., concerning the subject matters or activities in question. Such recognition presupposes not only that there is reason to believe that A has superior knowledge or understanding, but also that B is capable of recognizing A's superiority. Thus B must have a generalized capacity for judgment and must have or must potentially have access to enough knowledge or information about the subject matter in question to bring that capacity to bear on A's pronouncements and performances. The A-B relationship does presuppose differential knowledge or skill between A and B. But that differential cannot be so great as to deprive B of the possibility of making judgments.

Having made the judgment that A is an authority—that is having found reason to believe that A's pronouncements or performances have recurrently been of a comparatively superior quality—B will thereby have reason to accept A's individual judgments with less scrutiny than he gives the pronouncements and performances of non-A's. Thus he becomes "liable to" accept them in both the second and the third or probabilistic senses of "liable" noted above.

B may continue to be liable to accept A's statements and performances in both these senses despite occasional instances in which A proves to have been mistaken or inept. But we can envisage this latter possibility only because and only to the extent that B—or at least some among the

B's—in fact continue to scrutinize the merits of A's statements and actions. Having envisaged this possibility, it becomes clear that repeated mistakes or poor performances by A must either convince B to cease to recognize A as an authority or to suffer his relationship with A to deteriorate into something other than a relationship in terms of *an* authority.

The final point to be mentioned at this juncture can be put in terms of the second of those two features of Anscombe's argument that we anticipated above. Her fundamental concern in the paper we have been considering is *an* authority in respect to morals. This concern quite rightly leads her to emphasize that a person's moral beliefs, and the degree of wisdom and understanding that person evidences, are most importantly displayed in conduct, that is in the actions the person takes when confronted with moral issues. B displays recognition of A's standing as an authority primarily by acting in the ways that A's precepts and more particularly his practices suggest. This being the case, it follows that considerations discussed above under the heading of the internal logic of rule-governed conduct also apply to the A-B relationship. However well-grounded or enthusiastic B's acceptance of A's *an* authority may be, in every case that presents itself B must decide which modes of conduct are in fact recommended by A's teaching. For reasons already discussed, B cannot do this without engaging in some degree of critical reflection concerning those teachings. Whatever the intentions that set it in motion, this critical reflection will itself test B's continued acceptance of A's standing and it may contribute to a lessening of the distance between B and A. Indeed it may weaken the case for B accepting *any an* authority on the subject matter in question. This latter development is what we expect to take place in respect to morals, and it might well take place in respect to other subject matters and activities as well. Surely any *an* authority who is also a teacher will regard this as the optimum outcome of his relationship with B.

In Authority and the Exercise of Judgment

On the foregoing account of *an* authority relations, it is misleading to say that B "surrenders" his judgment to A; rather, B allows his judgment to be influenced by considerations that reach him by the vehicle of A's pronouncements and performances and in the context of the practice of authority. In short, B does *not* surrender his judgment. Rather, he *exercises* his judgment. *An* authority relations are distinguished not by the surrender of judgment on B's part but by the distinctive circumstances under which and the distinctive manner in which B exercises his judgment. The circumstances (given the practice of authority in B's society or subsocial milieu) are that B knows or believes (on the basis of information obtained directly or vicariously) that the quality of A's past performances has demonstrated his superior knowledge or skill concerning a subject matter or activity that interests B or with which B is otherwise involved. B's recognition of A's superiority in this respect provides B with a good reason to (supports his judgment that he should) give distinctively respectful attention to A's pronouncements or performances concerning that subject matter. It also gives B good reason to (supports his judgment that he should) believe, follow the example set by, and so forth A's statements and actions with less critical scrutiny of their merits than B would give to the statements and actions of persons not established (to his satisfaction) as *an* authorities and with less independent examination of the questions or issues involved than he would make if he were presented with the judgments of anyone else concerning them. If B refuses to accord such distinctively respectful attention to A's statements or performances, or if he refuses to accept or to act on those statements or performances with less scrutiny or independent examination than he gives when not presented with established *an* authorities, he rejects A's authority (or, perhaps, rejects the practice of *an* authority) and it becomes impossible for him to maintain an *an* authority relationship with A (or, perhaps, with any *A*). But the same result ensues if B ceases to make the kinds of judgments we have described. It follows that interpretations which equate good or right action with unqualified and uncritical submission to the beliefs and decisions of some other person are not interpretations of authority relations. Equally, arguments that object to *an* authority relations on the ground that they are destructive of individual autonomy either confuse *an* authority relations with something that they are not and cannot be (for example relations of dominance and submission or the sheer imposition of brute and alien forces) or rest on a conception of autonomy so tender, so virginal, that it could be instantiated only by an exceedingly jealous god. Finally, interpretations that stress the efficiency of participation in *an* authority relationships make a valid point so long as they recognize that the gain is relative or comparative; so long, that is, as they recognize the respects in which B's *qua* B's must continue to exercise critical judgment concerning the statements and performances of those they recognize as A's.

A possible response to the account, likely to be made by F-P theorists of the Oakeshott persuasion, is that, while perhaps accurate enough as an explication of what commonly goes on under the rubric of *an* authority relations, it shows that *an* authority relations are *authority* relations in name only; that *an* authority is categorially distinct from true or genuine, which is to say *in,* authority.

This objection is important at the present juncture because it implies that we cannot draw upon the foregoing analysis of *an* authority relations in order to further understand and assess the "surrender" of judgment in the case of *in* authority relations. If *an* and *in* authority are categorially distinct, characteristics of the former would be no more relevant to understanding the latter than propositions about the population of China.

It is manifestly a fact that the term "authority" is used of *an* authority relations. But if our account of this usage is correct, what is important about it is that the usage brings along with it the differences between the distinctively respectful attention that the B's are liable to give to *an* authorities and the kind of attention we all owe to one another under the norms of polite conduct. However we choose to label it, this is a distinct kind of relationship of considerable importance in human affairs. Given that the relationship is distinct and important, and given that it is commonly called a relationship between authorities and nonauthorities, it is less than clear why the theorist should treat it as anything other than just that.

Working from this premise, we return to *in* authority relations and an attempt to specify further the meaning of "by right" and "rightfully" as they attach to A's and X's by virtue of their standing in a practice of *in* authority rules. It will be helpful to begin by reconsidering the thesis that *in* authority yields rules to be obeyed, not statements to be believed.

This thesis rests on one of the important points of distinction between *an* and *in* authorities. In the former, A's authority is relational because he has it by virtue of the *recognized* quality of his performances. Joseph Raz to the contrary notwithstanding, in the absence of B's who give such recognition, *an* authority would be impossible.[12] But it is not a feature of *an* authority relations for A to intend that the B's *qua* B's *act* in a certain manner in response to A's performances. Nor does A's continuing as an authority depend on any action on the part of the B's. They may believe his statements, stand in awe of the skill of his performances, and do nothing more. Apparent counterexamples to this account either are spurious or are instances in which a single person both holds an office of *in* authority and is *an* authority on the subject matter dealt with by that office. The "doctor's orders" to patients that are in fact pieces of advice are an example of the former, and professors who require their students to repeat their teachings in order to pass an examination are sometimes (i.e., when the professor is genuinely an authority on his subject matter) examples of the latter.

By contrast, the rules and orders that are the usual devices through which A's exercise their *in* authority are directives intended by the A's to determine the course of action of the B's in a certain respect. If the B's do not understand this, and if they do not ordinarily comply, the authority of the A's will be lost. ("Usual" and "ordinarily" are in the previous two sentences in recognition of qualifications to the points the sentences assert. In addition to directives, *in* authorities issue permissions or powers which the B's are at liberty to use or not as they see fit. And as we argue later, occasional, even quite frequent, noncompliance does not necessarily destroy authority.) Thus it is (roughly) true that *an* authorities issue statements to be believed and not rules or commands to be obeyed. And it is also (roughly) true that *in* authorities issue rules to be obeyed.

Is it also true that *in* authorities do not issue statements to be believed? If so, it would follow that our account of the "surrender" of judgment to *an* authorities is irrelevant to understanding *in* authority relations. If the B's of an *in* authority relationship are not asked to believe anything, then considerations concerning the conditions under which belief is logically possible can hardly be helpful to understanding the role of the B's. Clearly, however, it is false to say that the B's are not asked to believe *anything*. At a minimum they must believe that there is a difference between rules that carry authority and those that do not, and they must believe that *these* rules carry authority. This being true, and it also being true that belief necessarily involves reflection and judgment on the part of the believing (or disbelieving agent), judgment is a necessary part of *in* authority relations.

It might be responded that the foregoing statement, while true, is trivial because it has no bearing on those aspects of *in* authority relations to which the thesis we are now considering (that *in* authority does not require or even solicit belief) is intended to apply. B must believe that A or X has authority, but he is explicitly not expected to believe, in the sense of thinking true, well-founded or justified, the *content* of the statements that A issues or in which X consists. As rules or commands, these statements are not eligible as subjects of belief. To treat them as eligible for belief or disbelief is to make a category mistake in the Rylean sense. As C. W. Cassinelli has put the point in question, A's possessing *in* authority is a circumstance logically entailing beliefs on the part of B's. But his exercise of that authority, in the sense of requiring or prohibiting this or that action of B, is a condition that excludes the relevance (though not the existence) of any and all beliefs (save the belief that the requirement or prohibition carries authority) to the decision whether to comply.[13] B "surrenders judgment," to repeat Friedman's words, in the sense that he "does not make his obedience *conditional* on his own personal examination and evaluation of the thing he is being asked to do. Rather, he accepts as a sufficient condition for following a prescription that it is prescribed by someone acknowledged by him as entitled to rule. The man who accepts authority . . . surrenders[s] his . . . individual judgment because he does not insist that reasons be given that he can grasp and that satisfy him, as a condition of his obedience.''[14] The corollary, of course, is that by "rightful" and "by right" it should be understood, not merely that A is entitled to issue the rule, but that he is entitled to do so without giving reasons for it and entitled to have B obey it despite B's not receiving any reasons for doing so beyond those provided by A's authority.

B's relations to *an* authority cannot be assimilated to the sort of respect owed under the rules of polite conduct. Similarly, *in* authority cannot be reduced to the case in which B does what A directs because B's independent examination of the merits of that action has convinced him that it is the best thing for him to do. On these interpretations, the distinction between authority and advice, counsel or even mere expressions of A's opinion evaporates. But this conclusion leaves open the question whether B's relation to *in* authority can be interpreted in a manner analogous to what we found to be yet another mistaken interpretation of *an* authority relations, namely that B has an obligation to believe what A says simply because A, *qua* an A who B recognizes as such, says it. Is the fact that a rule or command carries *in* authority itself a conclusive reason for B *qua* B to have an obligation to conform to the rule or to obey the command?

We argued that the defect in the analogous interpretation of *an* authority is that it destroys a condition of authority as opposed to mere compulsion or dominance—the condition, namely, that B must be in a position to judge the merits of A's pronouncements and performances. It might be argued, however—indeed this is exactly what Friedman and Cassinelli are arguing—that no such requirement obtains in the case of *in* authority. The requirement obtains for *an* authority because of the conceptual connection between that concept and concepts such as "true," "valid," "profound," "correct," and so forth, together with the fact that the latter concepts entail criteria, independent of A's views, by which A's views can be assessed. Because *in* authority has no connection with these or any comparable concepts, it entails no such requirement.

But this is false. Or rather, it could conceivably be true only on an understanding of *in* authority that is objectionable on normative grounds and is probably otherwise untenable.

In fact, of course, persons holding positions of *in* authority regularly act as if their pronouncements are true, wise, or otherwise substantively meritorious. But we can agree with F-P theorists that their position as *in* authorities does not itself entitle them to do so. We can also agree that no single such pronouncement can be shown to lack *in* authority merely (!) because it is not just, right, good, or in conformity with other normative standards. (We return to this last question below.) But there is at least one evaluative concept, or family of evaluative concepts, with which *in* authority pronouncements are necessarily connected. The most familiar member of this family is "valid," and the members of it most commonly employed in the kind of context we are considering are "constitutional" and "*ultra* and *intra vires*." Whatever other tests *in* authority pronouncements might be expected to meet, they must be shown to be valid in the sense of consistent with the "constitution," the "*grundnorm*," the "rule of recognition," or whatever, that is the source of the authority they are alleged to have.

To state this requirement, of course, is to state a tautology. An A or an X carries *in* authority only if it satisfies this test. Hence the theorists we have been discussing are likely to respond that their arguments encompass this point. But their arguments do not encompass all of the implications of this point for the question of "surrender" of judgment on B's part. The question whether a rule or command is valid is commonly difficult, often vexed. It is intimately connected, moreover, with the often equally vexed question of what actions the A or the X requires of or prohibits to B. The question whether A has authority to issue rule X is often undecidable apart from a determination of the range of actions it implies for B. These questions do not decide themselves. They are decided through the exercise of judgment by parties to the *in* authority relationship.

The interpretation of "surrender of judgment" that we are considering, then, must either deny the importance of these questions or turn their resolution entirely over to the A's. Cassinelli apparently leans to the former alternative. "The recipient [B] must . . . realize that the communication [from A] is an imperative, that the governor does not intend to convince, persuade, or bargain. However, he need not understand precisely what the communication is saying, and he can even misinterpret it to the extent that he believes it to say something which the governor did not at all intend. The governor's exercise of authority is not undermined by obscureness and misunderstanding. The recipient must only be aware that he is being told to do something."[15]

Taken literally, this passage suggests that it does not matter how B (or anyone else?—need A himself understand it?) understands a rule or command. B need understand no more than that he is told to do something—anything whatever.

Unfair as it may be to Cassinelli, this parody brings out a main difficulty with "surrender of judgment" in the interpretation presently before us. Given that the A or the X is rarely if ever simply pellucid, simply self-explicating, this interpretation leaves us to choose among the following three alternatives: (1) it does not matter how B understands A or X or what actions he takes or refrains from taking, it matters only that he does *something* and that he does it *because* he knows that X has authority; (2) it matters how X is understood and what B does, but the question of the meaning of X is entirely for the A's, B's role being restricted to accepting their determination without question; (3) B must himself interpret (at least provisionally) X and hence must exercise judgment concerning it.

Alternative 1 is manifestly absurd. It makes the relationship between the rule or command and the content of B's actions purely random. Alternative 2 is that objectionable theory according to which A has unqualified authority to determine the scope of his own authority. Leaving aside normative objections to this view, there is a serious question whether it is, in any form consistent with continued use of "authority," even cogent. At a minimum B must *decide* what to do when faced with A or X. He "must" decide because if he does not do so we would no longer have authority and the action of discharging an obligation, but imposition or compulsion. There is also a question whether authority is sociologically possible on this understanding of the A-B relationship. We have argued that authority needs the support of some array of values and beliefs that has acceptance in the society or association of which it is part. For values and beliefs to give such support, a kind of congruence must be thought to exist between them and the actions and requirements of authority. The initiatives, the leadership, in maintaining such congruence may indeed rest largely with the A's. But the B's must believe that the congruence exists, and this belief requires judgments on B's part.

In reality, then, the only tenable alternative is 3—which is to say that the A-B relationship entails the exercise of at least some kinds of judgment on B's part. "Surrender of judgment" to *in* authority cannot cogently be interpreted in the manner we have been examining.

Can it be cogently interpreted as excluding B's judgments about properties of X's other than their implications for B's conduct and the validity of those implications? Do *in* authority relations as such require B to surrender his judgment concerning the justice, the desirability, the wisdom, and so forth of an A or X? That they do so is the proposition on which F-P interpreters of "surrender of judgment" (whether defenders or critics of *in* authority) have been most insistent. Of course, B may in fact make such judgments. But any such judgments that B makes are purely private; they are not only irrelevant but inappropriate to his public role as a participant in relationships of *in* authority. In respect to that role, B must understand that judgments about the merits of A or X are either irrelevant or vested exclusively with A. If this point is not sustained, F-P theorists argue, *in* authority evaporates and at most we have counsel, advice, persuasion or argumentation over the merits of courses of action. "Surrender of judgment" in at least this sense is a categorial feature of *in* authority relations.

The first step in interpreting this contention is to emphasize again some of the considerations discussed in chapters 3 and 4, considerations that call attention to the continuities between questions about the implications and validity of an X and questions about its merits. Without rehearsing those considerations in detail, the minimal and undeniable point is that decisions about validity and implication require judgments concerning intentions and thereby about the pro-attitudes of parties to the relationship. In this respect at least, the A-B relationship excludes unqualified "surrender" of judgment concerning normative issues on B's part.

Can we say more than this? Are there further respects in which normative judgments by B are required by or at least consistent with his role *qua* B? Can, must, B *qua* B make and act upon continuing assessments of X's without thereby denying the authority of the latter or taking his leave from the authority relationship?

We must first set aside the argument that attempts at such judgments involve some species of category mistake—that rules and commands simply do not allow of judgments about their merits. Rules and commands are directives; they prescribe to action. As such they are paradigms of statements susceptible of normative assessment. Of course the person making such assessments must consider the properties distinctive to rules and commands—cannot treat them as mere predictions of how A's or B's will act, or as pieces of advice, requests, and so forth. But if these properties are taken into account, the merits of rules *qua* rules can be assessed. Thus at most the point is that *acting on* judgments about substantive merits is excluded from the role of B. Although any A or X can be described or characterized in a variety of ways, at least some of which invite normative assessment, the only characterization relevant to the conduct of B *qua* B is that the A or the X has the standing of a rule that carries *in* authority. The due process rule, for example, might be characterized as a principle of great importance to legal systems, as an element of natural justice, as a recurrent feature of human arrangements, as a great bulwark of human liberty and dignity, as an unfortunate burden on the police, and no doubt in a variety of other ways, many of which express normative judgments. On the thesis we are considering, however, the sole characterization relevant to the conduct of B *qua* B is that the due process rule carries authority in the jurisdiction of which B is a part.

The availability of a variety of characterizations of the formulations that are X's is part of the reason why B's must exercise the self-discipline that Oakeshott emphasizes so strongly. If the one and only way to characterize the formulation were as an A or an X, then the only alternatives with which persons who are B's would be presented would be to obey or to disobey the A or X. The argument for self-discipline in effect contends that for purposes of action B's confronted with an A or an X must proceed as if B is the only role they play and as if the characterization "an A" or "an X" is the only characterization that they may consider. This is not "implausibly circumspect" (Oakeshott), it is impossibly limiting. There is no such thing as a person who is nothing but a B, and there is no such thing as a formulation that is nothing but an A or an X. In thought and action the several roles that any person plays and the several characterizations of which any formulation allows inevitably coexist and interact in a variety of ways. As important as they are, role conceptions and distinguishing characterizations do not and cannot (if only because they are commonly defined in part by reference one to the other) form hermetically sealed compartments or windowless monads that are or could be altogether isolated from one another.

It is in part for these reasons that human affairs do not present us with pure cases of *in* authority on the F-P model or instantiations of "civil" or "enterprise" associations in unalloyed form. It is largely for this reason that F-P theorists argue, often passionately, for "self-discipline." Arguments for self-discipline would be pointless if the allegedly irrelevant modes of thought and action were not so readily available and so tempting.

But there is a further reason for this circumstance, a reason that casts doubt on any tendency to dismiss the discrepancies between model and practice on metatheoretical grounds. The reason is that actual practice has commonly displayed a widely shared belief, held on normative grounds, that there *ought* to be interpenetration and interaction, that the roles and kinds of characterizations *ought not* to be treated as totally distinct. In its most emphatic form the belief is expressed as the conviction that citizens have a positive *duty* to make continuing assessments of the substantive merits of X's and a positive duty to make action on these assessments an integral part of *in* authority relations.

In principle this duty could be discharged in a manner consistent with the interpretation of "surrender of judgment" characteristic of F-P theorists from Hobbes forward. X's and proposed X's would be assessed for the purpose of deciding whether they should achieve and should retain authority, not whether they should be obeyed as long as they have authority. The B's are not to surrender their judgment as to the merits of X's; they are only to surrender the prerogative of acting on those judgments as long as the X's carry authority. Or more exactly, they are to surrender the prerogative of basing decisions about obedience and disobedience on judgments about merits while continuing to claim that their actions are taken *qua* participants in the practice of *in* authority in question.

6 Authority, the Merits of Rules, and Civil Disobedience

Our explorations to this point soften the appearance that *in* authority is incompatible with individual autonomy or agency. Authority and authority relations are not reducible to argumentation over the merits of decisions and policies, to persuasion, advice and counsel, to requests and pleas. And the difference does consist, at least in important part, in the fact that participants in a practice of *in* authority have an obligation to conform with the requirements of *intra vires* rules and commands, an obligation that cannot be fully analyzed, explained or justified by reference to participants' assessments of the merits of such rules and commands. But authority and the obligations that it entails are also distinct from arbitrary, brute, or merely coercive impositions of alien forces or powers. Obligations obtain only if rules and commands have been adopted by designated officeholders through an established procedure and only if promulgating those rules and commands is within the authority of those officeholders. Nor is there any incompatibility between the concept (or the practice) of authority and arrangements that invite, encourage or even require subscribers to take an active, critical role in formulating, adopting and changing the content of the rules and commands they have an obligation to obey. Because a practice of authority does circumscribe, does place limitations upon, the propriety of acting on certain types of judgments, individuals who accord supreme value to such action may find authority unacceptable. Philosophical anarchism is not an absurd, groundless position. But practices of authority have sometimes provided important advantages to their members and might continue to do so. For this reason, and because authority only limits, does not exclude or destroy the exercise of individual judgment and action on judgment, persons who value judgment and action on it might rationally choose to subscribe to such practice in order to gain those advantages. On the basis of our discussions to this juncture, in short, it appears that the theory of authority does not itself yield a conclusive argument for or against rejecting authority as such.[1]

We have not, however, completed the task of conceptualizing the limitations that *in* authority places on individual judgment and action, and we

have only begun to interpret and assess the significance of those limitations. We continue these efforts in the present chapter. The first step
will be to examine Joseph Raz's distinctive conceptualization of the limitations. We then assess his (and other F-P) account(s) of those limitations
in light of the fact that practices of authority sometimes lose the support of
their (erstwhile) subscribers owing to the latter's disapproval of the content or consequences of the rules and commands those practices promulgate. We conclude by considering the conceptual and normative
merits of theories that have influenced and been influenced by such historical events, namely theories of revolution and of civil disobedience. In
this last stretch of the discussion the primary question will be whether the
distinctive contentions of the theory of civil disobedience are compatible
with the basic F-P argument that authority is an attribute of a system of
rules and offices.

Rules and Commands as "Exclusionary" Reasons for Action

The upshot of Raz's analysis of authority is essentially
identical to the position of Richard B. Friedman. "There is a sense in
which if one accepts the legitimacy of an [in] authority one is committed
to follow it blindly. One can be very watchful that it shall not overstep its
authority and be sensitive to the presence of non-excluded considerations. But barring these possibilities one is to follow the authority
regardless of one's views of the merits of the case (that is, blindly). One
may form a view on the merits but so long as one follows the authority this
is an academic exercise of no practical importance."[2] Again, and introducing language distinctive to Raz's formulation, "accepting authority
inevitably involves giving up one's right to act on one's judgment on the
balance of reasons. It involves accepting an exclusionary reason."[3]

The novel feature of Raz's presentation of this substantively familiar
position is a distinction between levels or kinds of reasons for action and
especially the notion that certain kinds of rules ("mandatory norms") are
not only (1) reasons for action in the sense of considerations that require,
recommend or justify a particular course of action, but (2) are reasons for
or against acting on other reasons. The fact that Johnny is hungry and
likes fruit are reasons of the first or "primary" sort for him to eat an apple
from the fruit bowl. The fact that his mother said that he was not to touch
the apples is both a "primary" reason for not eating one of the apples and
a "secondary" reason that "excludes" consideration of primary reasons
that conflict with it.[4]

Without summarizing the entire account of practical reasoning of which it is part, Raz's argument is that the distinctive property of rules and commands that carry authority is that they function as second-order reasons which do not "outweigh" primary reasons but exclude consideration of (at least some) primary reasons in deciding what to do. Authority presents itself as necessarily unacceptable to persons who value personal autonomy primarily because they (we) mistakenly think of all reasons for action (and hence of the autonomy that consists in acting on the balance of reasons) as primary reasons that should be weighed against one another. Hence they find themselves in situations in which authority orders them to act in a manner which, on the balance of primary reasons, they regard as wrongful or otherwise rationally unacceptable. But when they realize that rules and commands provide considerations which, while reasons for action, are different in kind from primary reasons, this appearance vanishes. "To accept an [in] authority . . . is not to act irrationally or arbitrarily. The need for an [in] authority may be well founded in reason. But the reasons are of a special kind. They establish the need to regard authoritative utterances as exclusionary reasons."[5]

Raz presents several examples and arguments intended to explain and establish his distinction.[6] For present purposes the most relevant of these involves an order, validly issued by a commanding officer, requiring a soldier (Jeremy) to perform an action that Jeremy judges unjustified by the balance of "primary" reasons for and against it. Jeremy nevertheless decides that he ought to obey the order.

Raz rightly says that Jeremy's resolution of his problem is quite typical. But does that resolution reflect an (at least implicit) recognition of the distinction between primary and exclusionary rules? Clearly Jeremy makes the command the decisive factor in reaching his decision. But does this show that the commander's order is something other than a primary reason which Jeremy judges to outweigh the primary reasons against the action? Raz's first move is simply to assert that interpreting the order as a primary reason to which decisive weight has been accorded would be to disregard "Jeremy's own conception of the situation. . . . [Jeremy's] claim is that the order is a reason for him not to act on the merits of the case . . . [,] that whatever his view of the case it should not affect his action, that all or most of the other considerations [other than the order] are to be excluded from the range of facts determining his action."[7] Needless to say, this assertion (concerning an example of Raz's own construction) does nothing to establish the distinction for which Raz is contending. Thus far, decisions such as Jeremy's could perfectly well be explained as resting on the view that the orders of commanding officers should be obeyed because the primary reasons for maintaining authority are so strong that they are virtually always decisive or because the commander is a recognized *an* authority on the subject matter of the action and hence his judgments can be counted on to give a correct assessment of the balance of primary reasons.

Raz's next move is to appeal to the ambivalence or dissonance commonly experienced by persons in situations such as Jeremy's. After altering the example in ways irrelevant to our (and to his?) purposes, he observes that Jeremy is "torn between conflicting feelings." Obeying the order deserves praise, but doing the action required by the order is wrong and blameworthy. The "action can be assessed in two ways that lead to contradictory results."[8] In order to account for the continuing ambivalence, Raz argues, we need his distinction between two *kinds* of reason. And the recurrence of such ambivalence shows that his distinction is implicit in our practice of practical reasoning.

Unfortunately for his argument, this move on Raz's part calls our attention to one of the features of authority relations that refutes his argument. Assume that Jeremy accepted Raz's distinction, that is, that he accepted the "general principle of practical reasoning" which (according to Raz) that distinction embodies and which "determines that exclusionary reasons always prevail when in conflict with first-order reasons."[9] If so, ambivalence or dissonance on Jeremy's part would be irrational and hence inexplicable as a feature of reasoned conduct. Jeremy would know with entire certitude that obeying the order was the right thing to do. He would know this by virtue of his knowledge that the considerations that appeared to urge disobeying it were in fact irrelevant to the decision. Jeremy would experience no more ambivalence over having set those considerations aside than he would experience if he had not counted the letters in his commander's name as a part of deciding what to do.

Jeremy's ambivalence, rather, is understandable precisely because the reasons for action that he finds in conflict are of one and the same *kind* (are commensurable) and hence can *genuinely* conflict with one another. Perhaps Jeremy thinks that there are good reasons for having authority in the military and believes that such authority is impossible if there is not a general pattern of compliance with rules and commands. These considerations provide him with reasons for doing what authority commands even though he dislikes the required actions. But if he dislikes the content or consequences of those actions, he also has reasons not to perform them. Resolving—as best he can—the matter on the balance of reasons does not alter the fact that there are reasons that genuinely count against the decision he reaches. And if those reasons are strong, Jeremy will continue to feel their force during his action and after he has acted. On Raz's argument this experience would be an impossibility. Because Raz is correct that the experience is commonplace in practices of authority, an analysis of such practices must reject Raz's proposed distinction.[10]

In Authority and Judgments concerning the Secular Tendencies of Rules and Commands

We can reject Raz's distinction between kinds of reasons without adopting the view that the decision whether to obey an *intra vires* rule or command must be based entirely on the merits of that particular directive. Raz concedes that his proposed distinction "is not reflected in any straightforward way in . . . ordinary language" and also says that it "has not been recognized and discussed by philosophers."[11] But both ordinary language and much philosophical discussion recognize, or rather insist upon, reasons for action that are like Raz's mandatory norms in that they require or justify *classes* of actions, not just this or that action by an assignable individual under particular circumstances. "Principles," "rules" and "maxims" are the obvious examples, it being part of the very meaning of these concepts that they are general in something like this sense.[12] "Laws ought to be obeyed" and "Rules and commands invested with authority ought to be obeyed" are instances of such principles or rules of conduct—instances that are widely accepted. More important at this juncture, they are instances of such principles or rules that must be accepted in some form if there is to be a practice of authority. Having found Raz's and other F-P accounts of them unacceptable, it remains to seek an alternative analysis.

Let it be conceded that when B *qua* B encounters a valid X he has an obligation to conform to the requirements of that X. Let it further be conceded that this obligation is entailed by the fact that X carries authority in the jurisdiction of which B is a part—specifically, that any judgments B may make concerning the merits of X will not diminish his obligation to conform with it. A question that even these far-reaching concessions leaves open concerns the relationship between such particular obligations, taken as it were one by one, and the fact that the association in question includes *in* authority such that there are X's and the socially established role of B.

There is reason to think that there is a positive relationship, that may be more than merely empirical (contingent), between the judgments of the class of actors B concerning the merits of the rules X and the fact that the association includes *in* authority such that there can be X's. A reason for thinking these things presents itself if we consider the following commonplace occurrence: when the B's of a practice of *in* authority persistently make severely adverse judgments of the X's of that practice, it commonly happens (sometimes in an astonishingly short time, sometimes not for an astonishingly long time) that the authority of the A's and X's diminishes and may disappear. How should we conceptualize this commonplace?

One possibility is suggested by a familiar feature of the recent history of a number of political associations, a feature that seems to have developed in part as a response to such occurrences. Numerous associations have institutionalized procedures that allow the B's to express and otherwise to act on their dissatisfactions with the merits of X's *without* challenging their standing as such or questioning the obligation to conform with them. Perhaps the most dramatic of these devices is elections, that is, devices through which those who hold positions of authority (and hence can be held responsible for the content of the X's) can be voted out of office. Their exercise of authority can be assessed, and perhaps rejected, without challenging authority in the sense of the standing of the practice itself. The B's may continue to conform to X's the substance of which they strongly disapprove, and may well do so primarily because the X's have been invested with authority. But their willingness to do this is likely to be enhanced by the fact that changes in the A's and X's can be effected without challenging the practice of authority. More important than the contingent matter of the "likelihoods" involved, this latter argument is a part of the widely accepted rationale for obedience in a number of associations. Where this is the case, an explicit, more than merely empirical, link has been made between obedience and a kind of judgment about the merits of X's.

By no means all associations with *in* authority have adopted such devices, and not all those that have done so have succeeded in forestalling challenges to authority resulting from widespread, secular dissatisfaction with the merits of the X's. Where such challenges occur on any substantial scale one can of course say that *in* authority has been destroyed and *in* authority relations terminated in the association. But that this is an appropriate way to characterize what has happened does not alter what such occurrences establish, namely that widespread and continuing approval, or at least the absence of overly emphatic and insistent disapproval, of the X's is a condition of *in* authority (and hence of any "surrender of judgment" thereto). In short, the existence of *in* authority is a condition of decisions to obey X's simply because they carry authority, but widespread and continuing approval of the substance of X's is a condition of the existence of *in* authority.

If this relationship is merely empirical, if it is no more than a correlation between types of occurrences that are unconnected in the ideas and patterns of intentional action of participants, it poses no very serious problem for F-P theory or the accounts of "surrender of judgment" that we are considering. A theory of authority cannot be expected to identify all of the empirical conditions that are in fact associated with the existence of authority, much less to work all such conditions into the account of what authority is and is not.[13] But the relationship may be more than merely correlational; it may even deserve to be treated as a kind of logical or conceptual relationship. As a next step in inquiring into the relationship, let us consider two possible analogues to it.

The proposition "A intends to do X" does not entail the proposition "A will do X." A might fail to do X on a number of occasions without casting doubt on the statement that he had intended to do X. Yet if A did not ordinarily do what he said he intended to do, and did not explain what had intervened to prevent him when he did not, others would begin to treat his statements of intention with suspicion and would ultimately disregard them. More generally, if most people did not do what they intended to do most of the time, our concept of intention would not be what it is.

Here is another possible analogy. The statement "A has a right to do X" does not entail "A thinks having a right to do X is advantageous to him." A might find the right disadvantageous, might forego exercising it, waive it, etc., on a number of occasions without thereby casting doubt on the standing of the right. But if A recurrently judges that having the right disadvantages him, it becomes inappropriate for others to go on saying that X is a right of A's.[14]

The use of "intention" and "rights," we are suggesting, brings with it the presumption of certain conditions; the recurrent absence of those conditions would alter the use and the meanings of the concepts. The conditions are not merely correlated with the use of the concepts, they are part of their use. A person who did not understand the connection between the concept and the conditions would not fully command the concept. Putting the matter yet one more way, if Jones says that he intends to do X and then does not do it, his auditors will expect an explanation. This is not because (without positing further facts) Jones had committed himself to do X such that he is subject to criticism if he fails to do it: rather it is because it is part of the notion of intending that one ordinarily does what one intends. Similarly, if Jones attributes rights to Smith which disadvantage the latter, others will expect an explanation. ("What is the point of asserting Smith's right to do X when he doesn't want to do it?") If no explanation is forthcoming, and especially if Jones persists in such statements without providing plausible explanations, others will conclude that Jones suffers from confusion about the concept of a right. (An example of an explanation would be: "It's true that exercising the right to do X is a burden on Smith in this case, but ordinarily it is valuable and so it is correct to insist on it now.")

Is the relationship between *in* authority and widespread and continuing approval of the content of X's like that between intention and performance and between having a right and generally approving of having it? Could the members of an association go on saying "Every rule and command that this practice of authority has produced is offensive to us" without thereby denying the authority of that practice? Is there a *conceptual* difficulty about saying, without further explanation, "We detest the content of every X that this practice has produced but we do not question their standing as X's"? (Cf.: "We never do anything we intend to do, but our intentions are intentions for all of that"; "We abhor every right that we have, but they are nevertheless our rights.") Quite clearly, statements of this kind would be conceptual absurdities in respect to *an* authority. "We (the community of persons interested in art history) think that all of Sir Kenneth Clark's statements on the subject are rubbish but we do not question that he is an authority concerning it" is absurd because one part of the statement denies the basis of what another part of it asserts. Can the same be said of analogous statements about *in* authority? Is continuing, generalized approval, or at least the continuing absence of generalized and vigorous disapproval, of the content of X's the "basis," or one of the "bases," of the *in* authority of A's and X's?

Strongly disposed as we are to answer this question affirmatively, we doubt that conceptual or any other mode of analysis will yield an undisputed answer to it. The question can be raised in a useful form by employing such analysis, and we hope that the foregoing discussion has allowed us to formulate it in an accessible manner. But it seems undeniable that it is a question about which there is a good deal of cogent dispute—and hence undeniable that practice supplies the conceptual resources necessary to conducting cogent dispute.[15] Argumentation concerning it is at least in part argumentation over how the several concepts at issue should be used, how their interrelationships and implications should be construed.

In Authority, Revolution, and Civil Disobedience

Given this circumstance, it will be useful to enlarge the discussion to include questions of a more explicitly normative character that have had a central place in virtually all of the great theories of authority in the history of political philosophy. We do so by examining a distinction that makes little or no appearance until recent times but is now widely familiar, that is the distinction between a revolutionary and a civil disobedient stance toward authority.

As different as they are in vital respects, these two positions agree that the B's *qua* B's not only can (logically) make continuing assessments of the merits of X's without thereby leaving the authority relationship but that they have something approaching a duty to do so. In this sense they agree that such judgments are a part of a practice of *in* authority. Advo-

cates of these positions also commonly agree to the importance of the
distinction between the merits of particular X's taken singly and "a long
train of abuses and usurpations"—though they may disagree over the
weight to assign to this distinction.

The chief difference between the positions concerns the uses to which
their proponents are prepared to put judgments about the characteristics
of X's. The revolutionary brings such judgments to bear on the question
whether to overthrow the regime that has yielded the unacceptable X's.
The civil disobedient, by contrast, contends that such judgments can
(logically) and should (normatively) be considered in determining B's obligations vis-à-vis particular X's the authority of which he does not deny
or seek to destroy (indeed the authority of which he could deny or seek to
destroy only at the cost of ceasing to take a civil disobedient position).
The civil disobedient, in other words, makes assessments of X's a part of
the practice of *in* authority in the further sense of making them both
logically relevant and normatively appropriate to decisions about and
action on B's obligations vis-à-vis X's.

Although civil disobedience has been intended by most proponents and
practitioners to throw up a less radical challenge to authority than does a
revolutionary posture (indeed has often been intended in part as a kind of
defense of or protection for authority against revolution), many theorists
of authority have responded more negatively and more vigorously to it
than to the revolutionary position. The reason for this, though not far to
seek, is of some importance to the issues we are considering. Revolutionaries (as distinct from anarchists) are not opponents of or commonly
even skeptics about authority, they are opponents of this or that practice
of authority. When they have torn down a practice of authority that in
their judgment has produced a long train of abuses and usurpations, they
set about to replace it with another such practice—this time one they
expect will produce desirable X's. What is more, revolutionaries have (all
too) commonly understood authority as excluding the B's of the new
practice from acting—except in revolutionary ways—on their assessments of the merits of the X's of the new practice. It may be at least in
part for these reasons that those who find themselves contending against a
revolutionary movement seldom bother with the argument, frequently
made against civil disobedience, that it contravenes the logic of authority
relations. Rather, they defend the merits of the practice of authority that
the revolutionaries have called into question.

This tendency, no doubt, is to be understood in large part in terms of
pragmatic considerations. It may be silly to try to still a revolutionary
movement with arguments about the logic of authority relations. A group
of people who are convinced that they are faced by tyranny or gross and
persistent injustice are not likely to be deterred by the contention that

their efforts to rectify the situation involve some species of illogicality or (in Hobbes' word)[16] absurdity. But thoughtful revolutionaries are not restricted to a purely pragmatic response to such arguments. They might, for example, take the position that "authority" and "obligation" are systematically subordinate to "just," "unjust," "right" and "wrong," and hence that there can be no absurdity in meeting the requirements of the latter when they conflict with the requirements of the former. But there is another position open to them, namely the position implied by the analogy we have suggested between "authority" on the one hand and "intention" and "rights" on the other. On this second position, persistent and strongly felt disapproval of X's need not mark a generalized subordination of authority relations to justice, rights, welfare, or any other distinct consideration. Rather, it might mark the end of the set of authority relations in question. It warrants, and therefore *ought to* mark, the end of the practice of *in* authority that has produced the unacceptable X's. Anyone who goes on defending that practice is defending power or force of tyranny, not authority. Anyone who objects to the position of the revolutionaries is thereby advocating not "surrender of judgment" to authority but abject submission.

A far from insignificant part of the history of thought and action concerning political authority testifies to the acceptance of this latter understanding of the matter. Of course it must always be difficult to specify abstractly and prospectively how strong or how well grounded the disapproval of the X's must be in order that it warrant the claim that authority has ceased. Yet to deny that this possibility is part of the notion of *in* authority is to render incomprehensible salient and dramatic moments in the history of authority.

From both a moral and a logical point of view the explanation for this fact might be said to lie in a feature of "authority" that has recurred in various forms in this discussion. On the lips of anyone but a declared anarchist, the concession that a rule or command has authority advances a *reason* why B's *should* conform with it. Now the fact that "authority" offers a reason for acting has been defended on a wide variety of grounds. These have ranged from the alleged origin of authority in divine will, in nature, or in immemorial tradition through notions about consent and contract and on to various versions of utilitarian reasoning. The differences among such arguments are of course of great importance (we will be considering some of them in part 2). Among other things they influence judgments about the *prima facie* strength of the reason for action that authority attributions provide. But the differences do not affect the conceptual fact that to attribute authority to a rule or command is to give a reason for obeying that rule or command.

If authority attributions are reasons for action, it follows that they

conform to the logic of that notion. Contrary to Raz, the reasons valid
authority attributions provide for obedience are susceptible of comparative assessment; they are susceptible of assessment as more or less conclusive, more or less weighty, strong, convincing, etc. than other reasons
that might be given for this or that mode of action in response to X's.
Such comparative assessment, moreover, can lead to the conclusion that the
reason "authority" provides for obedience is so much weaker than reasons for competing modes of action that it is unreasonable to act on it.
Arguments for revolution are arguments to exactly this effect. The reasons that authority provides for obedience are judged by the revolutionary
to be so weak, so unpersuasive, that it is no longer reasonable to act on
them. If this judgment comes to be widely accepted, "authority" as it
attaches to the practice in question has lost, if not its "basis," at least one
of the properties it must have to affect action, namely standing as a reason
on which associates recognize that they should ordinarily act. With the
loss of this property, we are suggesting, the authority of the practice has
disappeared.[17]

It is important to note that the *concept* of authority, understood as
(among other things) providing a reason for certain classes of action,
remains available. One of the things that successful revolutionaries typically go on to try to do is win acceptance of the view that the concept has
positive application in the association they have newly created. They try,
that is, to arrive at the circumstance in which the attribution of authority
to X's is once again viewed as a cogent, weighty, persuasive, indeed
ordinarily conclusive, reason for obedience. To the extent that they succeed, *in* authority and *in* authority relations will be established in the
society or association.

On this interpretation, judgments about the merits of the secular tendencies of X's, and action on those judgments, are an integral part of *in*
authority relations. This is true in a sense connected with, but going
beyond, those entailed by problems about the validity and about the
interpretation of particular rules. Widespread and successful action on
adverse judgments concerning X's, it is true, may put an end to the
practice of *in* authority that yielded those X's. But neither such judgments
nor the actions taken on them can be adequately identified, characterized
or assessed apart from the fact that they occur in and in respect to a
practice of *in* authority. Understood in this way, action on judgments
concerning merits is restricted in that disobedience is warranted primarily
if not exclusively to destroy a practice of *in* authority that has yielded
unacceptable rules and commands. But the judgments that lead to such
action are and must be a feature of the ongoing interactions that make up
the authority relations.

The civil disobedient position abandons the restriction that disobedience should be considered only to bring down a practice of authority. Disobedience can be characterized as civil only if its objective is to remedy unacceptabilities in A's and X's *without* bringing down the practice. If the disobedience does lead to the destruction or even the serious weakening of the practice of authority in question, the action is considered a failure. It is for this reason that most proponents of the position have argued that the action must be nonviolent, public as opposed to secretive or conspiratorial, and done with the expectation that arrest and punishment will properly ensue.[18]

All of these requirements, as well as the statements that the disobedient makes about and as a part of the act of disobeying, are intended to manifest respect for the practice of authority that is being disobeyed. Indeed it has commonly been argued that the disobedient action is taken in part for the purpose of protecting the practice of *in* authority against the demise that likely awaits it if the train of substantively unacceptable A's and X's continues unchecked. Civil disobedience, in short, is an action taken by persons self-consciously acting—and intending to continue to act—the role of B. It is an action intended to remedy substantive unacceptabilities while protecting authority against revolution.

Needless to say, the claim that civil disobedience is an action done out of respect for and in defense of authority, even the claim that it is an action done by B's identifying themselves as such, meets strong resistance. "An open refusal to obey an unjust law," Herbert J. Storing wrote, "shows the highest respect for law in the same way that an open insult to a degraded woman, with a willingness to be slapped for the insult, shows the highest respect for womanhood."[19] Civil disobedience, in the less highly charged language of the F-P theorist, is a withdrawal from the practice of authority, a termination of the authority relationship on B's part. It may or may not have further consequences, and any consequences it proves to have may be beneficial or deleterious, but it is not an action taken from within the authority relationship itself. That relationship simply does not accommodate the degree or extent of judgment, or at least action on judgment, on B's part that the theory of civil disobedience seeks to accord. Whatever the intentions of civil disobedients, their position is at best a recommendation for a substantial change in established understandings and practices of authority and at worst an argument that we should do away with *in* authority.

There are, of course, elements of recommendation and persuasive definition in any theory of authority. As noted, practice is neither so uniform nor so clearly delineated as to permit of an analysis of what authority is and is not that will not be open to cogent objection. It is nevertheless tolerably clear that the theory of civil disobedience is congruent with salient features of major instances of the practice of *in* authority. Itemizing the main points of congruence will put us in a position to summarize and draw conclusions from this exploration of the "surrender of judgment."

Civil disobedients do not deny that there are distinctive characteristics to questions about proper action in a practice of *in* authority. They do not argue that the proper response to a rule or command can or should be settled exclusively by assessing the merits of that rule or command. They accept that the role of B is a distinctive social role, one defined by quite definite requirements and prohibitions. It is a role that is incomprehensible apart from structured, rule-governed relationships with A's and X's, that is with other statuses, roles and rules that have a social standing which cannot be fully analyzed in terms of the merits of any instance or collection of instances of A's and X's. Civil disobedients manifest their acceptance of these understandings in the following ways:

1. By treating questions about subscription and obedience, non-subscription and disobedience, as distinct and distinctively important questions—questions that require serious concern and sustained, reflective attention. (One might say that civil disobedients have shown their sense of the distinctiveness of these questions precisely by elaborating a notion of *civil* disobedience.)

2. By accepting that there are circumstances in which well-grounded adverse judgments about the merits of X's do not provide a sufficient justification for disobedience. The distinction between a single unjust or otherwise objectionable X and a recurring pattern of such rules and comments is perhaps the most dramatic manifestation of this view, but in almost all versions of the theory it is accompanied by less categorical maxims counseling restraint and circumspection when deciding whether to engage in civil disobedience.

3. By accepting a variety of constraints on the modes of conduct that will be employed in the course of disobedient action. Among the more important of these are that the action will be done openly, not conspiratorially, and without the use of physical violence.

4. By insisting that well-founded adverse judgments about a series of X's, although perhaps justifying disobedience that can reasonably be expected to assist in bringing about the alteration or repeal of those X's, do not deprive the A's of the authority to attach and enforce legal sanctions for disobedience and do not justify the B's in resisting or even objecting to the application of sanctions for their disobedience. Well-grounded adverse judgments about X's, in other words, do not themselves (directly) deprive the latter of their authority. The only implication that follows immediately from such judgments is that the obligation to obey the X's, which ordinarily follows (the civil disobedient insists) from the fact of their authority, is called into question as a conclusive reason for obeying

them. It remains *a* reason for obedience to which the serious-minded B must give considerable weight (which it does not do, for example, for the revolutionary). But if the judgment that the X's are strongly objectionable conjoins with a number of other judgments about matters such as the likely consequences of the acts of disobedience, including the likely effects of acts of disobedience for the viability of the practice of authority, that judgment is accepted as contributing to a justification for disobedience.

Given these characteristics and commitments, it is hardly surprising that civil disobedients have been attacked for what they concede to authority as well as for what they seek to withhold from it. The items just iterated comprise a far from modest list of concessions to a manifestly dangerous institution. Surely few if any committed anarchists would give over their hostility to authority simply because civil disobedience became an accepted part of authority relations. A showing that the idea of civil disobedience is compatible with *in* authority will not itself settle the question whether the practice of *in* authority can be justified. (One of the reasons for the foregoing judgment deserves emphasis at this juncture. The theory of civil disobedience does not itself establish criteria by which to judge whether laws and commands are acceptable. It contends that judgments about the merits of rules are internal to authority relations and that action on such judgments should be of a certain character—should be limited in certain ways. Theories of civil disobedience, however, are often intimately connected with proposed criteria for judging the merits of laws and commands. A well-known example is the argument of John Rawls—an argument that effects a very close relationship between the theory of civil disobedience and the theory of justice. But the assessmental criteria connected with a theory of civil disobedience could as well be utilitarian, natural rights criteria, religious criteria, and so forth. Thus the arguments of this chapter need supplementing by a theory that specifies and orders the criteria that are to be employed in judging the X's. We attempt such a theory in part 2 in the limited [but not unimportant] sense that we propose a necessary condition—namely compatibility with individual agency—which any system of *in* authority rules must satisfy. [We do not attempt to identify a single substantive criterion or set of criteria—for example, the greatest happiness of the greatest number, Rawls' difference principle or other egalitarian principles, Nozick's natural rights—the satisfaction of which would be a sufficient condition of the acceptability of any given rule.] If accepted, the criterion there offered would further limit the range of thought and action appropriate to participation in authority relations. It would give preference to certain criteria of judgment in the process of deciding whether the authority of an X provided a good reason for obeying it.)

It is nevertheless undeniable that a practice of authority which incorporates the theory and practice of civil disobedience allows a wider scope to B's judgments and action on those judgments than is permitted by F-P theory. But does such a practice deserve the name of a practice of *in* authority? An understanding of *in* authority that permits an affirmative answer to this question renders the practice of authority substantially less objectionable to us (who, despite finding the anarchist position not only rational but attractive, do not subscribe to it) than it presents itself in F-P accounts. We can hardly pretend that our answer to analytic questions is free of the influence of this normative position. But there are considerations of a tolerably neutral character that support a conceptualization of *in* authority that will accommodate civil disobedience.

These considerations can be abbreviated as follows. The theory of civil disobedience accepts that questions about the merits of X's can only arise and can only be addressed and resolved where there are certain institutionalized relationships and shared understandings. These relationships and understandings consist in rules of several types, of values and beliefs that are widely shared among the members of the society or association in question, and of more or less distinct roles, statuses, and recurrent patterns of action that have grown up around and in respect to those rules and beliefs. Now if there are any useful short answers to the question "What is a practice of *in* authority?" as good a candidate as any is that such a practice *is* just such a constellation of interconnected rules, beliefs, statuses and roles and the thought and action that characteristically take place in and in respect to that constellation. The fact that civil disobedience presupposes and accepts such a constellation argues persuasively that it is a mode of thought and action internal to the practice of *in* authority.

Summary and Concluding Remarks

We summarize the foregoing discussion by reviewing the several respects in which *in* authority relations do *not* entail a "surrender of judgment" on B's part.

1. The B's must make the judgment that their society or association includes *in* authority.

2. The B's must judge whether putative X's are valid and must determine the actions that valid X's require of them.

3. Judgments about validity and implication require assessments of intentions and pro-attitudes and hence involve questions about the desirability of X's viewed in terms of their substance or content. The con-

tention that such questions *ought not* to be raised betrays awareness that they can be raised and that it is commonly thought appropriate for (if not a duty of) the B's to raise them, to answer them, and to act on their answers to them.

4. The duty to raise and answer questions about the merits of X's could be discharged without considering whether to disobey them. This stance would itself imply acceptance of a judgment, namely, that the B's *qua* B's should not connect judgments about merits with the question of obedience or disobedience. But such a connection is, in fact, commonly made, and it is legitimated in differing ways and degrees by theories of revolution and of civil disobedience. These theories effect more-than-contingent connections between judgments about the merits of sequences of X's and questions about obedience and disobedience, and hence between such judgments and the continued existence of *in* authority. Surrender of judgment concerning these questions would mark not the continuation or strengthening but the termination of the *in* authority relationship.

In sum, the notion that "surrender of individual judgment" in any of the senses we have considered is a defining (or any other kind of) feature of the practice of *in* authority is, at the very least, seriously misleading. The exercise of judgment about these several kinds of questions plays an absolutely central part in the practice of *in* authority. So far from excluding such judgment, the practice of authority would be impossible without it and is incomprehensible without recognition of it.

Notwithstanding its clash with a long tradition of interpretation and theorizing about authority, this conclusion is hardly surprising. It is unsurprising because the practice of authority is a normative practice; it is a practice that is a source of warrants for and justifications of the actions of participants. The fact that a rule or command has authority provides B with a reason for conforming to it. The same fact is understood to warrant the A's and the other B's in expecting B to conform to X and in some circumstances in punishing any B who refuses to do so. And so forth through a considerable list. This being the case, the idea that a subclass of participants in the practice—that is a subclass of the agents for whom the practice provides reasons for action—must or should give up the prerogative of judging and acting on their judgments is a kind of contradiction in terms. On the one hand, persons in this subclass are said to be agents whose conduct is subject to reasoned guidance, to assessment, and to various kinds of guilt and innocence, praise and blame, remorse and satisfaction; on the other, it is said that they must give over to others those very processes of judgment in the absence of which the former set of characterizations has no application. It is not the practice of authority that generates this impossibility, but imposition and domination seeking to clothe itself in the normative garb of authority.[20]

We do not intend to accuse all theorists of "surrender of judgment" of proposing or apologizing for domination and imposition. The notion of surrender of judgment achieved its prominent place in the literature of authority out of attempts to analyze an important characteristic of authority relations. Such relations form a distinct, rule-governed practice; a practice consisting in established rules, statuses, roles and widely accepted values and beliefs, and of the patterns of thought and action that take place in, and that variously influence and are influenced by, the rules, statuses, roles and beliefs. Participation in the practice involves (to varying degrees) following the rules, playing the roles, occupying the statuses and accepting and acting on the values and beliefs in which the practice consists. Thus participation in the practice *is* thinking and acting within the limits thereof; it is thinking and acting within the constraints and the guidelines that its rules, roles, and so forth establish. There are modes of thought and action that are permitted, some that are encouraged, some that are required; there are others that are tolerated, that are discouraged, and that are prohibited. Our explorations in the foregoing pages have been of some of the requirements and prohibitions, some of the inducements and dissuasions, that have been salient in notable instances of the practice.

In this perspective the notion of surrender of judgment might be understood as referring to the acceptance, by participants, of this not inconsiderable array of constraints, limitations and directives. If these rules, roles, beliefs, and so forth are a feature of practice, then acceptance of and conformity with them is necessarily a feature of participation in it. There are many thoughts and actions that are excluded, many inclinations and desires that must be set aside or pursued in some other context or forum.

Neither the reality nor the importance of these characteristics of the practice of authority should be denied or minimized. But it is profoundly misleading to conceptualize them as involving a "surrender" of judgment by participants. The characteristics, rather, are and could only be products of, are and could only be sustained by, the continuing exercise of judgment by participants. The practice is not an alien, external force that imposes itself like a *deus ex machina* on the lives of participants, it is part of the patterns of thought and action in which those lives consist. If participants cease to follow the rules, refuse to play the roles, reject the values and beliefs, the practice is gone. Because there is no such thing as following a rule, playing a role, or accepting a value or belief without the continuing exercise of judgment and action on judgment, surrender of judgment and action on it would mark the end of the practice.

7 Power

The relationship between power and authority has been a matter of sharp controversy among social theorists at least through the better part of the present century. In the view of a number of influential writers—for example Max Weber, Roberto Michels, G. E. G. Catlin, Bertrand Russell, David Easton, Sebastian de Grazia, Talcott Parsons, several jural theorists in the tradition of Austin, most writers of a Marxist orientation—authority is a type, a species or a manifestation of power. It is power "exercised in accordance with a convention" (Catlin), "power based on esteem" (de Grazia), "exercised ascendance; a manifestation of power" (Michels), "institutionalized power" (Parsons), or, as in the Marxist view of capitalist societies, power all but plain and simple with no more than the most transparent cloak of rationalizing ideology thrown over it. On each of these understandings, if "power" and "authority" are not simply interchangeable terms, at least there is an intimate conceptual relationship between them. A person's ignorance of power would betoken the same condition in respect to authority, and it would be a conceptual impossibility for there to be authority apart from power. The relationship between the two, moveover, is typically portrayed as hierarchical in the sense in which a genus (in this case power) is superior to any one of its species (in this case authority). (Thus, as already implied, there can be no authority without power, but for some of the writers just listed there can be power without authority.)[1]

The foregoing understanding of the matter has been contested by an account according to which "power" and "authority" are, conceptually, altogether distinct. Possessed of a pedigree that traces at least to Socrates' argument with Thrasymachus and that is especially marked in the Thomist and neo-Thomist traditions of political and religious thought, this position has found numerous and distinguished proponents in recent years. Hannah Arendt, Michael Crozier, Bertrand de Jouvenel, Richard B. Friedman, Carl J. Friedrich, H. L. A. Hart, Michael Oakeshott, Yves Simon and Peter Winch have argued that, however important it may be politically or in some other perspective, there is no more than an empirical relationship between power and authority.[2] Someone who understands power has thus far understood little or nothing about authority as such (and vice versa), and while the two frequently coexist and influence one another in important ways, instances of power but no authority and of authority but no power are altogether to be expected.

Our present interest in this set of questions arises from our concern to understand and assess authority. Of the various means that A might employ to influence B's action, power and authority are the two that are most commonly assimilated. If clarity concerning rules, offices and "surrender of judgment" is the most important desideratum of an account of what *in* authority is, analyzing its relations with power is the most vital task in determining what it is not. From this perspective, which must limit the range of our effort to analyze power, it is tempting to argue that the considerations advanced in the previous chapters are themselves sufficient to settle the issue in favor of the second of the two schools of thought just sketched. We have argued that A's having authority to promulgate X provides him with a warrant for doing so; and B's recognition of A's authority itself provides him with an obligation, and hence a weighty, ordinarily conclusive reason for accepting and conforming with X. If this contention is correct, the argument that authority is a species of power appears to be a variant of the indefensible (though hardly extinct) view that might makes right.

Unfortunately this last inference, though by no means groundless, is an oversimplification of a rather more complex matter. Authority *is* importantly distinct from, cannot be reduced to or equated with, power. But the two are importantly related—related in ways that militate against treating either in isolation from the other. The assertion that authority is categorically distinct from power, while plainly an improvement on the contention that it is reducible to or at most a sort of species of power, shares with the latter the vice of deflecting our attention from the details of the relationship between the two.

Power and Force

Rejecting the reductionist thesis, but nevertheless wanting to explore the relationship between the two concepts, we must obtain some degree of clarity concerning each concept taken alone. We have been trying to clarify "authority" in the previous chapters, but "power" remains almost entirely unexamined in these pages. Fortunately, the latter concept has received a good deal of attention in recent years. The results achieved by other investigators will do much to lead us to a more tenable position than the two we have noted thus far.

We begin by noting a feature which, at quite a high level of abstraction, is common to both "power" and "authority" and has been a major influence on writers who assimilate the two concepts. The feature concerns the post or station typically occupied by the two concepts. As noted, "power" and "authority" (and a considerable further array of concepts such as influence, leadership, persuasion, manipulation) both refer to attributes by which or processes through which one person or group of persons (A) is able to affect the thought and action of others (B). There are of course a great variety of cases in which such effects occur, a great diversity of instances in which it is impossible to understand what B has thought, said, or otherwise done apart from the direct or indirect effects on him of something that A has thought, said or done. It is therefore less than surprising that there is a considerable diversity of lower-order, less widely ranging concepts that figure in talk about the actions and interactions by which such effects are brought about. A can aid and abet, bid and ban, cajole and coerce, tempt, taunt and threaten B and B's conduct. As foolish as it would be to deny the differences among these processes, we will not understand the tendency to reduce power and authority to some common denominator without attending to the fact that both are used to generalize over some more or less encompassing range of those differences. B did X because A, whose authority he respects, directed him to do it; B did X because A, whose power he fears, directed him to do it.

The similarity in form of these two explanations for B's conduct masks very important differences that are among the central concerns of this chapter. Indeed, each statement taken alone requires a good deal of unpacking. Our immediate task is to identify at least a few of the complexities involved in saying that B's thought or action occurred because of A's power.

The fact that such explanatory statements appear to be causal in character has tempted a number of students of power to analyze them by analogy with causal explanations of occurrences in inanimate nature. A prominent case in point is the widely discussed analysis of Bertrand Russell. Although Russell defined power as "the production of intended effects," he thought of power and power relations as the social phenomenon most closely akin to energy and its effects on matter. His book was intended to show, in his words, "that the fundamental concept in social science is Power, in the same sense in which Energy is the fundamental concept in physics." "The laws of social dynamics," he went on to say, like the laws of physics, "are the laws which can only be stated in terms of power, not in terms of this or that form of power."[3] Students of power in this or that society might have to attend to the distinctive forms, and the traditions and conventions that partly explain them, that power takes in that society. But the true social scientist, understanding that social science no less than physics or chemistry must seek general laws, must get beneath such features of local history to power in its most basic character, that is as a kind of energy or force that is effectively in the service of A's intentions.

Of course there is an analogy between statements about energy in physics and statements about power in social science. The basis of the analogy is the commonality mentioned above, that both concepts are sometimes used to understand or to explain the effects of A's thought, action or perhaps mere existence on B. Nor is it difficult to understand that a theorist in quest of "general laws" of social life would be attracted to this analogy.

But Russell's own definition of power does much to weaken (if not to render useless) the analogy he wants to pursue. The specification that the effects of power must be intended—and hence that power and power relations involve an agent capable of and in fact forming and acting upon intentions—itself introduces a range of complexities that have no place in the analysis of energy and its effects upon matter.

There are many additional disanalogies. Russell's definition has merit as an account of important uses of the concept of force. Moreover, it can hardly be denied that the *word* "power" is commonly used in a manner indistinguishable from uses of "force," "violence" and even "strength" and "energy." There are nevertheless important differences among the *concepts* that these words most frequently mark. These differences are slurred over by Russell's discussion.[4]

In most general and basic terms, we will argue, power is a feature of interactions between or among two or more agents or groups of agents (A and B) each of whom (or which) are capable of and are in fact acting intentionally. Except in special senses to be discussed below, it is not a feature of the action of one agent (A) acting intentionally upon or against a subject or object who or which is incapable of such action or not in fact engaging in it in the relation with A in question. A may use *force* on or against an object in inanimate nature and may do so in order to produce certain intended effects. He may also employ force against a person ordinarily capable of action. He may do so if, for example, he acts on B without B's foreknowledge (A approaches B from the rear and violently pushes him so that his body crashes into C) or with such overwhelming violence that responsive action on B's part is impossible. As most recent analysts have agreed, however, "power" can no more be assimilated to "force" and "violence" than to the yet more primitive "energy" by analogy with which Russell tried to analyze it. Robert Dahl's account, although objectionable on other grounds not relevant here, is representative of many in this regard. Power has been exercised, Dahl argues, to the extent that A successfully gets B to do something that he (B) would not otherwise do.[5]

Of course force and violence play a part in power and its exercise. The capacity or wherewithal to use force and violence often, perhaps even typically, are vital to power relations. The (minimal) thrust of Dahl's definition, and of the more general point that power is a relation among agents acting intentionally, is rather that B must be aware of, must in some measure understand, and must act intentionally in response to the intention on which A is acting in seeking to exercise power over him (B).

A Schema for Analyzing Power and Power Relations Power as Intentional Action and Interaction

As we shall shortly see, this analysis is controversial in several respects. We proceed by elaborating it in schematic terms and then by testing the schema against competing accounts. Insofar as possible we restrict ourselves to issues that have a bearing on the relationship between power and authority.

In skeletal form, the basic elements of power relationships are the following: (1) A forms a purpose or objective and the intention to act to pursue it; (2) the purpose or objective may consist exclusively in, but in any case cannot (in A's view) be satisfactorily achieved without, getting B to act or to refrain from acting in a manner (X) that (3) A has reason to believe B is disinclined to do. (4) A directs or otherwise indicates that B should X and, in order to overcome his disinclination, (5) threatens B with some consequence (Y) that (6) A believes B will dislike, if B does not X (or, perhaps, offers or promises to provide B with some good that B desires if he X's). (7) B then decides whether to X. (8) If or to the extent that B decides to X despite his continued aversion to it and because he wants to avoid (or obtain) Y, A has successfully exercised power over B. (9) If B decides not to X, or if he decides to X for some reason other than to avoid (or obtain) Y, A has attempted to exercise power over B but has failed. A may then try additional threats, he may give up or redefine his objective, or he may continue to pursue the objective by means other than the exercise of power, for example persuading B to X by giving reasons not involving the threat or offer of Y, manipulating B or his circumstances, or (if B's *doing* X is not essential to achieving the objective) bringing some species of force directly to bear on B such that X is brought about without B's agency (for example, B's body is physically moved in the manner that A desires, B is hypnotized or drugged and then stimulated to X, and so forth), or by obtaining authority over X and commanding him to X.

Each of these elements (and the distinctions among power, persuasion, manipulation, force, and authority that arise in connection with them) presents itself in a considerable variety of forms. The foregoing brief remarks about them could profitably be elaborated at some length. Manifestly we have to elaborate on the distinction between authority and power. Beyond that, we restrict ourselves to further comments that bear on the basic idea that power relationships are among agents interacting intentionally.

Dahl's version of point 3 provides a good starting place. He argues that X must be an action that B would not "otherwise" do, that is would not do in the absence of A's initiative and threat or offer. This phraseology correctly suggests that A does not literally compel B to X. But it also allows us to speak of power when A's actions affect B only in the sense that they alter his circumstances sufficiently so that he is faced with the decision whether to X. Although it has a point to which we will have to attend, this formulation is too weak to convey the character of what are at least the most important cases of the exercise of power. It is not merely that it would not have occurred to B to X, it is that B has a positive aversion to or dislike for doing X. In this respect Peter Bachrach and Morton S. Baratz are closer to the mark with their argument that "in order for a power relationship to exist there must be a conflict of interests or values between two or more persons or groups. . . . [I]f A and B are in agreement as to ends [which, on Dahl's formulation, they might prove to be once A had brought the question of doing X to B's attention] B will freely assent to A's course of action."[6] B does "freely assent" in the weak sense that he is not literally compelled to X, but his assent is based, not on any value he assigns to X independently of A's threat to Y, but on his desire to avoid Y. This point has important bearing on the distinction between power and authority. As we see in further detail below, B's doing any particular X out of respect for the authority of A's command is not based in any direct way on his desire to avoid the sanction Y which A has attached to B's refusal. But neither need it be based (contrary to what Bachrach and Baratz seem to imply[7] and what Talcott Parsons explicitly affirms concerning both power and authority)[8] on the value that he had placed or has come to place on X itself. Although the latter consideration may play a role, B's decision to obey can be based on his respect for the system of authority and the obligations he has as a participant therein.[9]

But Dahl's formulation, if interpreted to include the Bachrach and Baratz point about conflict of interests or values, does have the merit of encompassing cases that seem to be excluded, or at least obscured, by our initial list of conditions. The list at least tacitly suggests that there must be a direct, an unmediated, relationship between A and B in respect to X and Y. It suggests that A must communicate a directive to do X and a threat or offer of Y directly to B and that B must respond to that X and Y. This construction makes it difficult to deal with cases of what might be called the indirect exercise of power. Sometimes A attempts to get B to do X by altering the circumstances or arrangements under which B would otherwise be thinking and acting. To take a deliberately simple example as a starting point, assume that A and B each operate a service station in a certain neighborhood. As B knows, A would like to eliminate B's competition. Instead of persuading B to go out of business ("the work is bad for your health," "if we continue to compete we will both go broke"), arranging to bring authority to bear (for example, having B's property rezoned), or exercising power as we have thus far analyzed it (say threatening to start a price war), A convinces the only wholesale supplier to cut off deliveries to B. Has A exercised power over B?

A's action has "produced intended effects," and one of the effects it has produced is that B has gone out of business, something (we will assume) that B not only would not otherwise have done but that he very much did not want to do (thus satisfying Dahl's definition with the Bachrach and Baratz amendment). On the other hand, B has not decided to go out of business as a direct, intentional response to a harm he knows to have been threatened by A. In an important sense B has not decided to do anything. A's action has made it impossible for B to do otherwise than go out of business.

Owing to the last-mentioned feature of the example, there is good reason for treating A's action as an exercise of force or manipulation, not of power. (The terminology is of secondary significance. What matters is that we recognize the differences, above all the conceptual differences, between this kind of case and cases which involve a decision on B's part.) Let us therefore alter the example so that A (without first explicitly threatening B) obtains priority in the delivery of (potentially or actually) limited supplies and that B learns of this action. B can continue in business, but his decision to do so is made under circumstances that have been significantly altered by A's action. Here, although A has not threatened B directly, it is an intended result of A's action that B is threatened by a harm and B must make a decision that he would not otherwise make. About this kind of case, of which there are of course a plentitude of varied instances, it seems best to say that power has been exercised by A over B. As indicated, we will refer to such cases as the exercise of indirect power. (Note that in both cases A might well have exercised direct power over the supplier, the zoning board, etc.).

Competing Schemas Harmful but Unintended Consequences
as a Criterion of Power

To recognize the "indirect" exercise of power opens
up a wide array of questions concerning the basic idea that power relations are among agents interacting intentionally. We turn now to recent
analyses in which these questions have been explored in ways that challenge the adequacy of the schema thus far presented.

Bachrach and Baratz were primarily concerned to call attention to what
they called the second "face" of power and power relationships. They
stressed that power is commonly used by A's not only to get B's to do
something that they do not want to do but to prevent B's from doing what
they very much want to do. In particular they emphasized that A's use
power to keep questions and issues off of "the agenda" of their society or
association, thereby forestalling if not eliminating the possibility that
those questions will get decided in ways contrary to the interests or desires of the A's.

We may begin to illustrate this "face" of power with our earlier example. Imagine that B decides that he would like to open a service station in
the same neighborhood as A's. On inquiry into the possibility of doing so,
he finds that A has priority in the delivery of limited supplies and that in
the past A has used that advantage to drive competitors out of business.
He seeks an understanding with A but finds that the latter will not so much
as discuss the arrangement. B's letters to A go unanswered, he encounters difficulty in reaching A by phone, obtaining an appointment with him,
and so forth. And if he does succeed in contacting him he receives the sort
of response (to shift to a more interesting example) that antipollution
activists are reported to have received from the managers of the United
States Steel plant in Gary, Indiana: " 'The company executives . . . would
just nod sympathetically and agree that air pollution was terrible, and pat
you on the head. But they never did anything one way or the other.' . . .
What U.S. Steel did not do was probably more important to the career of
Gary's air pollution than what it did do."[10] Here the A's exercise power
over the B's without, apparently, doing anything at all. Given their position, the A's are able to prevent the B's from achieving their objective
simply by sitting tight. And when the B's give up their project in frustra-
tion and despair, it can be said that they have had power exercised over
them despite not having done an X that they would have done.

There is no doubt that the political importance of this "second face" of
power exceeds the attention it had explicitly received prior to the work of
Bachrach and Baratz—and hence the attention it had received from students of power whose formulations influenced the above schema. Nor is

there any doubt that the "second face" of power is often peculiarly difficult to identify in empirical social scientific study. If an issue never makes it onto "the agenda," never surfaces explicitly, the analyst on the lookout for explicit actions and threats may never learn that its emergence was prevented by an exercise of power on A's part.

It is less clear that any significant conceptual shift occurs when "power" is used in identifying and analyzing this "second face." The alleged distinction depends on the difference between explicit, manifest, or perhaps affirmative actions and refusals to perform such actions. This difference is no doubt important in many contexts. As disgraceful as it was that people stood by and watched the murder of Kitty Genovese, their fault was less grave than the fault of her murderer. But they were grievously at fault. And our insistence on saying so removes any doubt that refusals to act fall within the class of intentional actions. A's refusal to give up his *de facto* control over scarce resources is every bit as intentional as his efforts to obtain that control to begin with. The refusal of U.S. Steel to cooperate to reduce pollution levels was every bit as intentional as their decision to adopt industrial practices that created the pollution problem. (And if their refusal to cooperate was accompanied by explicit or implicit threats against those who might attempt to induce them to cooperate—antipollution activists, the city or state government, local politicians, trade union leaders—then their intentional actions deserve to be called exercises of power in our sense. On this point, see below, chap. 7, n. 20.) Bachrach and Baratz and those who have followed their lead apply the concept of power in ways that enrich the empirical literature on the subject. But their analyses neither propose nor effect conceptual change.

Another contemporary student of the subject, however, namely Steven Lukes in the book from which we just quoted, explicitly challenges the conceptualization that has dominated recent discussions and that we have been developing here. Lukes launches his proposal from the platform provided by the Bachrach-Baratz position (which he calls the "two-dimensional" view of power). He agrees that Bachrach and Baratz do not escape the idea that power relations are among agents acting and interacting intentionally. Moreover, he is entirely willing to go on using "power" of such relationships (that is, he is willing to use it in the manner analyzed by the schema set out above). But he contends that its use should be extended to cases which involve no intentional—or, in his terms, no "conscious"[11]—action on the part of A, of B, or indeed of either A or B.

Lukes develops and illustrates his "three-dimensional" or "radical" view of power by reference to Crenson's analysis of the "unpolitics" of air pollution. He agrees that much of Crenson's explanation for the difficulties encountered by antipollution activists in Gary is framed in terms of the two-dimensional view of power. As he interprets Crenson's discussion of the events and "nonevents" in Gary, however, he finds that the two-dimensional explanation is an incomplete account of them. This is primarily because it fails to explain the fact that antipollution activists were unable to generate anything like widespread or intense concern about pollution and hence were unable to develop strong popular support for the antipollution measures they proposed. Despite objectively high and dangerous pollution levels, the bulk of the Gary populace remained largely indifferent to them. Antipollution issues were kept off the agenda not only by the devices discussed above but by some yet more subtle, difficult to discern, and effective process that prevented the development of concern over them.

In Lukes' view, indeed, this process was so difficult to discern that the B's were not aware that it was taking place and so subtle that the A's were not aware that they were "employing" it. Lukes nevertheless insists that it involved the use of power—this time in his three-dimensional sense. (Or rather, because the verbs "employ" and "use" seem out of place, it would be better to say that the process "involved" or "included" power.) What is the evidence that some such process was at work? What are the criteria in terms of which we can determine that the process involved power? On Lukes' (initial) account, the answer to both of these questions is the same. The evidence that power was at work is that, objectively speaking, the interests of one class (category?) of people (which the analyst has identified) were well served by existing arrangements, policies, or whatever; the interests of another class of people (identified, once again, by the analyst) were badly served by them. In short, evidence that outcomes, effects, or consequences (of what?) were or are (systematically?) unfavorable to the objectively defined interests of one category of a populace, but (systematically?) advantageous to the interests of another category of that same (?) populace, is *sufficient* grounds for the conclusion that power has been at work in the relations (?) between the members of the two categories. Specifically, there need be no evidence that either A or B has acted "consciously" to bring about the result in question ("I propose to speak of the exercise of power whether by individuals or by groups, institutions, etc., and whether consciously or not")[12] and hence no need for evidence that A has intentionally threatened B with Y in order to get him to do X or that B has knowingly or intentionally responded to a threat-supported directive from A.

Power and Objectively Defined Interests

As Lukes has in fact developed this interpretation of "power," the controversial notion of objectively defined interests (and hence of "false consciousness" on at least some interpretations of that splendid *trompe l'oeil*) is crucial to it. His acceptance of this notion allows him a truly wonderful convenience: he can assert that the interests of whole categories of people have been served or disserved without acquiring evidence that they have had any such thoughts about themselves. Whether its political implications are radical-progressive, radical-reactionary or altogether indeterminate, this convenience could only be treasured by any social scientist who has struggled with the difficulties of finding out what large populations of highly idiosyncratic human beings think about themselves and their situations.

Later we will see that this convenience is bought at a high price in terms of clarity concerning "power." But let us first follow Lukes' development of his argument somewhat further. In Lukes' own understanding, the notion of objective interests is vital to his argument because it allows him to claim that our item 3 is a feature of and is in fact satisfied by the three-dimensional concept of power. His reasoning is as follows. As illustrated by the example Crenson provides, the preponderance of the populace of Gary showed no signs that they were unhappy about the levels of air pollution in the city, gave no explicit evidence that they would have "done otherwise" than accept those levels and the industrial practices that produced them. As Lukes puts it, the "relevant counterfactual" that he (somewhat surprisingly) admits is necessary to demonstrating that an exercise of power has occurred is not supplied by observable conflict between A and B.[13] But given the premise that the levels of pollution are, objectively speaking, contrary to the interests of the B's (and given a further unstated premise that people ordinarily act on their interests such that we need an explanation when they fail to do so), *something* must explain the fact that the B's do not act to protect those interests. That "something," Lukes proposes, is the power of the A's. Once the A's have been deprived of their power, the familiar argument seems to run, the B's will once again act on their own interests.

Power and Responsibility, Praise and Blame

There are difficulties with the notion of "true" or "objective" interests, and we will have occasion to return to some of them below. But these are by no means the only difficulties with Lukes' proposal. Evidence that one group of persons is systematically disadvantaged by, but not in fact objecting to, a practice or arrangement may be a good reason to *suspect* that power is being exercised over them and to seek evidence that confirms or disconfirms that suspicion. We can also agree that such evidence will often be difficult to ferret out.

But the way we have just put the matter is incompatible with the point that gives distinctive character to the three-dimensional view of power. It is a distinctive feature of the latter that evidence that one person or category of persons is advantaged, another disadvantaged is not a *symptom of* the exercise of power but the *criterion* by which to determine *that* power has been at work.

So understood, the analysis is deeply implausible. It implies, to take an admittedly extreme example, that there is no conceptual impropriety in explaining differential advantages resulting from purely natural conditions or the workings of purely natural forces in terms of power. If greater exposure to sunshine makes the residents of San Diego healthier than the residents of Seattle, the difference can *therefore* be conceptualized as a consequence of power.

Lukes, however, draws back from this implication. Having set out his three-dimensional view in the terms we have recounted, in a final substantive chapter he criticizes the Althusserian Marxist Nicos Poulantzas for making a "conceptual assimilation of power to structural determination."[14] He correctly argues that making this move serves (among other things) to render it impossible to attribute responsibility for the consequences of the exercise of power. To avoid this result, he amends his initial account to say that we can "identify a given process as an 'exercise of power'" only if "it is in the exerciser's or exercisers' power to act differently" than he, she or they in fact did.[15] This addition to the account clearly excludes the workings of natural forces from the realm of power. More important, it is specifically intended to exclude cases of action (including knowing inaction) in which A could not have done otherwise than he did because he "could not be [could not have been] expected" to know that his doing X would have adverse consequences for B. To use the example with which he himself illustrates this point, prior to the time that it was known that cigarette smoking causes cancer, the fact that the objective interests of cigarette smokers were adversely affected by smoking would not itself have warranted us in saying that the cigarette manufacturers exercised power over their customers. (But now that this fact is known, are the adverse effects on the customers *sufficient* to warrant the conclusion that the manufacturers are exercising power over the customers?)

It seems, in short, that there is little satisfaction to be gotten from attributions of power that do not carry with them attributions of responsibility (and hence assignment of praise, blame, etc.). And to bring these latter concepts into the picture we do need some sort of evidence about the conscious states of those alleged to have exercised power. At a minimum, we need to know that they could have known but did not in fact know that their "actions" caused harm to the B's.

In conceding this point, Lukes blurs the clarity and weakens the significance of the distinction between his three-dimensional view of power and the views, or rather—since the two-dimensional view is conceptually indistinguishable from the one-dimensional variety—the view, against which he is arguing. But he endeavors to minimize the concession, to save as much as he can of the three-dimensional view. He does so by narrowly restricting the evidence about conscious states that is required in order to attribute responsibility to the A's. We do not need to know that A acted intentionally or even knowingly to harm or disadvantage the B's. We need only know that A *could have* known that his actions would harm the B's and in this sense could have chosen to act otherwise. The notion that the A's could have acted otherwise than they did allows him (convinces him that he is entitled) to ascribe responsibility, praise and blame to A's who he not only admits but insists are not consciously acting to bring about the consequences for which he holds them responsible.

Power, Strict Liability, and Negligence

Viewed from the perspective of its connections with and implications for the concept of responsibility, Lukes' proposal concerning power can usefully be compared with the notions "strict liability" and "negligence" as they are used in legal and (to a much lesser extent) moral practice. These concepts are used to ascribe a special kind of responsibility (special at least in the sense that the kinds of punishments that can be imposed are narrowly limited by it), despite the absence of a number of the conditions that such ascription ordinarily presupposes. In the case of strict liability, in H. L. A. Hart's words, "it is no defense that [1] the accused did not intend to do the act which the law forbids and [2] could not, by the exercise of due care, have avoided doing it."[16] The notion of negligence works the same way in respect to 1: an accused can be convicted of, say, "manslaughter by negligence" despite the entire absence of intention to kill. But 2 drops out; the accused can successfully defend himself against the charge of negligence by showing that he had taken "due care" to determine whether his contemplated act would or would not be likely to cause death. His negligence, if such there was, consists in failing to take such care.

In the early stretches of his discussion Lukes' (implicit) use of "responsibility" closely approximates "liability" as it is employed in the notion of strict liability. And one has the impression that he ultimately draws back from this use for the same reasons that, as Hart argues, many jurists and legal philosophers have found the latter notion distasteful and even "odious."[17] Although initially attractive from a number of "social" or "utilitarian" perspectives, the notion so deviates from deeply normative conceptions of the individual and individual freedom as to be unacceptable. Whether for this or some other reason, Lukes then enters the modifications we have examined, modifications that bring his discussion of responsibility closer to the use of that concept in the law of negligence. The A's must be "conscious" of what they are doing at least to the extent necessary for the question of "due care" to have application to them.[18]

The law of negligence, however, is not concerned with power or its exercise. A main question that emerges from this discussion of Lukes' analysis of the power of the A's concerns the advantages and disadvantages of thinking of it on the model of negligent conduct. (Additional questions arise concerning his analysis of the B's.) We can pursue this question by referring to Crenson's probing study of the "unpolitics" of pollution in Gary.

If we read Crenson's analysis with Lukes' proposal in mind, three possibilities present themselves as ways of characterizing the A's and what they did and did not do. We identify and examine these in the course of the remainder of this chapter.

1. The A's were knowingly and intentionally acting to achieve or maintain some objective, and their actions included attempts—whether direct or indirect—to get some number of persons (B's) to do or refrain from doing various X's by explicitly or implicitly threatening them with various Y's. Some at least of those affected by the actions of the A's were aware of this and knowingly and intentionally responded—whether directly or indirectly—to them.

As we read Crenson, and as Lukes seems to agree, a good part of what occurred in Gary in the period in question is best understood in these terms. The moguls of U.S. Steel knew perfectly well that their industrial practices produced levels of pollution that were seriously harmful to the health and well-being of the entire populace of the city and area. Although small and politically ineffective, the antipollution forces had seen to this much. ("The company executives . . . would just nod sympathetically and agree that air pollution was terrible.") Whether out of a crass, selfish desire to maximize profits, to satisfy distant stockholders, and so forth, or perhaps in the sincere belief that they were contributing to GNP, to the fight against unemployment, or to maintaining a free enterprise economy, they employed such devices as were available to them to resist efforts to change those practices. Possessed of a good deal of the wherewithal necessary to make highly credible threats and to offer inducements that were difficult to resist,[19] the exercise of both direct and indirect power—as that concept is analyzed by our initial schema—was prominent among those devices. They may have used it subtly and indirectly, but they used it liberally and effectively.[20]

2. A second possibility is that some number of A's were "exercising" power in Lukes' third-dimensional sense; that is they were acting "negligently" in the sense that emerged from our examination of Lukes' pro-

posal. Information about the harmful effects of their industrial practices was available; hence a condition necessary to their deciding to alter those practices was satisfied. But they had not taken the trouble, had not exercised the due care, to acquire that information. Thus they could not be said to be knowingly and intentionally acting to cause harm to the populace and could not be said to be exercising power in the sense of our schema.[21] And because many residents of the city did not know that they were being harmed, made no objection to the practices that harmed them, it would be wrong to say that they had been subjected to power in the sense given by our schema. But because the actions of the A's (including their refusals to act) did in fact harm those residents, we can say that those actions constituted an exercise of power in Lukes' third-dimensional sense, and we can say that the B's were subjected to power in that sense.

As an analysis of what occurred in Gary, especially as an account of what was done by U.S. Steel, this account is implausible on its face and receives little if any support from Crenson's investigation. It is unlikely in the extreme that U.S. Steel officials were unaware of the information about pollution levels or of the judgment that those levels were seriously harmful. (They may have rejected, sincerely or otherwise, the latter judgment, but either assumption removes them from the distinctive aspects of Lukes' schema.) It is more plausible that some more or less substantial proportion of the population was unaware of or unconcerned about that information and judgment. And they may have been and may have remained in that condition in part because U.S. Steel exercised its power (in our sense) to prevent the media, the unions, the school system, the local political leadership, and so forth from making the information and the judgment available to them. But here again use of Lukes' extended sense of "power" to analyze the situation serves to distort rather than to clarify it.

Reflection about the Gary example suggests that we are in fact unlikely to identify cases of substantial, continuing exercises of power in Lukes' extended sense. If the information that a policy or a practice is seriously harmful to large numbers of people is in fact "available" in any useful sense of the term (which would not include, for example, the sense that it was deeply implicit in the results of basic scientific research but not yet derived or applied to the industrial or technological practice in question), it is likely to be brought to the attention of those following that policy or practice. And from the instant that they have that information they fall out of Lukes' category of "negligent actors." (It is for this reason that the law of negligence typically finds its applications to episodic incidents, to cases in which an agent or agency harms others by a particular act in the performance of which he, she or it did not exercise due care.)

But there are almost certainly some cases that meet Lukes' requirement. Let us assume so and ask whether it would be appropriate to think of them as instances of the exercise of power. One of the general reflections that Hart drew from his examination of the law of strict liability and negligence will put this inquiry in an appropriate perspective:

> Human society is a society of persons; and persons do not view themselves or each other merely as so many bodies moving in ways which are sometimes harmful and have to be prevented or altered. Instead persons interpret each other's movements as manifestations of intention and choices, and these subjective factors are often more important to their social relations than the movements by which they are manifested or their effects. If one person hits another, the person struck does not think of the other as just a cause of pain for him; for it is of crucial importance to him whether the blow was deliberate or involuntary. If the blow was light but deliberate, it has a significance for the person struck quite different from an accidental much heavier blow. No doubt the moral judgments to be passed are among the things affected by this crucial distinction; but this is perhaps the least important thing so affected. If you strike me, the judgment that the blow was deliberate will elicit fear, indignation, anger, resentment: these are not voluntary responses; but the same judgment will enter into deliberations about my future voluntary conduct towards you and will colour all my social relations with you. Shall I be your friend or enemy? Offer soothing words? Or return the blow? All this will be different if the blow is not voluntary.[22]

Of course Lukes does not say that exercises of power in his extended sense are "involuntary" on the models of muscle spasms or movements that occur under drugs or hypnosis. But he makes it a defining feature of such actions that those who perform them do not know or intend the very results which put the actions in the category of power. And he is insistent on holding the actors responsible for these results. When they object, as they surely will, that they did not know that their actions would have the effects that they proved to have, Lukes (one imagines) will indignantly rejoin, "But you could, and should have known. And since you did not take the trouble to find out, we will hold you responsible for the harms that you have in fact caused."

It is undeniable that this is an intelligible, even a familiar response to negligent conduct. It is exactly the response we make to the roofer who (to use one of Hart's examples) injures someone by thowing debris onto a sidewalk below and then claims that he did not know that anyone was passing. But would we, should we, say that the negligent roofer had exercised power over the injured party? What exactly would saying this add to the statement that the passerby had been injured as a result of the roofer's negligent actions?

A part of the problem here stems from the general implications of

Lukes' willingness to break the connection between power, responsibility and intention. As angry as we may rightly be with the negligent roofer, our human reactions to him would, and should, be quite different than our reactions to persons who hurl objects on passersby with the intent of harming them. Lukes could of course preserve this distinction at the level of the kind of blame to be attached to the two cases. But for him to do so would be to concede that power of the third-dimensional kind is less blameworthy than power of the sort identified by our schema. He does not address this point explicitly, but the tone of his argumentation suggests to this reader that he would resist such a concession.

But there is a further difficulty, one that bears more directly on questions about "power" and how it is or should be used. Consider the distinction between a negligent roofer and a person who periodically hurls objects from his roof with the intention of deterring others from parking in front of his house. We suggested that it would be odd to say that the negligent roofer exercised power over the passerby. This is because, although he undoubtedly harmed the latter, not only did he not intend to do so, he had no intention to affect the passerby or his actions in any way. But the unattractive character who has now entered our deliberations has very definite intentions in respect to passersby. True, he may not intend to harm them; he may even regard his actions as unsuccessful if he does harm them. But he is willing to take that risk in order to achieve the objective he has in view.

It is the writer's linguistic intuition that the concept of power embodies the distinction just exemplified. It does so by requiring evidence that A acted with the intention of getting B to do or to avoid doing X by threatening him with Y. Whether this intuition is correct, the distinction is of manifest importance. If we adopt Lukes' proposal to use "power" in ways that obliterate the distinction, we will merely have to draw that distinction anew within the confines of the concept of power. This, in fact, is a good part of what Lukes accomplishes with his distinction between one-dimensional and three-dimensional views of power.

3. We come now to that third possible way of characterizing what the A's of Gary did and did not do that we anticipated above. In negative terms, the A's were neither acting knowingly and intentionally, as in 1, nor "negligently," as in 2. We should consider them, rather, as responding to, as acting more or perhaps less self-consciously on, values and beliefs that make up the authoritative in their society or subsocietal milieu. Perhaps we should even understand them as responding to those yet more deeply buried influences that were discussed in chapter 4, those which Wittgenstein talked about as "general facts of nature." Consideration of this possibility will bring us back to the notion of objective interests and will help us to identify important insights that lurk beneath the details and the stipulations of Lukes' discussion of power.

Power and the Authoritative

Let us consider two possible variations on interpretation 3:

3*a*) A believes that his actions or practices are valuable. Criticism of them is common enough, but he does not respond to it by claiming ignorance of consequences. Rather than offering excuses, he defends, justifies, perhaps even celebrates what he is doing.

3*b*) A's actions are of a type that he never seriously or even explicitly questions; they are "taken for granted" or "hardly ever given a thought." If A is criticized for them, he will be surprised and will find it difficult to respond without first forming or reviving a judgment concerning them.

An instance of 3*a* is provided by attitudes toward industrialism that prevailed until recently (and that have by no means disappeared). Industrialists and the bulk of the populations of industrialized societies have of course been aware that most factories produce large quantities of smoke, dust, and other yet more noxious effluents. Nor was Rachel Carson the first to realize that these effluents have harmful effects or the first to point out that the harms done by at least some forms of pollution (as we now call it) are distributed unevenly among the members of the societies that they afflict. Until quite recently, however, critics of these industrial practices, some of whom have been very forceful (Engels, Dickens, Steffens), had only modest success in arousing opposition to these among their consequences. Industrialization was widely viewed as a great human achievement, one that signaled a triumph over nature and promised an end to scarcity, to brute human labor, and to many other evils. Its unpleasant, even many of its undeniably harmful consequences, were judged to be a small price to pay for the great good that it produced.[23]

Insofar as industrialists, financiers, politicians and so forth knowingly and intentionally sacrificed the express interests of some segments of the populations of their societies, knowingly and intentionally persisted in practices that systematically harmed some segments of the populace more than others, *and* knowingly and intentionally employed threats against those who sought to end those practices, it is quite correct to say that they exercised power over those whose express interests were sacrificed. It is quite correct, that is is to say, that they exercised power in the sense given by our schema. But two connected features of this situation deserve emphasis. The first is brought out by the fact that those who used power felt little guilt or remorse about doing so and that there is little evidence that they were widely criticized or condemned for doing so. "Power" is by no means an unequivocally pejorative term. Where power is used to bring about "progress," to achieve "liberation," to serve the common good or the public interest, and so forth, even if there is recognition that doing so involves disserving or sacrificing some merely private or perhaps "unprogressive" interests (note that there must be such recognition if we are to talk about power in our sense), it is commonly judged to be an innocent if not a positively good thing.

The second point about 3a that deserves emphasis is as follows. Let us imagine that the Rothschilds, Carnegies, Rockefellers, DuPonts, Krupps, etc., accepted the objective theory of interests that is an essential feature of Lukes' three-dimensional view of power. If so, they might well have denied that they were exercising three-dimensional power over anyone. They might have conceded that their actions harmed the subjectively defined interests of some individuals; but it is likely that they believed those actions served the true, the genuine, the long-term, or the objectively defined interests of the latter. Indeed it is highly likely that the moguls of the U.S. Steel in Gary took exactly the same view. Is it not, they would likely ask, objectively true that a high rate of unemployment is the greatest ill that can befall the working class? Is it not also objectively true that antipollution regulations would increase unemployment? And if "negligent" disservice to the objectively defined interests of an individual, a group or a class is enough to show that power has been exercised in the three-dimensional sense, is not knowing and intentional service of those same objectively defined interests enough to show that power has not been exercised in that same sense?

The first moral to be drawn from 3a is that it is less than obvious that the one-dimensional and the three-dimensional views of power are as easily compatible and complementary as Lukes appears to think.[24] On the one-dimensional view, "power" can be used only if the B's themselves manifest their objection to X and their awareness of the threats that the A's are employing to induce them to do X. The A's may be able to justify X, but it will be clear that it is an exercise of power that they are justifying and the justification will be in the face of B's objections to it. By contrast, on the three-dimensional view of the same case the A's may cogently deny that they are exercising power at all. By retaining a tie between "power" and the interests of the B's, but sometimes allowing, sometimes depriving the B's of distinctive standing to define their own interests, Lukes creates the possibility that an action is an exercise of power in one of the senses he accepts and is not such an exercise in another sense that he accepts. Of course Lukes intends his third-dimensional sense to extend the use of "power" so as to capture cases excluded by the one-dimensional view. Hence it is not surprising that his analysis yields this result in the general form in which we have just described it. It is important to note, however, that in the example under discussion "power" in Lukes' three-dimensional sense is arguably more constricted than it is in the one-dimensional sense. As noted, it seems to permit A to escape from the charge that he or they have used power over B by contending that, whatever B may think, A's actions in fact served B's true or genuine interests. If this is correct, Lukes will either have to show that the A's are objectively mistaken about B's objective interests or be put in the awkward position of recapturing the example as an instance of the exercise of power by returning to what he had insisted was an excessively narrow conception thereof.

We presume that Lukes would opt for the first alternative and set about to demonstrate that B's true interests were truly what he (Lukes) believed them to be. The question whether A had exercised power over B would resolve itself into the question of who (other than B, the latter's views having already been dismissed as irrelevant) had the objectively correct understanding of B's objective interests. This realization calls attention to the price a theory of power must pay in order to get the convenience afforded by an objective concept of interests. Whatever else we might think about this outcome, it will not enhance the prospects of clarity about "power" or agreement as to whether power has been exercised in this case or that.

We are now in a position to draw this discussion to a conclusion as regards the specifically conceptual issues raised by Lukes' proposal and the challenge it throws up to the schema advanced here. There are three main difficulties with his proposal. First, it is largely unnecessary because most of the types of cases that he seeks to bring under the rubric of power are readily accommodated by the one-dimensional view of it. Second, to the extent that the extension he proposes captures new cases, it does so at the cost of weakening if not breaking the connection between "power" and "responsibility" and hence "power" and praise and blame. Finally, the proposal inflicts upon the concept of power the notorious difficulties of achieving agreement concerning the objective interests of the B's. For these reasons the proposal should be rejected.

The arguments against Lukes' conceptualization of power are also considerations in favor of the analysis that we presented at the outset. In particular, they are considerations in favor of the basic notions (1) that power relations are among agents who are acting and interacting intentionally; and (2) that these are relations in which A employs threats or threatening inducements in order to bring B to do something that he does not want to do or to prevent him from doing something that he wants to do. Lukes agrees that these are basic elements in the standard uses of "power," and his attempt (which is the most extended and forceful of a number of analogous efforts) to devise uses of the concept that eliminate or substantially alter these elements yields numerous difficulties and few if any advantages. Hence we conclude that the schema we developed at the outset holds up as an account of what are and should be the basic elements in the concept of power.

We have not, however, examined Lukes' discussion in the foregoing detail merely to reject his conceptualization and to affirm our own. As already suggested, there are important insights embodied in his arguments, insights that are obscured by his explicitly conceptual proposals and that should be more accessible now that we have analyzed the latter. The insights in question will be developed, *inter alia,* in the following chapter. We introduce them here by referring to an instance of our long-postponed category, 3*b*.

Gentlemen of the 1940s and 1950s doffed their hats on meeting ladies, opened doors for them, helped them with their coats, met the costs of meals and entertainments shared with them, and so forth. Although clearly a learned (if not a positively unnatural!) pattern of conduct, from their adolescence forward these actions were "second nature" to males brought up to be gentlemen in the (rather thin) sense in question. Persons with such upbringing were familiar with alternative patterns of conduct, and if questioned about their own pattern they may have been able to produce an argument in its defense, possibly even an argument that their actions were a kind of duty. But in fact they rarely argued for or even gave active consideration to these actions, and they would probably have been initially puzzled by questions concerning them and at least vaguely annoyed by challenges to them.

Certainly these "gentlemen" would have been surprised by the suggestion—easily derivable from an application of Lukes' conceptualization to the example—that these actions of theirs represented an exercise of power over women—a reaction that would likely have been shared by women who had learned to take these courtesies for granted. For the reasons indicated, this reaction would have been well grounded. On the assumption we have built into the example, it is simply not helpful to treat it as a case of the exercise of power. (There are, of course, plausible assumptions in terms of which such gender-based role differentiations are quite properly analyzed as instances of power relationships.) But in saying this we do not mean to deny that the beliefs and patterns of conduct under discussion had significant effects on those involved in them. The effects that they had, moreover, were systematically different as between men and women, different in ways that were (and are) harmful to the latter. They contributed importantly to definitions of the statuses and roles of men and women, definitions that severely restricted the conceptions of self, the opportunities, the choices, and so forth that were in fact open to women.

The phenomenon that this example represents (and that in general category 3*b* is intended to encompass) is of undeniable social and political importance. It is this phenomenon, we suggest, that Lukes seeks to bring under the rubric of power by extending the latter to a third dimension. His desire to extend "power" in this way takes its plausibility from the restrictions and constraints that these patterns of interaction impose upon, from the harms that they do to, the B's. Or, to use an amended version of the very general formulation we used at the outset, its plausibility stems from the consideration that the interactions between A's and B's help us to understand why the B's act in ways other than those that we expect of them. Although much too limited an analogy with ordinary senses of "power" to warrant Lukes' proposed extension of that concept, this consideration is sufficient to indicate that analysts of "power," of "authority" and of the relationships among them will do well to provide a place for and otherwise to attend to the significance of the phenomenon in question. We propose to provide a place for it under our rubric of the authoritative (and to a lesser extent under the rubric of "general facts of nature"), and we attend to its significance in the next chapter.

8 Power, Authority and the Authoritative

Much of the discussion in the previous chapter focused on the actions of and interactions among individual persons. Our basic schema has A forming a purpose or objective and the intention to act on it, adopting a plan of action designed to accomplish the purpose, and acting on that plan in part by attempting to exercise power over B. It then has B evaluating A's action and reacting to it in the light of his own purposes and by framing and acting on his own intentions. Of course the placeholders "A" and "B" can accommodate groups, associations and other collective actors or agents. But the thrust of the discussion is, at least tacitly, individualistic in character.

We do not intend to abandon this focus, this perspective. To do so would make power relationships as we in fact encounter them inexplicable. Agamemnon learned to his regret that Achilles was a man who responded with particular intensity to attempts to exercise power over him.[1] Henry VIII had a similar experience with Sir Thomas More. We will not understand the interactions between these figures, or indeed the countless other more mundane interactions that are the stuff of the phenomenon of power in human affairs, if we treat as irrelevant the distinctive characteristics of the individuals among whom they occur.

Power as a Collective Phenomenon

It is clear, however, that this perspective deflects our attention from vital aspects of power and its exercise. As the later stretches of the previous chapter began to suggest, power relationships, even when they take the form of interactions restricted to two individuals, involve more than the distinctive characteristics of those individuals. There are several respects in which, or perhaps several levels at which, this proposition is true. Each of these concerns a sense in which power can be said to be a collective phenomenon. We will begin by briefly identifying three such levels and then explore them and their significance in the course of the present chapter.

The first operates at the level of the individual actors themselves. To understand the conflict between Agamemnon and Achilles, we must understand the distinctive character and personality of each. But to do so, and especially to understand the ways in which their characters and personalities were manifested in that conflict, we must attend to the values and beliefs that they shared as members of the culture that Homer depicts. To mention only the shared beliefs and values most salient for our purposes, that culture gave an honored place to assertive, aggressive conduct, to moral and physical courage and vigor, and to a kind of heroic virtue that can be achieved only by someone who risks conflict with other individuals who are pursuing the same ideals. Achilles is deeply memorable because his brooding, sulky aggressiveness is his own, is distinctive to him. Yet we cannot even imagine such a character in the context of, say, the culture of the Hopi Indians with its insistent demand for complaisance and self-effacement.[2] The power relationships between Agamemnon and Achilles, we might say, were a collective phenomenon in the sense that they took place between individuals who were the individuals that we know them to have been in part because of characteristics of the collectivity in which they lived their lives.

The second level concerns the degree to which the values and beliefs of a collectivity encourage or reward, allow or tolerate, discourage or exclude the exercise of power itself. The culture presented in the *Iliad* clearly did the first of these in that success in attempts to exercise power over worthy protagonists was deeply admired. (Of course vigorous and successful resistance to such attempts was also admired and in part for this reason the attempts commonly failed.) Hopi culture clearly does the last of the three. Isolated attempts at the exercise of power might be initially successful because the individuals affected would be reticent about resisting. But willful, insistent conduct of the kind that the exercise of power ordinarily involves would be strongly disapproved and would lead to censure and the ultimate isolation of anyone who persistently engaged in it. As to the middle range of the continuum we have set out, we suggest below that a number of contemporary Western societies fall somewhere within it. Power is not rejected as it is among the Hopi, and it is celebrated only if it is seen to be in the service of some collectively valued objective other than amassing power itself. It is sometimes mildly disapproved, sometimes tolerated as a necessary element in politics or some other dimension of life, sometimes admired or at least envied. At this among our levels, in sum, power is exercised or not by distinct individuals within society, but it is a collective phenomenon in that widely shared beliefs and values encourage, support or deter its exercise by individuals.

A third level at which power is a collective phenomenon is given by its exercise on behalf of or in the name of a society or other collectivity. Here it is likely to be exercised by an agent who occupies an office or a status and plays a defined role, both the status and role having more or less explicit recognition in the collectivity. It is power that is collective in this sense that is most difficult to distinguish from authority and hence will require our closest attention here. It will be important, however, to bear in mind that power that is collective in this third sense is almost certainly collective at the other two levels as well. The use of *power* (as distinct from other devices for affecting thought and action or bringing about intended results) by those who act on behalf of the collectivity must have at least the tolerance of the collectivity. And persons who occupy collectively recognized offices and statuses and play more or less established roles remain individuals whose beliefs and values, objectives and intentions, will be incomprehensible apart from the authoritative in their society.

The Exercise of Power as a Mode of Giving Reasons

By way of introducing a larger theme that we develop in what follows, let us put a general point implied by the foregoing remarks in the following terms: The exercise of power might be understood as an attempt by A to affect B's thought and action by giving B a distinctive species of *reason* for thinking and acting in the manner that A wishes. A does not want to bring X about by forcing or coercing B; rather, he wants B to *do* X. B can be said to do X only if he makes a decision to do it. Hence A can succeed in his project only if he provides B with some species of that genus of considerations that is the usual (if not a conceptually requisite) basis of decision; he must, that is, provide B with some species of reason for doing X.

This understanding, or something akin to it, underlies the familiar proposition that power is not a substance or quality that A possesses (as he might possess a weapon, a high IQ, or a well-stocked wallet), but a relation between A and B, a relation that depends (both logically and practically) on B's responses to A's actions. Whatever A's resources— whatever his strength, wealth, arms, cunning or what have you—his power over B can only be as great as B allows. This is because B must treat A's threat-supported directives as convincing reasons for doing the X's that A demands.

Although based on a distinction that is tolerably clear in its abstract formulation, this account is likely to be resisted because it is so common for the exercise of power to be more or less intimately related to the use of force and coercion. It is true that B must decide to do X. But if he decides to do X out of *fear* (as we often—and with good reason—say) of the Y with which A has threatened him, there is likely to be resistance to saying that he did X for a reason. Or, more accurately perhaps, there is likely (and understandably) to be resistance to saying that A has affected B's conduct by reasoning with him about doing X. Power relationships might properly be said to require decisions or choices by B, but the latter should not be understood as based on or resulting from a reasoned exchange between A and B.

Part of the problem here is that power relationships occur over a range differentiated by the character of the Y with which A threatens B and with the degree of choice that Y actually or realistically leaves open to B. If Y is "an offer that cannot be refused" on the Mafia model, we would say it provided B with a reason for doing X only if the other alternatives were deeply and morally repugnant. By contrast, where Y is a minor disadvantage or inconvenience, there would be little objection to thinking of it as a reason for doing X, one to be considered along with other reasons in a deliberative process.

To put the matter this way highlights the significance of the several levels at which the exercise of power is a collective phenomenon. A must decide upon an objective, must decide to use power to achieve it, and must select a Y with which to threaten B. In turn B must evaluate A's objective and, more important here, A's choice of power as a means of pursuing it and the choice of a particular Y as a means of exercising power. If B finds that A's decisions and choices are outside of the permitted range, he will not respond to them as providing him with reasons for doing what A directs him to do. Hence it will be impossible for A to achieve his objective by exercising power over B. In short, as with any attempt to give an agent reasons for thinking and acting in a certain manner, the exercise of power presupposes shared values, beliefs and conventions that give such notions as "thought," "action" and "reason" a foothold and yield criteria by which individuals may judge any reasons for thought and action that are in fact given.

This understanding brings "power" close to "authority" as we have analyzed the latter concept in previous chapters. "Power" and "authority" share not only a post or station in our discourse but also the quality of being interwoven with the web of conventions that partly constitutes the practices, associations, societies, cultures and even civilizations in which they fill that post or station; they are interwoven with what we have been calling the authoritative.

**Power and Authority in Collective
Life** Hannah Arendt's Theory of Power

The foregoing remarks require a good deal of elabora-
tion. As a first step in providing it, we examine the treatment of power by
a theorist, namely Hannah Arendt, who pressed (with her wonted resolution) the understanding of power as a collective phenomenon well beyond
the point to which we have thus far taken it. Because Arendt's formulations also have the effect of underestimating and obscuring the differences
between power and authority, examining those formulations will help to
prevent an imbalance in this regard that is an inevitable concomitant of
her approach to it and that has already begun to develop in the present
analysis.

Arendt distinguishes sharply between strength and power. As she uses
the term, strength is an attribute of individuals. It allows those who possess it to bring "force" to bear on nature, on fabricated objects, and on
other persons treated as objects. But individuals as such do not have or
exercise power, and power relations do not occur among individuals.
Power "springs up" when, and only when, people "act in concert."
Those coalescences of opinion, belief, and the will to act on them that
occur among the members of a political community are defining features
of power. Power and its exercise are neither an end of political community
nor a means by which such a community pursues its ends. Rather, power
is an attribute of such a community, a feature without which a community
cannot continue for long (if indeed it can exist at all) and that obtains only
as a feature of political communities.[3]

On this view, power must of course presuppose many of the conditions
that are requisite to political community. Of those conditions, Arendt
emphasizes shared opinion and belief. More particularly, she emphasizes
the belief that there is a set of arrangements and institutions, those
through which the political community ordinarily acts in concert, that
deserve the respect, support and loyalty of the members of that community. Power, Arendt argues, needs no independent, no distinct or distinctive justification. Or rather, it allows of no independent justification. It
takes *its* justification from the justification for political community and the
distinctive value of the kinds of action (including the exercise of power)
that are impossible apart from such a community. What power urgently
needs is legitimacy. The members of a political community must accord
the institutions and arrangements through which they act politically that
distinctive respect and allegiance which are the hallmarks of the recognition of authority. Power and authority not only appear (and disappear)
together, they are so deeply interdependent as to stand (on Arendt's
account) in what must be regarded as a symbiotic relationship. A struc-

ture of authority, grounded in beliefs about religion and tradition, provides a legitimated setting of institutions and practices in which action in concert occurs. Action in concert in that context *is* power. Not surprisingly, therefore, "institutionalized power in organized communities often appears in the guise of authority."[4]

All of this is salutary in the links that it forges between power and authority and between both of them and the web of beliefs, values and conventions that make up the authoritative in a society. But there is a serious difficulty lurking here. Anxious to celebrate the "action in concert" itself, anxious to establish it as the preeminently human dimension of life, Arendt says remarkably little about the recipients of these actions in concert, of the B's in the power relationships that are created by actions by the A's. Now action by A (whether an individual, group, or other collectivity) is manifestly a necessary condition of the exercise of power. But it is not a sufficient condition of its exercise. Not all cases of action, even action that is collective in Arendt's sense, are cases of the exercise of power. To repeat, power is a relational term that presupposes some agent or agents over whom the power is exercised. If the A's of the community of Roland Park come together in a setting of institutions to which the accord authority and unanimously decide to adopt the golden retriever as the official Roland Park dog, there has been action in concert but no exercise of power. It is a further condition of the exercise of power that some B's object to what the A's have done but accede to it in order to avoid the Y with which the A's threaten them. If B is perfectly happy with the choice of golden retriever, or if B's preference for community dog is the Irish setter but he accepts the golden retriever because he has been assured that the community bird will be the tufted titmouse, the A's have not exercised power over him.

Can the A's be said to have exercised power over B if B accepts their decision because of the legitimacy (in Arendt's sense) that it obtains from the intimate relationship between power and authority? Because of the relationship between power and the authoritative? We begin with the first of these questions.

✓ By stressing the relationships between power and authority Arendt does recognize, albeit obliquely, that power involves B's who judge themselves to be adversely affected by its exercise. If there were no B's (so defined) involved, if all those involved or affected were enthusiastic about the X, questions about the legitimacy of X would no more *arise* than questions about its justifiability. She recognizes, in other words, that the exercise of power raises normative issues that are not fully settled by the value to the A's of action in concert. Moreover, there is merit (as well as much mischief) in her argument that *justification* for power must be partly in terms such as the value of political community and the unique opportunities it presents for action in concert. The merit of this argument (probably not the one Arendt saw in it) derives from the very fact that B objects to the specific content of X and complies with it because of his aversion to Y. This being the case, if the action of the A's is to be justified to B, the justification will have to be cast in some terms wider than those referring to the Y itself.

Could the imposition of X through the threat of Y be rendered legitimate? As we have been construing the concept of power, there is nothing in that concept itself, no connection between "power" and concepts such as "right" or "wrong," "obligation," "duty," "ought" and so forth out of which an argument for the legitimacy of imposition could be formed. On this view of the matter the exercise of power by one private individual, taken simply as such, over another taken the same way, cannot be characterized as legitimate. "Power" is all there is to work with in forming the wanted argument for legitimacy, and it is of no help.

This feature of the situation, together with the view that "authority" *is* used to give legitimation to the X's that A's require of B's, does much to explain and to give cogency to the argument that power and authority are categorially distinct. But it also explains why Arendt posits an intimate relationship between power and authority. For the reasons we have mentioned, Arendt thinks power is an indispensable feature of fully human affairs. In order to defend it against the weighty objections that it quite properly elicits, she (1) glosses over its effects on B, (2) seeks to legitimize such of those effects as she does implicitly recognize by defining power as an attribute of collective action, and (3) makes an intimate association between it and a phenomenon, namely authority, that is not only an attribute of collectivities but one that gives legitimacy to demands that collectivities impose on their members. These maneuvers are not without their warrants. Their warrants are provided by two considerations: first, both power and authority are relations among agents who have values and beliefs, form interests and desires, and frame and act upon intentions and choices; second, these latter operations are incompehensible apart from the shared conventions of some social entity that is identifiable and with which the agents in question do in fact identify. These commonalities between power and authority, particularly evident in respect to power exercised by and on behalf of collectivities, provide warrants for making a close association between the two concepts.

But exactly how should that association, however "close," be conceptualized? For reasons already noted, attempts to identify the two, to reduce the one to the other, must be out-and-out mistakes or mere stipulations for which there is little to be said. Arendt does not make this mistake. But it is also a mistake, we want to argue, to associate them as closely as Arendt does—to suggest, as she does, that there is no such thing as power without authority or authority without power.

Continuing to leave *an* authority out of the picture, there are plenty of instances of constitutions, rules and offices (and persons who occupy the offices) that have *in* authority but no power whatever.[5] There are (unfortunately) a yet greater abundance of cases in which there is very considerable power, including power in something that is at least uncomfortably close to Arendt's sense of action in concert, but no authority over the B's whose thought and action are affected by the power. Leaving aside the conceptually peculiar but interesting anarchist view that all governments belong in the latter category, it surely is the proper way to classify any number of gangs and terrorist bands and not a few groups that have somehow managed to appropriate the control of states and governments.[6] True, such instances of power without authority would be impossible apart from the relationships between the powerholders and what they do, on the one hand, and, on the other, shared beliefs, traditions and so on that obtain in the societies and cultures in which they exercise that power. Even the most brutish power is not "brute" in the sense in which philosophers have sometimes used that term.[7] But the fact that neither authority nor power are "brute" (which, after all, does not distinguish them from much if anything else) hardly warrants us in associating them as closely as Arendt does.

Power, Authority, and Punishments

There is a better case for saying that authority and power are both *effective* (in getting the B's to do the X's) only if they are in fact associated with one another in something like the manner Arendt suggests. Or perhaps we should say that neither power nor authority can be effective for long unless a mutually supportive association develops between them. There may be counterexamples to this contention, but the assertion does help us to focus the most difficult conceptual issues concerning the relationship between power and authority, issues raised by punishments and other sanctions. If we are correct that there can be authority without power and power without authority, it follows that in principle there could be authority relations that can be understood without reference to power and vice versa. We can understand that A has authority, and that B does or does not do X because of A's authority, without referring to the power (or lack thereof) of A or anyone else. And the parallel proposition will be true of power. The proposition that neither authority nor power alone can be effective, or can be effective for long, is in effect a denial of this claim. It says that we cannot understand the thought and action of the B's, or at least that we cannot understand their thought and action over any appreciable stretch of time, without attending to *both* power and authority.

Richard B. Friedman throws up a fundamental challenge to the latter (Arendtian) proposition. He contends that the question whether in fact the B's do X is irrelevant to our understanding of what authority is and does. "Authority" he argues, does not imply or explain effectiveness. The fact that "a person has the right to rule does not mean that those under his jurisdiction acknowledge his title to ascendancy over them, so that his command may be either ignored (in which case he lacks influence of any sort) or else obeyed, but out of fear, prudence, hope of reward, etc. . . . Likewise, a person who holds a position which entitles him to use force to secure compliance with his decisions may be obeyed because he is recognized to be entitled to command or for the very different reason that he exercises the force he rightly possesses. That a person possesses the authority to use force does not alter the fact that if he does use force to extract obedience his subjects are not then obeying him out of respect for his authority. That force is rightfully or lawfully exercised does not alter the cause of obedience, thought it may justify the use of coercion."[8]

Taking Friedman's remarks about force to apply to power as well,[9] he is saying that the differences between power and authority concern the character of the reasons that they respectively give for B's doing X. This difference being categorial, nothing but confusion can result from saying that authority is impossible without power or power without authority. As already argued, Friedman is clearly correct about this to the extent that there can be authority without power and vice versa. But he is too short with (which is not to say he is wrong about) both the conceptual implications and empirical consequences of situations in which A's authority includes the right to threaten, and in fact to impose, *punishments* for disobedience on B's part. Where this is the case (and of course it is commonplace as regards the political authority of governments), and where the threat of such a punishment is in fact attached to the rule or command to do X, the exercise of authority and the exercise of something that is at least very much like power become conceptually linked. Y cannot be called a punishment (except in a metaphorical sense) apart from A's having authority to threaten it and to in fact impose it. But a punishment is still a harm for all of that. If the reason, or one of the reasons, for B's decision to obey X is to avoid the threatened punishment of Y, then B's action cannot be explained without reference to A's authority. Yet, because A has used the threat of an imposed harm to get B to decide to do X, B's action cannot be explained without reference, if not to A's power, at least to something that is not easily distinguished from power. For the moment we will designate that "something" power* and we will try to determine whether power* is a more than notional entity.

In the kind of case we have been discussing, the exercise of power* and the exercise of authority appear to be inseparable. If A had power but no authority he could threaten B with a harm but he could not threaten B with a punishment. If A had authority but no power* he could assign a punishment for failure to do X but he could not credibly threaten B with that punishment. Thus the union of power* and authority appears to make possible a kind of act on A's part that (logically) could not be performed in its absence. It also appears to establish conditions necessary to what would otherwise be (assuming that the reasons for an action are part of its character as an act) logically impossible acts by B. Assume that B respects A's authority, acknowledges that it entitles A to promulgate rule X, and hence accepts that he has an obligation to do what X requires. But X is unattractive to him and he finds himself backsliding. He then reflects that A also has the authority to assign a punishment for the nonperformance of X, has in fact assigned punishment Y, and is well supplied with the wherewithal (power*) to impose Y on him if he does not do X. He then decides to do X. His decision is based on a combination of reasons, namely (1) that he has an obligation to do it, (2) that he will rightly be subject to punishment if he does not do it, and (3) that it is highly probable that he will in fact suffer the adverse effects of Y if he does not do it. It may very well be that the removal of any one of the three elements of this combination would convince him to omit doing X. If A has no authority to command X, then both X and the threatened Y are mere impositions and B will indignantly resist them. If A has promulgated X but has not assigned Y (or has assigned it but, despite enough power* to do so, in fact never imposes it), B (whose character is in less than perfect array) will backslide and omit to do X. If A has promulgated X, assigned Y, but lacks power* to impose it, B will backslide. On these assumptions, and, again, on the assumption that the reasons one has for an action make up a part of its appropriate descriptions, A's act of doing X would be impossible apart from the union of power* and authority in A and A's actions. It begins to look as though power* is more than notional.

Those who hold that power and authority are categorially distinct will respond that the foregoing account in fact supports their analysis. However entwined the account may show power and authority *in fact* to be, they will (cogently) argue, the account itself is able to and in fact does distinguish those features of the example that involve authority and those that involve power. One version of this response would be that the entire business of assigning, threatening and imposing sanctions (including punishments) is a part of power relations, not of authority. If or insofar as B does X out of a desire to avoid Y, his action is to be explained by his distaste for Y and his fear of A's capacity to impose it. This argument is unacceptable because it is unable to distinguish between a punishment and other forms of harms. There is, however, a better-formed objection, one which focuses on the word "credible" in our example. It is a part of A's authority that he is entitled to assign punishments for failure to discharge the obligations that are attendant upon B's recognition of A's authority. But the question whether A can make those sanctions credible, whether B will believe, and will act on the belief, that the punishments will be effectively imposed in any particular case, has to do with power, nothing whatever to do with authority.

Indeed one might go further. One might join with Kant and Hegel and those who have followed them in arguing that if B's concern about sanctions is genuinely a concern about *punishment,* A will have no need to make the threat of punishment credible. B himself will positively insist that the punishment be imposed when he fails to do X. So far from feeling threatened by Y, B has a right to it and A fails in his duty to B if he does not administer Y to him when B—in that interesting phrase—"has it coming to him." If B does not take this view of the matter, that is proof both that he does not accept A's authority and that his doing X must be understood as submission to A's power.[10]

The Kantian-Hegelian extension of the counterargument may seem too far divorced from what actually occurs in known practices of authority, too aridly formalistic (or moralistic) to deserve serious consideration.[11] Later we suggest that something like its central contention may nevertheless be important to a satisfying resolution of the difficulty that seems to be emerging. But let us set that question aside for the moment and ask what is to be said about the relationship between authority and power in respect to punishments.

The discussion thus far does indicate a main reason why it has been so difficult to settle, or at least to still, the controversy over the relationship between authority and power. On the one hand, (1) the notion of a punishment is conceptually inseparable from the notion of authority, and (2) it can hardly be denied that the fact that punishment Y has been attached to rule X gives B a reason for doing X that he would not otherwise have. Moreover, (3) this reason is of a kind—namely the desire to avoid a harm attached to not doing X—that is strikingly similar to the kind of reason B has for doing what mere powerholders direct him to do. Theorists who focus on these three features of authority relations are likely to conclude, with some show of justification, that in cases involving assigned punishments authority and power are conceptually interwoven. On the other hand, (a) punishments are conceptually distinct from unauthorized harms, (b) a punishment is legitimate or not altogether apart from whether it is imposed, and (c) those who are B's in authority relationships have an obligation to do X and an obligation to submit to Y if they (guiltily) do not do X—an obligation that obtains quite apart from the probability that A will in fact administer Y to them. Theorists who focus on features $a-c$ of authority relations are likely to conclude, with justification, that authority and power, however important the empirical relations between them (indeed because of the importance of the empirical relations between them) are conceptually distinct.

As a matter of strict conceptual construction, the arguments for the latter view are compelling. The strongest element of the argument against it, namely, the third of the three reasons mentioned on the other side of the controversy, establishes no more than an analogy between punishments and the harms threatened by persons with power but no authority. That analogy may be vital to understanding various political and psychological dynamics of authority and power relations. But it leaves us unable to deal with major implications of (well-grounded) talk about punishments, implications that simply cannot be derived from talk about the harm threatened by persons attempting to exercise power. Thus as a conceptual matter our theoretical entity power* proves to be purely suppositious and we can dispense with it.

Power and the Authoritative

It would be as uninstructive to leave the matter with this conclusion as it would be mistaken to deny the validity of the conclusion. There are a number of reasons for saying this. Examining them should allow us to draw the results of this exploration of authority and power together and to move on to the relationships among authority, power and the authoritative.

One of the reasons for the conclusion concerns the question of the conditions under which authority and power are efficacious (in the sense that attempts to exercise them do regularly bring about the desired conduct on B's part). Friedman is surely correct that we should not confuse answers to this question with, should not substitute answers to this question for, an analysis of "authority" and the distinctions between it and related concepts. Identifying the conditions under which authority is effective or ineffective presupposes an understanding of what authority is and is not such that we can decide whether "it" has or has not been effective. But neither do we want to fall into an Oakeshottian conceptual essentialism that disjoins the analysis of "authority" from patterns of thought and action that are prominent in practices that include the phenomenon of authority.

Here is a familiar example of such a pattern. If the rules and commands of a practice (however impeccable their formal credentials) rarely bring about the desired response on the part of the B's, both participants and observers are likely to say such things as that A's authority is or has become purely formal, is or has become *de jure* but not *de facto,* has fallen into desuetude, and so forth. A writ that will not run becomes a "writ," not a writ (and maybe a laughingstock); a law that is violated with impunity becomes a dead letter. Assume that we want to understand this pattern. Assume further that we accept (as we do) the arguments (1) that authority and power are conceptually distinct and (2) that questions about efficacy concern either B's rectitude in discharging his undoubted obligations or A's power, not authority. On these assumptions, the arguments we have accepted positively require that we attend to relationships between power and authority.

There are further reasons for attending to those relationships, reasons that are especially important in respect to understanding the exercise of authority and power in and by communities and associations. These further reasons will take us back to Arendt's arguments and to the insights implicit in Steven Lukes' discussion of power. They concern the senses in which the exercise of power (as well as of authority) would be impossible if its use were not more or less actively accepted and supported by some substantial segment of the members of the community or association over whom it is exercised.

The proposition that power requires the acceptance and support of the B's may appear to be sharply counterintuitive. By our own hypothesis, B is disinclined to do X and is subjected to threats in order to overcome his disinclination. Are we to assimilate submission to threats and acceptance and support? It will be instructive to consider the treatment of this matter in various versions of class analysis from Marx (if not from Thrasymachus) forward. According to the simplest versions of class analysis there is a two-tiered class or caste structure consisting in one class that exercises power over the other. Acceptance and support come all but exclusively from the former; opposition, resistance, or at best grudging submission all but exclusively from the latter. Both patterns of conduct are to be understood in terms of action taken to advance class-specific interests. This analysis is perhaps most convincing when applied to power exercised by one more or less distinct community over another, with the first understanding the second to be importantly external to itself, for example a colonial or imperial power over a colony or other conquered people, a slave-holding society over its slaves, perhaps a political class over members of the community who are excluded from all or most of the political process (noncitizens in the classical polis?). Some such arrangement may be assumed in Arendt's discussion, and it is certainly a feature

of Lukes' account of power in the third dimension. (The foregoing speculation about Arendt is suggested by her lack of attention to the position of
the B's in the power relationship.)

As a number of more subtle versions of this mode of analysis have
emphasized, however, if we are talking about power, not force, it cannot
be the case that acceptance and support come exclusively from the A's.
This is because the exercise of power involves the exercise of agency on
the part of the B's. The B's must *decide* to do the X's. If the B's never
decide to do the X's, the A's will always fail to exercise power over them.
Thus the B's must accept and support the power relationship at least to
the extent of giving consideration to and sometimes acting on the reasons
(the Y's) that the A's give them for doing X. As Antonio Gramsci and
those influenced by him (for example Eugene Genovese) have emphasized
in their important theory of hegemonic relations, even in a class- or
caste-ridden society this feature of power relations produces complex
patterns of consensus and dissensus that extend across class lines. Even
in societies marked by sharply drawn and strictly maintained class or
caste distinctions, the A-B power relationship is partly constituted by a
more or less elaborate web of norms, beliefs, and accepted patterns of
action that are at least partly shared among the A's and the B's. If the
strands of this web were to unravel entirely, the exercise of power would
become altogether impossible. If the pattern of the web becomes so confused or so internally contradictory as to be difficult to comprehend and to
act within, the exercise of power will become difficult and problematic.[12]

Most analysts of power relations who have made use of notions such as
class and caste would concede that there are power relations among the
members of a class or caste as well as between castes and classes, and
some of them might even concede that there are power relations among
the members of a class or caste as well as between castes and classes, and
some of them might even concede that there are power relations that can
just as well be discussed without reference to the class or caste structures
of the society in question. Bourgeois exercise power over other bourgeois
as well as over the proletariat, women over other women, colonials over
other colonials, slaves over other slaves. And there may be power relations in, say, avocational groups or families that simply do not have
much to do with the class or caste relations that dominate the society.
Insofar as this is the case, experience with such power relationships may
in some measure prepare participants for acceptance of power as a feature
of the larger society in which they live. But theorists of class structure or
hegemonic patterns nevertheless insist that the dominant, the most important, power relations in the society are between classes, and that the
A's of that relationship are found all but exclusively in one class or caste,
the B's in another. On this view, the beliefs, norms, values, patterns of

acceptable action, and so forth that are shared across class or caste lines are, to one degree or another, constrained or restricted by the system of class or caste relations that is the basic feature of the society. Most important, because any given person is unlikely to shift back and forth from the role of A to the role of B (at least in respect to the most significant power relations), class- or caste-specific understandings and modes of interpreting and applying the shared norms are almost certain to develop. Thus we have class-specific subcultures and class-specific mentalities ("the working-class culture," "trade union consciousness," "the culture of poverty," the "slave mentality," the "white man's burden mentality," etc.). The classes or castes are locked into interdependency one with the other, and they could not relate to one another—through power or in any other way save possibly brute and episodic uses of force—if there were no commonalities among them. But the common features are put to systematically different uses from one class or caste to the other. The B's accept and support power as a feature of their society in no more than the weak sense that they participate in power relations, make the decisions that such relationships require, often do X to avoid Y, and so forth. Their constant concern is to limit and to frustrate the exercise of power, and they put the commonalities to this use to the greatest possible extent.

As theorists of hegemony have emphasized, and indeed as the analysis of power that we are developing requires, the B's in a hegemonic system do manage to extract some advantages from power relationships. It is partly for this reason that they prefer power relations with the A's over "relationships" in terms of the strength, force or violence of the A's. But because it is systematic that they obtain fewer and less attractive benefits than the A's, they are unlikely to regard the power and the power relationships that they experience with much enthusiasm.

This need not be the case with participants in power relationships in which persons and groups shift readily and regularly from the role of A to that of B and back again. A group finding itself a B in respect to a particular transaction or interaction will of course try to limit the efficacy of A's power in that transaction. But the group might well recognize that it is by the exercise of power that it has won and can hope to win many of its own advantages; hence it might well recognize that it is to its advantage that the exercise of power continues to be an accepted mode of action in the society. If the National Rifle Association threatens to organize opposition to Senator Church's reelection in retaliation for Church's vote for gun control legislation, Church may try to render their threat ineffective by mobilizing support from gun control groups. But Church knows that he will not get far with his favorite legislative proposals unless he can sometimes exercise power over those who oppose them. Hence Church will try to resist the power of the NRA without calling into question the idea that the exercise of power is an acceptable (or at least an indispensable) feature of the political process. The NRA can be expected to take a similar position, as can a considerable array of other participants who believe that, on balance, they stand to benefit from the fact that power relations are a feature of political (or economic, or religious, or university, etc.) life. *These* shared values, beliefs, attitudes and so on give a kind of acceptance and support to power relations that is much more positive, that goes much beyond, the support provided by the commonalities that class theorists recognize in the societies they study. Power and power relations of any sort would be impossible without the support of *some* set of commonalities, but the kind of support the exercise of power receives (and hence the specific character of power and power relations) varies with the set of commonalities that in fact supports them.

We can take this matter a step further by considering the possibility that Senator Church, the NRA, the antigun lobby, and indeed the totality of agents in the society are of an Arendtian, a heroic, cast of mind. It is not merely that each of them expects to come out of the set of its power exchanges with a net gain in terms of the particular interests and objectives at issue in the exchanges taken one by one. Rather, all of them believe that the "action in concert" which such participation involves is itself a good, one that is not reducible to consequences for particular interests and objectives. Let us, indeed, consider the possibility that they regard such action in concert as integral to the realization of a fully human existence. On this assumption, power and its exercise would not only be accepted and supported, it would be viewed with the greatest enthusiasm, it would be "gloried in." The practices, arrangements, patterns of acceptable action in which it consists or which are necessary to it would be defended against all challenges and protected against all attacks. "Power" would shed the mildly pejorative connotation that it carries in much liberal and pluralist thought and become an honored, a celebrated feature of community life.[13]

As noted earlier, emphasizing the foregoing kinds of considerations tends to bring power and authority very close together. Not only do both occupy the same post or station in our discourse, neither could fill that post or station if it did not derive acceptance and support, as a feature of community life, from values and beliefs that are widely shared and acted upon by members of the community. Despite the vital differences between them, many if not most of which concern the normative claims that attach to the actions of the A's *qua* A's, they are both a part of the axiology of a community or association. For these reasons, and because in fact the exercise and effects of power and of authority are so often intimately related, it is dubious indeed to seek to understand, and certainly to seek to theorize about, either of them in isolation from the other. Although conceptually distinct, power and authority are so intimately related that the study of one must illuminate the study of the other.

In this respect there is much to be said for Arendt's approach to the two concepts. But her approach also carries substantial dangers; or rather, her writings on the topic realize and manifest serious analytic and especially normative defects. These defects result from inattention to differences among the senses in which authority, power, and the authoritative provide the B's with reasons for action. We conclude with this point.

From an analytic perspective, the most important difference between power and authority can be stated as follows: Owing to their connections with the authoritative, the B's may have reasons for accepting and in various other ways supporting authority and power (either or both) as features of the practices in which they participate as members of a community. The exact content of these reasons varies with the content of the authoritative. Regardless, however, of the specific content of the authoritative, every B who accepts authority *thereby* acquires an obligation (though not a conclusive, all-things-considered reason) to conform to any rule or command X that is *intra vires* in the jurisdiction of which he is a member. By contrast, and again regardless of the content of the authoritative, acceptance of power as a feature of one's practices does not yield an obligation, indeed does not *itself* give B any kind of reason whatever, for doing any specific X. (The notions *intra* and *ultra vires*, of course, have no application to the exercise of power.) Rather, the very fact that A seeks to get B to do X by exercising power over him may itself (and despite B's acceptance of power as a feature of his society) be plausibly regarded by B as a reason to avoid doing X if he can possibly find a way to do so (a reason that competes with the reason for doing X that is supplied by the threat of Y). As with Achilles in the example mentioned early in this chapter, B's acceptance of power does give him a reason for not objecting, categorically as it were, to A's attempt to use power; unlike the comparable case in respect to authority, however, he has every reason for taking whatever other steps are available to him to render A's attempt unsuccessful. (Of course there are likely to be "side constraints," constraints coming from principles or commitments independent of B's acceptance of power, that will limit the means B will employ in trying to frustrate A's attempt.) Needless to say, the exercise of power would be very difficult, would succeed only rarely and episodically, in a society in which few if any of the putative or potential B's accepted it. But the truth or falsity of this generalization in no way vitiates the conceptual point that acceptance of power is itself no kind of reason for submitting to any particular exercise of power. Authority, as we might put it, has a deontological quality that power altogether lacks.

The chief defect in Arendt's analysis is that it obscures this difference. Correctly emphasizing that the acceptance of both authority and power is grounded in the authoritative, she incorrectly infers that the logical or normative force of this grounding extends to particular exercises of power and submission thereto. Thus she says that the exercise of power needs and can have legitimacy, but neither needs nor can have any justification independent of the justification for the political community itself. B can object to doing the X's he is directed to do by those in power only if he is prepared to object to the political community itself. We have suggested that this account is mistaken even in regard to authority; that B's recognition of the authority of X does not deprive B of the possibility of cogently objecting to discharging his obligation to do any X. And we have suggested that this analytic mistake carries normative implications of no mean importance. The parallel analytic mistake in respect to power is more blatant. If accepted and acted upon, its implications would produce nothing less than a moral enormity.

The final point in this connection takes us back to the important considerations implicit in Lukes' notion of three-dimensional power. Recall that the most plausible construction we were able to make of this notion was in terms of our category 3b as exemplified by a certain mode of relationship between "gentlemen" and "ladies." Recall also that we objected to treating that example and the category it illustrates as a species of power. We might now restate our objection by insisting that not all of the relationships and interactions that are influenced or even controlled by the authoritative should be thought of as relationships and interactions in terms of power and authority. Some relationships and interactions, including some that observers may judge to be systematically disadvantageous to one of the parties or set of parties to them, take their character more or less directly and entirely from the authoritative itself. "Gentlemen" and "ladies" of the 1940s and 1950s understood themselves to be following the rules of polite conduct, rules that were a direct reflection of beliefs concerning sex differences and received evaluations of those differences. They did not understand themselves to be exercising or obeying authority, exercising or yielding to power. The reason why a gentleman helped a lady with her coat was that it was proper to do so; the reason why a lady welcomed and indeed expected such assistance was that it was proper for her to receive it.

The important point that Lukes makes is that such widely accepted beliefs, values and patterns of conduct are far from innocuous. They may contribute importantly and positively to the quality of life in the society or association; equally, they may be harmful, and they may well be especially and systematically harmful to one class or category of those who accept the beliefs and values and hence who willingly, even enthusiastically, participate in the relationships that are structured by the beliefs and values. But the harmful effects of the arrangement are not the result of power. Indeed one might well say, as some feminists can be read as saying about relations between gentlemen and ladies, that such relationships can be especially harmful precisely because they are not understood as relationships in terms of power. As we have just argued, if the B's understand that the A's are exercising power over them, they thereby understand that the only sense in which they have a reason for doing the particular things that the A's want them to do is provided by the credibility and seriousness of threats that the A's employ. And this means, most specifically and importantly, that the B's do no wrong, fail in no duty, have no reason for feeling guilt, remorse or shame if they succeed in resisting the demands of the A's. It also means (assuming that the exercise of power itself has that requisite degree of support in the authoritative discussed above) that the B's will regard themselves as justified in using power to counter the power of the A's. When women themselves question, reject, and overtly challenge the beliefs and values that support the rules of polite conduct in question, they create one of the conditions necessary to thinking of "gentlemanly" conduct as an exercise of power over them. And when they do so, it becomes possible for them to recognize and otherwise to act to resist that power.

It may be useful to develop this argument somewhat further by discussing again that people, the Fox, by reference to which we originally set out the distinction between authority and the authoritative. The culture of the Fox is likely to be attractive to anyone who is skeptical about authority. Because there is yet better reason to be skeptical about power, the attractiveness of the culture is substantially heightened if we interpret it, as it can plausibly be interpreted, as involving the rejection of power as well as of authority. Assuming the empirical accuracy of the accounts on which these interpretations are based, it appears that individual Fox rarely experienced a sense of being imposed upon by other members of the tribe, rarely found themselves required to do a substantively objectionable X merely or primarily because some other assignable person or persons had decided that they should or must do it. The interpretation we are making of those accounts also carries the suggestion that there was little if any of that deeper mode of disaffection or alienation that commonly develops when individuals find themselves at odds, perhaps without quite knowing why, with the values, beliefs and established patterns of action that limit, orient and organize day-to-day choices and conduct. Of course the Fox themselves might nevertheless have been unhappy about many aspects of their circumstances. Perhaps they suffered serious shortages of necessary or strongly desired goods. Or they may have been subject to periodic and destructive incursions by other peoples. But these dissatisfactions would not have been perceived as resulting from the wrongness, the injustice, or any other objectionable characteristic of the social and moral order that they shared among themselves and that they sustained through their own patterns of interaction.

It by no means follows that observers of Fox society are debarred from, deprived of the possibility of, cogently objecting to features of that society that were completely acceptable to the Fox. The consensus on basic values and beliefs that was apparently responsible for those among its attractive features that we have just mentioned might be viewed as unfortunate and harmful. Someone of an Arendtian cast of mind would surely object to the content, the substance, of the values and beliefs. How can life have any savor, how can it be genuinely human, in a society that forbids the quest for and the exercise of power, authority and leadership? Indeed someone of a strongly altruistic bent might enter a related objection. Are not authority and even power means of doing great good for others and for society? Would there be any real possibility of effective service in Fox society? Others might observe that various of the desiderata valued in the society were in fact distributed quite unevenly among its members; that elders, or males, or those of special physical prowess, aesthetic appeal, traditional standing, or whatever, possessed more material goods, were accorded greater respect and prestige, and so forth. And they might point out that the taboo on power and authority had the effect of perpetuating such inequalities by depriving the disadvantaged or their champions of modes of action through which they might have eliminated them. Just as the inequalities between men and women in America and other occidental societies (to say nothing of oriental varieties!) in the forties and fifties were arguably more harmful to women *because* the latter did not perceive the inequalities as imposed by power, protected by authority, or even as harmful at all, so those Fox who did least or merely less well under established arrangements might have been held in the warm but stifling embrace of a system of beliefs and values that they accepted implicitly.[14] To say with Lukes that the *interests* of the least favored are disserved by the situation, and to explain that outcome in terms of the *power* of the most favored, is inappropriate not only for the reasons given earlier but because doing so deflects attention from the seriousness of the plight of the disadvantaged.[15] But to reject his conceptualization is by no means to deny the importance of his understanding that authoritative values and beliefs can be harmfully constraining and otherwise damaging in deeply insidious ways. Rather, to reject this conceptualization for the reasons given is explicitly to accept and to emphasize that very understanding. Later we will have occasion to see the importance of this understanding for the normative theory of authority.

9 A Brief Review and Some Comparisons

In a remarkably large number of the instances that we have examined, both members of the apparently conflicting assertions noted in chapter 1 have proved to be at least partially true. For example *in* authority does partly consist in and does yield rules to be subscribed to and obeyed. For some purposes, moreover, the statements in which such rules consist are not eligible subjects of knowledge or belief. At the same time, putative or intended rules can attain and retain standing as rules only if participants in the practice hold certain kinds of beliefs about them. Specifically, participants must know or hold the belief that there are criteria that distinguish rules which possess authority from those that do not, and that they know what those criteria are, that *these* statements are intended to and do in fact satisfy those criteria, and that the rules of the practice are, in their overall character and in the secular tendencies of subscribing to them, good or at least acceptable rules. In addition, we have argued that participants must accept some set of propositions (making up part of the authoritative) according to which rules are acceptable features of social life.

To take one further example, it is true that there is no single purpose or collection of purposes (or functions, or objectives, etc.) that are necessary or even in fact common to all instances of *in* authority. Yet considerations of purpose enter *in* authority relations through the medium of the rules that are so prominent in those relations. Considerations of desirability enter authority relations through these same media.

If these and our analogous contentions are correct, it emerges that F-P theory is correct in its insistence that rules, procedures, offices and subscription to them are the distinctive features of practices of *in* authority. This emphasis is the great strength of F-P theory. But the theory seriously underemphasizes a number of other characteristics of authority, characteristics that are central to authority precisely because they form conditions necessary to rules that actually *rule* human conduct. Among these are the substantive, purposive, and normative characteristics of rules, the role of officeholders in formulating and applying rules, and the decisions and judgments of the B's in recognizing, understanding, and obeying or disobeying those rules. Most important, the most prominent versions of F-P theory underestimate the place and significance of reasoned judgments—especially judgments by the B's—concerning the merits of the rules of their practice.

The question addressed in part 2 is whether a practice marked by these and the other characteristics examined is in principle a justifiable feature of human arrangements. In order to focus this question, and in the hope of putting it into an appropriate perspective, we conclude this review with a brief comparison between authority and two other moral and political practices, namely, justice and rights, with many of the same characteristics as authority.

All three of these practices have large and important deontological dimensions. Classes of actions within the practices are identified, ordered, and to a considerable extent assessed in terms of the relationships between the actions and the established procedures, offices or other institutions, and especially rules. In the case of authority, directives adopted by officeholders through the established procedures thereby acquire the standing of regulation or authorization-type rules. In all three practices disputed questions are treated, at least initially, as issues about what the procedures and rules are or should be. Thus procedures, offices and rules mediate relationships among participants and mediate between individual participants and actions the latter may be disposed to take or to avoid when considered under characterizations other than those supplied by the procedures, offices and rules.

Somewhat more specifically, *in* authority shares with a significant class of rights, and with justice in many of its legal aspects, a characteristic that H. L. A. Hart has called "content independence." The obligations that the rules of these practices entail for associates do not result directly from the moral or other worth of the content of the rules, but from the fact that they are rules arrived at or adopted by a certain established procedure. For example a wide range of rights and correlative obligations can be created (given the practice of rights) by promising and contracting, that is by employing certain procedures that are established as yielding rights and obligations. Similarly, the A's in a practice of authority can promulgate a wide range of X's merely by employing the procedures that have been established for so doing.[1]

The content independence of promising and contracting projects the personal characteristics of promisors and promisees into a prominent place in the workings of the practice of rights. The rights and obligations that get established are very much a function of interests and desires, objectives and purposes of the persons who avail themselves of the procedures. Similarly, the content independence of the practice of *in* authority gives great prominence to the characteristics of those who occupy the offices. Within the often broad limits set by the beliefs and values that inform the practice, those who occupy offices of *in* authority are entitled to invest an extraordinary diversity of rule formulations with authority and hence to create an extraordinary diversity of obligations for participants.

The difference between rights and authority in this regard, however, is of the utmost importance to assessing authority. In promising and contracting, the promisor or the contractor can obtain a right, and can create an obligation for the promisee or contractee, only if both parties (or their appointed agents) specifically agree to the promise or contract in question. By contrast, A's possession and *intra vires* use of *in* authority form the jointly sufficient conditions of X's becoming a rule that entails obligations for all subscribers. Given that the intentions, purposes, and other characteristics of the A's must be visibly at work in the processes of rule formulation, interpretation and enforcement, it would be a singularly dull lot of B's who did not therefore realize that the practice of *in* authority is a highly dangerous affair—an affair in which prudent persons will participate with a skepticism extending beyond the question whether the rules and the actions of the A's are scrupulously *intra vires*.

Whether "skepticism" as such is necessary, we have argued that the disappearance of critical examination of the merits of the rules marks the end of *in* authority. When critical judgment on the part of the B's has ceased, *in* authority and obligation have given way to something else—to manipulation, to coercion, perhaps to dominance and submission of which the extreme examples are master-slave relationships. If so, it is vital that we understand how critical judgment can be exercised in a practice of *in* authority. The internal logic of this process, the logic of understanding and following rules, has occupied us at length, and we will not further repeat our account of it. A prominent account of the external aspects of the process, usually with a strong S-P flavor, is that the rules of a practice of *in* authority are or at least should be assessed by reference to natural rights, the laws of nature or the principles of divine or natural justice. It should be clear from chapter 4 that we are not favorably disposed to these positions as such. But our argument concerning the role of widely shared values and beliefs in practices of *in* authority has important analogies with them. In common with their proponents, we deny that systems of procedures, offices and rules are *sui generis* or self-sufficient; we insist that rules and rule-guided conduct presuppose a wider setting of beliefs and values and that thought and conduct concerning rules is more or less continuously influenced by such a setting. The anatomy and physiology of any practice of *in* authority will be largely a function of the continuing interplay, taking place in the thought and action of participants, between the procedures, offices and rules and the wider context in which the former play their distinctive roles. In part 2 we argue that the possibility of justifying *any* instance of the practice of authority depends on the availability of this kind of interplay, and the justifiability or not of this or that instance of the practice depends on the particular form which that interplay in fact takes.

2.Justifying the Practice of Authority

Alexis de Tocqueville

Men would not have found the means of independent life; they would simply have discovered (no easy task) a new physiognomy of servitude.

10 Questions and Criteria in the Justificatory Theory of Authority

Can a practice with the characteristics we have been examining be defended; does it present a feature of human societies and associations that is in principle justifiable? Or has our analysis of what authority is and is not identified characteristics of the practice that ought to set us firmly against it, ought to convince us to exclude it from our arrangements entirely or to the greatest possible extent?

Metaquestions

We begin by noting a pair of somewhat curious characteristics of the history of these questions. On the one hand, the questions have achieved something of an honored place in the lengthy story of systematic, critical thinking about politics and morals. It would be no worse than an exaggeration to say that they have been an abiding concern of political and (to a somewhat lesser extent) moral philosophers. On the other, virtually all of the "major" philosophers who have considered these questions, and the overwhelming preponderance of the "minor" ones who have done so, have answered them in the same way in at least one important sense—that is, they have almost all urged acceptance of *in* authority as a valuable part of political and moral arrangements.

This pair of characteristics is curious for at least two, perhaps connected, reasons. First, given the absence of serious disagreement, it is odd that the questions have remained of such compelling interest. If we indulge the minor simplification that anarchism is the alternative or competing position,[1] it appears that theorists have found that position too weak to accept but far too important to dismiss (a stance to which we are strongly attracted). Although boasting few defenders of genuinely distinguished philosophical stature, anarchism can claim a truly stellar company of opponents. Second, if we are correct that authority is a manifestly dangerous institution, it is not only curious, it is disturbing that so few careful students of politics and morals (not a notably dull lot) have found it unacceptable.

From a certain familiar metatheoretical perspective, of course, the first of these curiosities is readily explained by the character of the questions themselves (together, it is true, with a certain special brand of dullness alleged to be characteristic of those with a taste for philosophizing). From the perspective in question, interest in the questions has recurred because they appear to be particularly grand and important but in fact are not genuine questions at all and hence cannot be answered. There are genuine and genuinely difficult questions about the proper scope of authority in this association or that, about how it should be organized and distributed here or there, about whether to obey it in particular circumstances, and so forth. But the idea that "it" could be attacked or defended wholesale, the idea that a theorist could somehow get philosophical purchase on the merits of authority as such, is simply a confusion.[2]

In its most unqualified forms, this position has little to recommend it.[3] Suitably reinterpreted, however, its contentions are not so much at variance with arguments we have employed here (especially the arguments of chapter 4). Taken together, the two may help to put our present concerns in proper perspective.

We have emphasized that the practice of authority has certain generic characteristics but no essence; certain generalizations can be made about the concept "authority" and about historical instances of the practice, but there can be no essentialist theory concerning "it." If so, perhaps encompassing justificatory questions have been difficult to put to rest because of the diversity of instances that have presented themselves under the concept. Failure to dispose of general justificatory questions indicates not that such questions are fatally confused but that the answers offered have concerned differing species of a divers genus. Despite some appearances to the contrary, theorists have not attempted to justify all of the features of all cases of authority against all possible objections; they have tried to defend authority as they knew and understood it (directly or vicariously) against the objections that were most pressing in the circumstances in which they thought and wrote. There are continuities in the history of this endeavor because there are generic or at least recurrent features of both "authority" and practices of authority: there is a lack of closure in that history because instances of the practice of authority are not identical one to the other. As a reaction to essentialism, a skeptical metatheoretical stance is fully justified; as a categorical objection to attempts at a more rather than less encompassing normative theory of authority, it is misplaced.

A version of this understanding informs the reflections that follow. We begin by delineating criteria for deciding whether *in* authority is in princi-

ple justifiable as a feature of human political arrangements. We then inquire into the conditions under which those criteria might be satisfied by
an instance of the practice. Because historical instances of the practice
are importantly diverse, we then ask which of those characteristics would
have to be present in order that a practice be justified by the proposed
criteria. The criteria we propose are not drawn directly from, and the
conditions and characteristics that we suggest might satisfy them are not
detailed descriptions of, any particular instance of the practice. But it will
be evident that our reflections on these matters are primarily influenced
by comparatively recent instances or putative instances of the practice.
Having developed such reflections in abstract terms in chapters 10–13, in
the final chapter we discuss the bearing of the reflections on practical
questions that arise in and concerning certain historical examples of the
practice.

Criteria for Assessing the Justifiability
of Political Authority Political Authority
and Individual Agency

From roughly the middle of the seventeenth century to
the present the most severe and unyielding objections to the practice of
political authority have been based on its alleged incompatibility with
individual freedom, with action grounded in the reasoned judgments and
decisions of the actor, and with the continuing moral integrity and responsibility of those who participate in it. Although pressed with especial
vigor by anarchist thinkers who have won limited acceptance of the conclusions distinctive to themselves, this array of (closely connected) objections reflects assumptions and beliefs that have been, and happily so in
our view, widely shared by modern thinkers about morals and politics.
Commonly manifesting themselves in political thought in the doctrine that
political societies ought to be in some sense free or voluntary associations, these assumptions have featured various versions of the idea that
individual human beings have the capacity for self-actuated, intentional
and rational conduct. More or less continuous and effective use of these
capacities, it is argued, is a condition of integrity, responsibility and a
morally and otherwise good life. This capacity for "agency" (as it is
sometimes called in the law and elsewhere), moral and otherwise, is the
single most distinctive and important attribute of individual human beings. Any practice or association that does not recognize, respect, and
allow the fullest possible scope to the agency of its members thereby
shows itself to be a tyranny, a despotism, or some other species of un-

acceptable arrangement. If political authority is incompatible with recognition and respect for the agency of those over whom it is exercised, it is therefore intolerable. Thus the question whether authority is incompatible with agency must be a primary concern of the justificatory theory of authority.

If the criterion just proposed can be clearly delineated and can in principle be satisfied by the practice of political authority, we would thereby have reason to expect that authority could also satisfy a number of other criteria plausibly proposed for judging its acceptability. A practice that respects the agency of its participants, for example, would thereby also respect many of the commonly cited examples of basic, natural or human rights. Again, while a practice that respected individual agency might commit occasional injustices against its members, its respect for agency would also constitute a commitment to basic aspects of the notion of justice.[4] Nevertheless, the notion of compatibility with agency could not provide a sufficient criterion for determining the acceptability of any instance of the practice of authority. Although the notion of agency is fundamental to rights and to justice, it is not equivalent to either of the latter. A practice of authority premised on respect for the agency of its members might violate their rights or commit injustices against them. Or it might unnecessarily harm, violate the rights of, or perpetrate unjust actions against the members of other societies or against persons who are members of the society of which it is part but not included in the practice of authority itself. Again, such a practice might so grievously misuse resources of the society as seriously to reduce the quality of life of its members (in respects other than the integrity of their agency)—doing so, moreover, in ways clearly traceable to the arrangements that make up the practice of authority itself. Such circumstances or developments might warrant the judgment that the practice in question, despite assiduous respect for the exercise of agency by its members, must be disobeyed in this or that instance or even abolished.

There are nevertheless good reasons for according the criterion of compatibility with individual agency pride of place (which is not to say exclusive place) in a justificatory theory of political authority. Perhaps the most obvious of these reasons is the one stressed by numerous anarchist writers, namely, that there are exceptionally good grounds for thinking that authority—perhaps uniquely among major human practices and arrangements—is *necessarily* incompatible with individual agency. A particular practice of political authority might or might not do well with the resources of its society, might or might not regularly act justly toward persons within or outside its domain. But there is reason to think that it is impossible for it to respect the agency of the preponderance of its own members. In sum, if the integrity of individual agency is properly valued and if there are substantial general reasons for thinking that political authority is incompatible with it, then the question whether political authority is in principle compatible with individual agency merits a special place in the justificatory theory of political authority.

But perhaps this matter of agency should *not* be accorded such significance. Granting that the capacity for agency is a salient and important characteristic of human beings, why should it be singled out for special concern? After all, human beings have numerous characteristics, some at least of which are, at most, indirectly connected with their capacity for agency. For example they are animate and sentient creatures with various undoubted biological needs; and owing to their psychological and spiritual makeup they are deeply affected by pleasure, pain and a great variety of other emotional and spiritual experiences. If political authority serves these other characteristics well, is it obvious that we should reject it because it conflicts with or ill serves the capacity for agency?

We take up particular versions of this question in the chapters that follow. At this juncture we restrict ourselves to the following preliminary considerations.

The questions just raised are certainly not to be dismissed. There have been an abundance of situations in which needs that have little if anything to do with agency have been so pressing, so urgent, that other considerations have given way to them—perhaps necessarily so, perhaps properly so. As a first response, let us note that if human agency *entirely* disappeared, if *none* of the persons in question were acting in a self-actuated, intentional and rational manner, questions of rightness and wrongness, propriety and impropriety, justification and disjustification would have no place. But it has sometimes seemed that human needs and desires could be best served by restricting the exercise of agency to a small proportion of the populace whose needs and desires are the object of concern—with the preponderance of that populace relegated to a passive role in deciding how to meet those needs. Is it clear that a practice of political authority with this characteristic would necessarily be unacceptable?

The question is badly posed. If the choice is formulated as between the *authority* of a few, on the one hand, and entire loss of agency for the many, on the other, we must reject the formulation as incoherent. It is true that persons or other creatures who or which are not regarded as agents may benefit from an arrangement. The traffic regulation requiring motorists to halt at stop signs provides my pet dog with the inestimable advantage of intervals when it can cross streets in comparative safety. Despite this benefit, we do not say that my dog has an obligation to obey traffic regulations. In saying that members of a practice of authority have obligations we attribute agency to them. It is part of the very distinction between a practice of authority and, say, a master-slave relationship or a relationship of sheer coercion or manipulation, that *all* members of the practice are regarded as agents.

As a first response to the objection, then, we must say that the question of respect for the agency of its members has pride of place in the theory of political authority because in the absence of such respect there can be no authority. If the anarchists are correct that authority is incompatible with the agency of any of its putative members, they are also correct that authority is an impossibility.

The Concept of Agency in Leading Theories of Authority

The most important modern defenders of political authority have accepted some version of the ideas we have been considering. Because they have done so, they have also had to concede that anarchist attacks on authority have been cast in relevant terms or categories. (It is no doubt in part for this reason that defenders of political authority—including the present defender—have found it difficult to dismiss the anarchist's challenge.) Of course defenders of authority have rejected anarchist conclusions; they have argued that a state with authority can respect, perhaps even contribute to, free, rational and morally responsible action on the part of its members. These efforts of defenders of authority have met with considerable practical success. Although they have failed to convince a persistent and sometimes vocal minority, the proportions of that minority have remained miniscule. The preponderance of virtually all modern populations have apparently accepted the view that states with authority can in principle be compatible with an acceptable minimum of individual agency on the part of their members.[5]

Unfortunately, if this acceptance has been or is based on the arguments actually advanced by the most prominent modern defenders of the idea of political authority, it is surprising and indeed disturbing. If judged—as they ought to be judged—from the perspective of more than minimal or token concern about individual agency, the most prominent of these arguments prove to be remarkably weak and unconvincing. True, these defenders commonly begin with a vigorous assertion of the beliefs and assumptions about individual beings that we have been discussing.[6] But they then proceed with astonishing rapidity, certitude and equanimity to an interpretation of authority that allows—or rather insists upon—far-reaching limitations on the exercise of the very capacities that those beliefs and assumptions announce and celebrate.

It has commonly been asserted that the practice of authority must find

181 Questions in the Justificatory Theory of Authority

its genesis and perhaps its continuing foundation in some species of voluntary act or acts on the part of those who participate in it. Some species of consent, agreement, acceptance, subscription or the like is taken to be at least a necessary condition of a state possessed of authority (as opposed to force or even power). Notoriously, even this requirement has commonly been interpreted to allow its "satisfaction" by "actions" that could be called voluntary only on exceedingly latitudinarian constructions of that concept. But it is probably true that most theorists of consent (and related notions) have stretched those concepts (and hence also "voluntary") primarily to encompass what they thought would be a recalcitrant minority of persons who could never be gotten to consent in anything approaching a direct or full-blooded sense (and, perhaps, that the persons in question thereby demonstrated that their consent would not be worth having). It is probably the case, in other words, that theorists of the voluntary origins or foundations of authority have assumed that a practice of authority does presuppose genuine acceptance on the part of a preponderance of its participants. Certainly the theorists we have in mind—Hobbes, Locke and Kant are obvious cases—made vigorous attempts to develop reasons for accepting authority, reasons that they thought *should* convince citizens to accept or consent to it.

Given the insistence that authority must be founded on some kind of voluntary acceptance, what is remarkable is how little this voluntariness is allowed to carry over to, how little it is projected into, the ongoing workings of the practice said to be justified by its voluntary foundations. As Rousseau scathingly pointed out, meaningful participation was all but excluded from the ongoing operation of even those practices said to be founded on consent.[7] The great bulk of associates were expected to contribute little if anything to decision making in the state; they were simply to accept and submit to whatever decisions were made by that tiny number of members who had acceded to offices of authority. Although entering the practice under the banner of free, rational and moral persons, in Rousseau's view their role in its ongoing operations was that of slaves who assert their agency only in initial consent and in the extreme act of revolt. Agency in a minimal sense may be present, and hence one of the minimal conditions of authority satisfied. But the scope allowed to agency is so limited, the possibilities of exercising it so restricted, that anyone who shares the judgment about human beings with which we began this discussion will draw back in horror from the practice of authority.

In short, it is wrong, at least in the sense that it is inadequate, for a justificatory theory to rest with showing that political authority can be sufficiently compatible with agency to warrant predication of authority at all. We might agree that authority can be predicated of a particular practice and yet deny that the practice is justifiable.

Once stated, this conclusion (and hence our first response to the view that agency is of little or no account) is obviously correct. The question of justifying *authority* can only arise if there is or at least could be authority to justify, that is if the concept of authority has application to some practice. If some measure of agency on the part of the B's is necessary to predicate authority of the association of which they are part, two things follow. The first is that a measure of agency on the part of the B's is also a condition that must be satisfied in order that the question of justifying authority can arise. The second is that if the presence of such a measure of agency is taken to be sufficient to justify authority, then authority would be just what Kant if not Hobbes in effect said it was, namely self-justifying. If some measure of agency is at once a condition of authority and the criterion by which the justifiability of authority is properly judged, then it is an analytic truth that any and every practice of authority is justified. The distinction between an analytic account of authority such as we have attempted above and a justificatory theory of authority collapses. Put another way, if correct our analysis of the role of B's judgments and action on judgments in a practice of authority, and the more general argument that the authority of X is a *reason* for B to conform to it, would be sufficient to justify the practice.

As we have occasion to see in more detail below, there is a sense in which this Kantian conclusion is correct. To anticipate briefly, when self-identified members of a practice attribute authority to it and its rules, it will ordinarily be the (intended) implication of that attribution that the practice is sufficiently justified that the members have an *obligation* to obey the rules. We will argue, however, that even in the circumstances posited this is only commonly the case, not necessarily so. There is logical space (often occupied by such locutions as "illegitimate" or *"de facto"* authority) for a person to recognize the authority of a practice and yet deny that it is justified.

Before taking up this complication, however, we want to insist that at the level of general theory there is and must be a distinction between authority and justified authority. This distinction should be drawn first and foremost in terms of *the extent to which* authority is compatible with the agency of its members. We suggest, in other words, that compatibility with agency sufficient to warrant predication of authority to a practice is not sufficient to justify that practice. (This is not to say that our analysis of the practice is irrelevant to deciding whether it is justified.)

We pursue this matter by considering two familiar rejoinders to Rousseau's objection, rejoinders commonly advanced by theorists content with the initial, or indirect, or generalized consent that drew Rousseau's scorn.

The first of these rejoinders has commonly gone roughly as follows: it is true that the exercise of agency enters authority relations primarily through the medium of a generalized assent to the practice of authority as such (and, of course, through the medium of the action of those relatively few persons who actually hold offices of authority at any moment in time). In respect to the day-to-day workings of the practice, the preponderance of subscribers must give over the prerogative of making and acting upon their own judgments concerning the rules and commands promulgated, the decisions and actions taken, by those who have authority. But to do so is not to give over their status as free, rational and moral agents. As important as it is, the practice of authority comprises but one aspect of the lives of those who (among many other things) are subscribers to it. The practice establishes and maintains certain very general conditions that may be vital to the lives of its subscribers, but all subscribers take innumerable actions, engage in a great diversity of interactions, on which authority has no bearing at all or only such limited bearing as is given by the aforementioned conditions. Subscribers to a practice of authority retain (so far as the practice affects the matter) their standing as agents in respect to that entire array of actions and interactions that are left unregulated by authority. So far from having become slaves who are implicitly at the disposal of some master or despot, they remain free beings who do as they see fit in all but narrowly circumscribed aspects of their lives. Subscription to authority does involve diminution of agency, but the diminution occurs in respect to so small a part of their affairs that talk of slavery is rhetorical excess.

Started by Hobbes, this argument has occupied a promiment place in F-P theory and in the loose congeries of theories making up liberalism. Because agency is a distinctively important human characteristic, and because it can enter authority relations (except in the thought and action of those in positions of authority) only in the form of the decision to accept or reject the practice itself, it is of great importance that the scope of the actions of authority remain narrow. Although accepting the necessity, even the considerable value, of authority, numerous versions of this pattern of thought (though not Hobbes' version) promote a skeptical, even a suspicious attitude toward it. Individual agency is residual because for most members it finds significant scope only where authority has not entered or acted. But if authority enters few dimensions of life, if it restricts itself to maintaining (notionally) "adverbial conditions," individual agency may retain a vastly more vital and prominent place than the strictures of Rousseau (to say nothing of those of anarchist writers) would suggest. Specifically, it may retain a place sufficient to allow clear-headed and self-respecting moral agents to accept the practice of authority.

The continuing theoretical and practical significance of this first rejoinder to Rousseau (or rather a special version of it) will emerge as we proceed. But taken alone it is at best a thin and unsatisfying response to the objection that authority destroys agency. Its inadequacy as a defense of authority, moreover, has become increasingly evident in the two centuries or so since Rousseau launched that objection. Under the best of circumstances it sharply circumscribes the scope allowed to agency by a practice of authority. It in effect says that individual agency (except in a terribly crabbed expression) can play no role in achieving the values and objectives specific to the practice of authority. Nor have circumstances remained favorable to it. The most obvious reason for the latter judgment is that the activities of state authority have steadily increased throughout the nineteenth and twentieth centuries. Virtually every society in the Western world now looks to such authority for resolution of an enormous array of issues and problems. If individual agency subsists primarily outside of the practice of *in* authority, one would be hard pressed to dismiss the conclusion (drawn and lamented by, for example, Hayek, Nozick, and Oakeshott) that such agency has suffered an enormous decline in contemporary Western societies.[8]

The second familiar rejoinder alluded to above can be understood in part as a response to the development just mentioned (but, perhaps, also as an influence partly responsible for bringing that development about). It seeks to justify the authority of the state in terms that give substantially less weight to its relationship with the agency of the preponderance of participants in the practice. Making use of understandings and arguments of a kind that have always been prominent in S-P theories, it stresses the contribution of authority to the production of some number of commonly valued goods (including, or rather especially, "public goods" in the technical sense). Authority does sharply restrict individual agency. But its costs in this regard are outweighed by the contribution it makes to such objectives as justice, order and security, social coordination, a greater degree of community, the reduction of objectionable inequalities, perhaps especially the more efficient use of productive and other social resources. For a variety of reasons these goods are held to be unobtainable, or obtainable only to an inadequate degree, through unregulated interactions among private persons and groups. The practice of *in* authority is a remedy for this difficulty. It yields offices and officeholders with the resources to pursue social goods, and it puts the remainder of the population under a clearly defined obligation to obey the rules that implement the decisions of those officeholders.[9]

As we have presented it thus far, this second rejoinder is straightforwardly teleological in character. And in some versions and applications its acceptance has had the consequences that thinkers of a deontological bent argue necessarily result from teleological thinking about practices such as authority. In particular, its acceptance has reduced concern for the effects of authority on individual agency and integrity. If equality and social justice are increased, if GNP goes up, if national resources are more efficiently used, if national defense is sturdy and effective, enlargements in the scope of authority are thereby justified. For example the ascendancy of welfare state and socialist type thinking about issues of social policy has been accompanied by a notable diminution in the suspicion with which authority is viewed, suspicion that has been a prominent and in our view a salutary feature of the Western political consciousness for several centuries.

We seem to be faced with a choice between theories that can only lament salient developments in the practice of authority and theories that give up serious concern for individual agency in favor of the very different benefits that those developments are alleged to provide. In a deeper sense, however, the views we have been discussing do not present us with any choice at all. This is because they share a crucial assumption. Just as in the United States it was said that partisan politics must stop at the water's edge, so the exercise of individual agency is said by these theories to stop at the threshold of the actual exercise of authority. And just as the relentless encroachment of cold war foreign affairs into domestic politics seemed to jeopardize partisan politics of a meaningful sort, so the apparently ineluctable expansion of the activities of state authorities has left the theories we have been discussing bereft of resources for reconciling authority with more than a minimal form of individual agency. In short, we are once again faced with the view that individual subscribers to the practice of authority must surrender their judgment and action on their judgment concerning the substance and purpose of the rules and commands that issues from the practice. And we now see that this view, with its Hobbist implication that the agency of most subscribers is largely residual (in the sense that they can act freely, rationally, and in a morally responsible manner only where authority has not in fact entered), leaves distinctive human qualities hostage to events as regards the actual scope of the exercise of authority in any time and place. Given the secular tendencies of the events that have in fact transpired, it comes as no surprise that many theorists committed to this understanding have been driven to ever more bitter lamentations. The normative theory of authority has become a vehicle for expressions of nostalgia.

Concepts of Agency

In the chapters that follow we examine this impasse, this dilemma. We inquire whether, and if so how, a practice of political authority could be compatible with forms of individual agency more robust than that minimally necessary to allow predication of authority. Can a practice of political authority be so arranged, understood and conducted as to accommodate—even encourage and otherwise facilitate—the active exercise of individual judgment, choice and decision in respect to the substance of the rules and commands that the practice involves and generates? Is it possible to participate in a practice of authority and yet be free to form, to act upon and sometimes to satisfy interests and desires, objectives and purposes that are affected by the content of laws and commands? Is it conceptually and morally appropriate for individual participants to regard rules and commands as presenting them with reasons for action, reasons—as with any consideration deserving the name—the merits of which they are to assess as an integral part of deciding how to act within the confines of the practice itself? Can a practice of political authority allow participants to do these things to a degree sufficient to hold them morally responsible for their actions as participants?

We argue that these objectives can in principle be achieved to an imperfect but nevertheless considerable extent, and advance some suggestions as to how this might be done. And we contend that to the extent that they can be achieved, these objectives must be achieved. A practice of authority can be justified only if it is understood, organized and conducted so as to maximize its compatibility with and contribution to the agency of its members. In most general terms, this must be done because the freedom, rationality and moral integrity of individuals is and ought to be a primary human value. More particularly, it must be done because the maximum possible scope for individual agency is and ought to be a feature of a specifically *political* existence.

Our argument for these assertions will depend heavily on the particulars of our use of the concept of agency in developing it. The remaining business of this chapter is to present some more specifically conceptual comments about "agency."

As familiar as it is among us (perhaps partly as a consequence of its very familiarity among us), there are a considerable variety of formulations of this notion. True, it is easy enough to find or to invent uncontroversial examples of the exercise of agency and yet easier to write scenarios in which its exercise has been prevented or restricted. In deciding to go to the concert rather than stay home and read the latest work on the theory of authority, I exercised agency; when I spoiled the Mozart with a series of violent sneezes, I did not. When Stalin ordered the death of political prisoners he exercised agency; when his thugs used overwhelming physical force to drag those prisoners to the place of execution they violated the agency of the prisoners.

The availability of agreed examples of agency and its denial is of course of great importance. If we could never agree on examples, the notion could not have the place in our thought that it in fact has. Agreed examples provide boundary or limiting cases within which discussions of agency in this or that context must remain. A political arrangement with the characteristics of Stalinism cannot be said to be compatible with the agency of those on whom it imposes; one whose members acted as free of constraint and compulsions as I do in going to the symphony would have to be said to be so. There is a distressing abundance of instances of the former type and hence many self-proclaimed practices of political authority are not that at all but tyrannies that could not possibly be justified. And there are other practices which satisfy the minimal conditions for predicating authority but which cannot be justified by defensible criteria.

But there are no practices of authority that present agency as clearly as our going-to-the-symphony example. Authority of any sort restricts, if not the choices members can properly make, at least the considerations they can properly consult in making choices. We have also seen that political authority is associated with power, with coercion, and with other kinds of influence that intrude and impinge upon the thought and action of participants. In our judgment these facts do not themselves justify the conclusion that authority and individual agency are incompatible. But they convince that deciding whether a suitably robust agency can be preserved in a practice of political authority is a complex business.

Owing to this complexity, and because we accept J. L. Austin's view that the presence or absence of agency must be determined primarily by identifying constraints and compulsions or their absences,[10] we must elaborate our notion of agency in the course of, along with, our examination of the kinds of constraints that practices of authority typically put on their members. An account of agency in the practice of political authority must be integral to a theory of authority not entirely brought to or imposed upon such a theory. It is for this reason that the notion will be worked out, *inter alia,* in the course of the following chapters. But there are further preliminary comments that should be made, comments about an influential notion of agency that is inadequate for our purposes but that will be instructive in pursuing those purposes.

One of the familiar versions of the argument that political authority must be compatible with agency comes down to us from Immanuel Kant. Compatibility with individual agency, or "autonomy" as Kant and his followers tend to call it, is the primary criterion for judging authority (and all other practices and arrangements). This is because authority is a moral practice and autonomous agents are a necessary condition of morality and moral actions. To be autonomous in the moral realm is to act on the basis of one's own moral will (i.e., in Kantian terms, *Wille* as opposed to *Willkür*);[11] it is to decide to act exclusively in terms of a moral duty that one has "legislated" to or for oneself. If such action is impossible, the practice of authority is therefore also an impossibility.

For reasons already suggested in another vocabulary, agency in something like this Kantian sense of self-chosen or self-legislated action is clearly a condition of the practice of authority. If participants are not in a position to "legislate" to their own action in something like Kant's sense, questions about authority cannot arise. But a condition of a practice is not the same thing as an adequate criterion for judging the acceptability of that practice. And in this case the Kantian notion of autonomy is inadequate as such a criterion.

There are several reasons that support this conclusion. The notion of Will in which Kant locates individual autonomy seems to make no necessary reference to the actuality of acting on that Will. Will may be a necessary basis of moral action. But because the Law that Will legislates must be cast in general terms, the agent must choose particular actions that are consistent with the Law in the various circumstances in which he finds himself over time. Second, the agent must be in a position actually to act on those choices. For example he must not be uniformly prevented from acting on them by other persons or uniformly required by other persons to take actions inconsistent with the Law he has promulgated to himself. That is, for a concept of autonomy to protect agency, it must itself morally exclude the kind of heteronomization that results when other persons control the agent's acting.

On the first point, there is serious doubt whether the choice of any particular action can be shown to be required by Will in the distinctive Kantian sense. Although Kant himself apparently believed that the Categorical Imperative is "practical" in this sense, the requirements of that Imperative—in particular its prohibition against allowing "contingencies" such as interests, intentions, objectives and purposes of any sort to appear in the formulation of any Law or Maxim—would seem to exclude deriving any garden-variety actions from it. (Something like this prohibition, the reader will recognize, is what Oakeshott seems to have in mind in his discussion of the Lex of a Civil Association.) As Robert Paul Wolff has argued in his analysis of Kant, Will (*Wille*) is a "pure Idea of Reason" that is entirely in the "noumenal" realm. The interests, desires, objectives and so forth that are features of garden-variety acting, by contrast, are features of the phenomenal realm. Because the two realms are categorially distinct, Will can play no role in the choice of a particular action. Given that reason is identified with Will, Wolff concludes, "The adoption . . . of ends is a non-rational process. . . . There are, in principle, no ends that reason requires and no ends that it rules out."[12]

On this interpretation, which seems to us to be correct, it also follows that the Kantian Will is irrelevant to determining whether our second requirement has been satisfied. If it is impossible to determine what actions are consistent with the Will, it is of course also impossible to determine whether other persons have violated an agent's autonomy by preventing him from acting consistent with his Will. But there is a further difficulty here. Let us waive the objection we have been discussing (Wolff's interpretation of Kant being controversial and in any case the notion of a purposeless law being, as we have seen, less than cogent) and note that on Kant's own view it is (not only) consistent with (but required by) the agent's autonomy that he Will the Law or Maxim that "all rules and commands issued by duly constituted authorities shall be obeyed without question."[13] Clearly, a notion of autonomy or agency consistent with this maxim cannot provide an acceptable criterion for deciding whether the practice of political authority is in principle justifiable. The agent who Wills this Maxim has "protected" his agency by turning it over, by "surrendering" it, to constituted authorities.

A further reason for rejecting the "Kantian" notion of autonomy concerns the much more demanding interpretations of that notion by some of Kant's followers rather than Kant's own discussion of it. We touched upon the difficulty in chapter 5 when we discussed Robert Paul Wolff's notion that B's autonomy is lost if he does X because someone he recognizes as an authority says that X should be done. A possible interpretation of this idea is that B acts autonomously only if he himself is the originator of the thought that X ought to be done or is the right action to take. If the thought comes to B from A, and if B then proceeds to do X, B's will has been heteronomized. A less extreme interpretation of the idea allows that B can retain his autonomy if the thought of doing X originates with A. But it insists that A's standing as someone with *in* or *an* authority must play no role, must have no influence upon, B's decision to do X.

The first version of the idea is implausible in the extreme. It renders autonomy incompatible not only with any species of authority but with most of what we know to be social existence and relationships. (Certainly it renders autonomy incompatible with acceptance of the authoritative.) Extreme romantic individualists such as Max Stirner seem to have entertained some version of this idea,[14] but it is doubtful that it can be expressed in an intelligible form. The second version is intelligible enough and does carry the implication that Wolff found in it when he was writing *In Defense of Anarchism,* namely that acceptance of authority by B and B's autonomy are incompatible. If we construe agency on this model of autonomy there is no possibility of justifying authority.

But there is no very good reason to construe agency in this way. Authority relations do inject distinctive considerations into the process by which B decides to do an action. Rather than deciding exclusively in terms of the merits of the action required by X (its merits considered apart from the fact that it is required by authority), B gives weight to the fact that a rule or command to do the action has been promulgated by an authority to which he subscribes. But first, as Kant himself would stress, it is B who accords weight to those facts. He will do so under the influence of a language and of shared values and beliefs that are part of his social and cultural milieu, but he himself will assess those influences and their bearing upon his decisions. Let us imagine, moreover, that his assessment of those influences has led him to the following convictions: he believes that authority is in principle a defensible human institution because it contributes importantly to, say, the assurance of justice; he is satisfied that the practice of authority in question is properly formed; he is convinced that this A has been properly invested with an office of authority in the practice in question and that promulgation of this X is within the authority of that office. The thesis we are considering argues that even under these conditions B's autonomy is necessarily lost not only if he gives, à la Kant, decisive weight to the authority of X when deciding to conform to it, but if he gives any weight whatever to that authority. You or I might think that B is mistaken in holding one or more of the beliefs that we have assigned to him. But assuming that he does hold them, for him to act on them in the sense of giving them weight in deciding about X presents a paradigm case of autonomous thought and action.

In sum, Kantian and neo-Kantian notions of autonomy do not provide an acceptable criterion for judging the justifiability of the practice of political authority. Either they are consistent with conditions that are unacceptable or they settle the question of the justifiability of authority by a species of conceptual fiat that has little to be said for it. We need an understanding of agency that has more content and hence offers both more guidance and more protection than the notion of a "Will" governed by a purely formal Imperative but that is less restrictive than the neo-Kantian conception offered by Wolff.

These reflections on Kantian and neo-Kantian interpretations of autonomy suggest the outlines of a more adequate preliminary construction of the concept of agency. To be appropriate to a theory of authority, "agency" must require action, not just thought or Will, and must direct concern to the content of the rules to be followed, the actions to be taken, and so forth. Although there is no objection to B's accepting and acting on rules and plans of action that originate with an A, the practice must conceive of B himself as an appropriate source of ideas for and initiatives concerning rules and plans of action. B *qua* B must regard himself, and must be regarded by the other members of the practice, as a contributor to the formation of rules, not merely a passive recipient who acts (within the confines of the practice of authority) *only* in the sense that he obeys X's exclusively because they are rules that carry authority.

Finally and most important, there is the question of the "weight" that B may properly give to the fact that a rule carries authority in a jurisdiction of which B is a part. In his work on anarchism Wolff argued that B loses his autonomy if he gives any weight whatever to this fact about a rule. In the view he there argued, B retains his autonomy only if he decides to do each and every X exclusively on the basis of his judgment of the content and merits of the act X requires or forbids.[15] So-called legal absolutism, whether Kantian or some other variety, contends that when B is considering a course of action that is required or forbidden by a legal rule, the *only* consideration to which he may give weight is that the action falls under the rule. F-P theorists, to extend the comparison to one additional position, argue that the legal absolutist is correct *if* B intends his action to be the action of a subscriber to the practice of authority in question. He may consider the merits of the action only if he intends to take his leave from the practice.

Legal absolutism is clearly untenable.[16] We have argued against the F-P position at various junctures in previous chapters, and we have begun to adduce arguments against Wolff's views. What is required, then, is a position that allows B *qua* B to treat the authority of X as a weighty reason (the basis of a *prima facie* obligation) for doing what is required by X but does not require him to accord absolute or conclusive weight to that reason. If such a position can be delineated, and if a practice of authority can in principle be compatible with it, then the practice would be compatible with a familiar and defensible sense of the concept of agency. Indeed the practice would be compatible with individual agency to the greatest possible extent consistent with the practice remaining recognizable as a practice of authority. In respect to much of the history of the theory and practice of political authority the foregoing "if-clauses" express counterfactual conditions. The primary question we pursue in the following chapters is whether, and if so how, those clauses could in principle be descriptive of an actual practice of political authority.

11 The Democratization of Authority

The root idea to be considered in this chapter is that authority will not diminish the agency of those who themselves possess that authority. If authority could be democratized in the sense of distributing it widely and more or less equally among the members of an association, the problem of reconciling authority and agency would be resolved or at least significantly relieved. Put another way, "democratizing" authority in this sense promises to protect and perhaps even to enhance the agency of the B's by eliminating or greatly reducing the significance of the distinction between the A's and the B's.[1]

Of course there is no single notion of democratizing authority and no one agreed-upon device for doing so. In the hope of keeping the discussion within bounds appropriate to present concerns we employ a rough (albeit not unfamiliar) distinction between restricted and radical proposals for, or restricted and radical forms of, democratizing authority. "Restricted" theories aim to maintain at least some distinctions between those who have authority at any time and place and those who do not. But they seek to reduce the number and sharpness of those distinctions in various ways, and to provide those who have little or no authority with devices for influencing and controlling those who have it. "Radical" theories seek to eliminate the distinction altogether or to reduce it to the minimal possible significance in political life. So much so that theories of this type might be thought to imply the elimination of authority itself—to imply that authority would have no place in a political order that was democratized in a truly radical sense. As we use the term, however, "radical" theories preserve authority in several respects, the most important being that once laws have been duly adopted they are invested with authority and all members have an obligation to accept and obey them for that reason.

Restricted Forms of Democratization

The single device most widely and heavily relied upon by "restricted" theorists is elections. The authority to make laws is invested in offices that are filled by the vote of an electorate consisting of a greater or smaller proportion of the populace. Where elections are more than a charade, the decision to invest a particular person with the authority of such an office is itself a decision that carries authority. Thus those who make up the electorate possess a kind of authority, and voting is an exercise of authority. In this (no doubt extended) sense of "authority," the (by now) most common form of democratization distributes authority widely and equally.

There are numerous variations on such arrangements and a wide variety of arguments for the basic device of elections and for this as opposed to that electoral scheme. Moreover, the basic device can be put to uses which, from the standpoint of democratizing authority, are more dramatic than selecting officeholders. Initiatives and referenda are perhaps the most salient instances. In addition to allowing the choice of officeholders, these devices invest the electorate with direct (albeit not necessarily sufficient) authority to make laws and other decisions. In some associations, such devices are put to very extensive use. Suffrage is broad, elections are held frequently and for a high percentage of the offices of authority, initiatives and referenda occur regularly concerning a wide range of issues. In many instances, moreover, associations supplement the devices we have mentioned with institutional arrangements intended to have related effects—for example decentralization of authority, the separation of powers, the proliferation of agencies and bureaus—all of which limit the authority of any given office and put at least some authority (beyond the suffrage) in the hands of a comparatively large number of people. What is perhaps more important, these devices and arrangements occasion informal interactions that may involve substantial proportions of the citizenry in one or another aspect of the exercise of authority.

As noted in chapter 5, even the most minimal of these arrangements (say plebiscitary or "Bonapartist" democracy) involves the citizenry or electorate in the exercise of authority in at least one respect: it is open to citizens to vote for or against candidates for office on the basis of judgments concerning the merits of the laws that the candidates have made or are expected to make. The use of this option may project a variety of effects forward and backward from the moments at which it is actually exercised. Voters may attend to the conduct of those in authority in ways they would not otherwise do, may try to influence those in authority between elections and other voters at the time of elections, and so on through a list of activities that regularly occur in democratic associations.

Owing to such activities, individual citizens may have influence on the content of the laws well beyond what they acquire directly from their "authority" as voters or even as officeholders. As a consequence, they may believe that their acceptance of offices of *in* authority beyond those they personally possess or can reasonably expect to attain derogates little from—may actually augment the efficacy of—their individual agency. Others who in fact have little or no such influence may nevertheless think that it is available to them if they choose to expend the energy and other resources necessary to obtain it. Hence they too may find acceptance of the practice of authority unproblematic or less problematic than it would otherwise be.

It can hardly be doubted that such arrangements and their various indirect and informal concomitants have often served, at least as a practical or psychological matter, to render authority more acceptable than it would otherwise be. Under such arrangements the rules that must be obeyed are less likely to present themselves as impositions of external, alien, or hostile forces. Accepting and obeying the rules may be justified in terms that refer to their particulars, in terms less abstracted from the contents of the rules than are arguments about some sort of initial or original consent (when? by whom? to what?), about abating contingencies (which? to what extent? at what cost?), or about the conditions alleged to be necessary to a certain kind of order or a certain mode of association. Insofar as the B's participate in the practice of authority in concrete, specific ways, the many ways in which that practice affects their lives become more familiar and more easily comprehensible to them. Authority and its interventions are not a *deus ex machina* descending arbitrarily or mysteriously from some other realm, they are an ordinary, a continuing, even a taken-for-granted feature of day-to-day affairs. To the extent that this is the case, one of the substantial arguments that authority is incompatible with individual agency is undermined.

As we had occasion to note in chapter 5, reasoning presuming such arrangements and the possibilities for action that they open up has become deeply embedded in thought and action concerning obedience, disobedience and many other matters central to the practice and the theory of authority. It would not be too much to say that the practice of authority as it presents itself in a large number of countries can no longer be understood without attention to assumptions stemming from "restricted" conceptions of democratization.[2] Given the continuous, active intervention of political authority in the affairs of most modern societies, it is not easy to see how it could be justified apart from some such assumptions.[3] When authority takes from one-fifth to four-fifths of the income of its citizens, conscripts those citizens into military service at substantial risk to their lives, requires them to educate their children within certain specified patterns, monitors and indeed controls their movements in and out of and perhaps within their countries—to mention only a few of the interventions that are routine in virtually all contemporary states—it needs bases of acceptance (if not of willing and enthusiastic support) that a distant, inaccessible authority structure is not likely to generate.

The advantages afforded by democratizing authority on the restricted model are in principle considerable and do much to relieve the difficulty that is our central concern. Nevertheless, even in states in which these advantages are genuinely available and substantially realized they do not and almost certainly cannot fully reconcile authority and agency. There are a number of reasons for this conclusion, some of which could lead us into relatively technical literatures concerning voting, majoritarianism, and individual and collective rationality. For our purposes the gist of the difficulties with and limitations upon restricted democratizations resides in the following characteristics of the democratic process on this model.

The A-B distinction retains great importance. Certain kinds of authority—particularly to vote—may be widely and equally distributed, but distinct offices of authority remain and the invariably smaller number of persons who occupy them at any moment in time have great advantages over the much larger number who do not. The voters elect and may otherwise influence the officeholders, but only on rare occasions can they control the details of the latter's day-to-day decisions and actions. If restricted democratization is combined with—and especially if it is thought to justify—F-P-like understandings concerning the surrender of judgment that is entailed by recognition of the authority of a rule, the B's will commonly find themselves in situations strongly analogous to that of the subjects in the insistently undemocratic state proposed by Thomas Hobbes. Second, the practice of widely distributing certain kinds of authority may reduce the value of any individual's share of that authority. The suffrage is the most dramatic case in point, with large numbers of enfranchised voters having concluded that their ballots count for so little that it is not worth their while to cast them. The same difficulty arises to a lesser degree concerning other devices for democratizing authority, for example creating numerous offices each with authority over a narrowly restricted range of questions (and perhaps in competition with other offices concerning even that range of questions) or a single office (such as a legislature) with a large number of officeholders who must reach agreement before action can be taken. Here again possession of the authority that the offices carry may be judged to so little protect or augment agency that few individuals can be induced to seek those offices. Finally, democratization in the sense of wide distribution of at least some authority almost certainly maximizes the incidence of publicly explicit disagreement among those who share the authority to make this or that class of decision. Hence it requires rules and procedures for reaching decisions in the face of disagreement among the A's. The most common such procedure in democratic societies is majoritarianism in some one of its variants, and majoritarianism will of course regularly leave large numbers of A's in the position of opposing decisions reached in (by) the very offices in the authority of which they share. All of these difficulties are maximized in the huge, diverse, and highly complex nation-states that dominate the contemporary political scene.

In short, attempts to reconcile agency with authority by introducing restricted forms of democratization are likely to diminish the value of the authority itself while reproducing, in what may seem to be only minimally altered forms, the very difficulties that the devices are intended to remedy. It is perhaps partly for this reason that theorists of a considerable range of political persuasions—for example, Oakeshott, Nozick and Robert Paul Wolff—have concluded that these attempts have been misguided or worse—that they have induced a misplaced complacency which actually compounds the difficulty of reconciling authority with individual freedom, rationality and moral integrity.

As real as are the difficulties with and the limitations upon restricted democratization, it remains the case that it has in fact contributed to easing the authority–individual agency problem. In most general terms it contributes to easing that problem simply because it *conceives of* citizens as participants in the day-to-day workings of the practice. Of course this conceptualization cannot itself assure that participation will in fact occur. But it gives standing to, it legitimates, participation and hence it delegitimates attempts to prevent or to restrict it. Although it is surely no panacea for the problem we are considering, there is more to be said for it than has been allowed by its most severe critics (such as those just mentioned). In order to appreciate both its contributions and its limitations we must attend not only to the formal devices that it employs—elections, referenda, etc.—but also to the patterns of informal political interaction that sometimes develop in part because of the institutionalization of those devices. As with any system of rules and rule-governed institutions and practices, we must look at the ways the rules and institutions that make up systems of restricted democracy are in fact used by the human beings who accept them.

Radical Forms of Democratization

We return to the informal workings of "restricted" democratic institutions below, where we attempt to integrate the foregoing considerations with arguments generated by an amended version of F-P theory. But first it is necessary to examine the possibility that democratization could provide an entire reconciliation of authority and individual agency, could produce a form of association in which, in Rousseau's famous words, "every person, while uniting himself with all, . . . obeys only himself and remains as free as before."[4] We must look, that is, at the arguments for radical democratization, for a democratization so far-reaching that it eliminates situations in which the A-B distinction is a distinction among members and all situations in which the authority of the association conflicts with the agency of any of its individual members.

As Rousseau's statement indicates, the objective of such an arrangement would be to banish altogether the sense that laws are imposed by others. We interpret this requirement to mean that all laws must be adopted through a process in which every citizen participates freely and on equal terms *and* that the content of every law must have the approval of every citizen. Citizens would not submit to or accept laws made by "others"; they would identify with laws made through a process in which they were full participants and with the content of which they were in full agreement. If those with an obligation to obey the laws participate fully in making them, and if unanimity is required for a law to be adopted, then it would appear that every citizen would indeed "obey himself alone" and would be as free as he had been before he entered into the arrangement.

Such an arrangement would of course reinforce and extend the benefits resulting from the conceptualization of restricted forms of democratization. It might also be expected to heighten what might be called the psychological advantages afforded by the latter. Having a yet greater and more decisive voice in the making of laws than in restricted forms of democracy, citizens might well identify more readily and more completely with those laws. The most original and powerful of the theorists of radical democracy, namely Rousseau, believed such an arrangement to be the only possible means of overcoming evils pervasive in modern societies— evils that make genuine authority impossible and the ersatz substitute for it entirely unacceptable. In his view the inexpungeable physical distinctness of every human person had been powerfully reinforced and augmented by beliefs and values that foster egoism and selfishness. The unremitting pursuit of purely private interests had all but destroyed any sense of commonality and common purpose, all but eliminated any sense of identification with entities larger than the individual self. As a consequence, even when conceptual and institutional barriers to participation had been lowered, laws necessarily presented themselves as serving the personal interests of those in authority. "Laws" were made either by individual despots or, in the case of associations employing some form of restricted democracy, by the "will of all"; that is by a mechanically aggregated sum of privatized individual wills. In neither case did they or could they have the slightest claim to the moral standing of genuine authority.

Given this dismal circumstance, Rousseau thought, a greatly expanded and invigorated participation in political decision making was at least a necessary condition of both authority and genuine individual agency. Involvement in such a process might induce participants to enlarge their vision, to appreciate the respects in which a citizenry makes up a distinctive whole with interests and objectives more significant than those of particular persons viewing themselves exclusively as separate and private individuals. Such a development had occurred in religious movements known to Rousseau, and he apparently believed that something approaching it had taken place in certain forms of the classical polis and in Geneva of an earlier day. Certainly we are familiar with such processes from revolutionary and anticolonial struggles, some of which may have been influenced by Rousseau's ideas. Thus his argument is not without cogency and even a degree of empirical support. Its recurrent appeal since Rousseau advanced it is easy to understand.

Even if we accept the notion of agency implicit in it (which anticipates Kant's autonomy), however, there are well-tried objections to the argument. Perhaps the most familiar of these objections is that the scheme is hopelessly impractical as a political proposal in the world of the modern nation-state. In a state or other association of any size, it would be impossible for everyone to participate as intensively as Rousseau's scheme would require. And if this difficulty could somehow be overcome, the sheer number of participants would all but guarantee dissenting votes— and hence the impossibility of action—on any but the most innocuous of proposals.

These difficulties are anything but merely "practical" or "mechanical" in character. If we continue to treat voting as the exercise of a kind of authority, under such an arrangement each and every citizen is in a position, by virtue of his authority, to impose his will on all the others every time he casts a dissenting vote. And if participation consists primarily of voting (as for example in Robert Paul Wolff's weekly electronic referenda),[5] the arrangement might constitute a modest improvement on the once-and-for-all consent that has satisfied a number of contractarian theorists and that drew Rousseau's own contempt. It would not, that is, involve citizens in the day-to-day patterns of informal political interaction which can build understanding and acceptance of the outcomes of formal processes. Also, the fact that a citizen supported a proposal when it was under consideration would not be a good predictor of whether he would continue to approve of it after it had been adopted and its effects had become evident. Thus if the arrangement were thought to justify surrender of judgment once a law had been adopted, it (the arrangement) would augment imposition and the loss of agency.

Radical democratization, then, will not itself adequately reconcile authority and individual agency. It is intended to induce participation that is more widespread, vigorous and efficacious than is encouraged or even allowed by more restricted modes of democracy. But in an association of any size the two desiderata are likely to conflict with one another. Either the participation is intense but less widespread and the arrangement becomes hard to distinguish from restricted democracy, or it is widespread but lax or thin, thereby failing to enliven identification with and acceptance of substantive outcomes. And in both cases its formal properties leave the association subject to the veto power that the scheme puts at the disposal of all members.

Democratization and the General Will

Rousseau was neither unfamiliar with the objections just discussed nor especially sanguine about overcoming the problems that prompt them. But he did evolve a conceptualization-*cum*-theory intended to deal with the more important of the objections at the level of ideas. Because his thinking introduces crucial complexities in the issues we are considering it will be instructive to examine it further.

The centerpiece of his construct is his famous—or notorious— distinction between the Will of All and the General Will and his intimately related notion that under certain circumstances citizens must be "forced to be free." The famous distinction took its moral and political importance from the combination of what he believed to be a fact and a fundamental moral principle. The fact was the prevalence of egoism and privatization. The principle that made this fact important is that a law can be acceptable to a self-respecting agent only if it meets moral standards over and above the requirement of adoption through a process involving free and equal participation. A law is morally acceptable (is a *law* in the proper sense of being entitled to authority) only if it is directed to, and only if it in fact serves, the interests of individuals *qua* members of the association or collectivity, not those interests that they have as private individuals.

Very roughly, laws that serve the interests of members *qua* members (citizens) express the General Will, laws (or putative laws) that serve private interests can express no more than the Will of All. In a perfectly functioning association, it is true, this distinction between the two

"Wills" would have no application. Participants in the lawmaking process would support only those proposals that serve the interests of the citizenry as such. As noted, Rousseau seems to have thought that a fully participatory process is a strongly contributory if not a necessary condition of achieving such a state of affairs. He reasoned that it is through involvement in such a process that the individual can be sustained as a moral being who makes the good of the citizenry the good of all his actions *qua* citizen. We must leave aside difficulties in making the transition from an amoral populace to a predominantly moral one—difficulties that call for the obscure but apparently unique and crucial talents of the Legislator. Assuming a solution to those difficulties, intense and continuous involvement in a participatory process is (in Rousseau's own view) nevertheless no more than a necessary condition of the requisite mode of moral personality. Some participants may remain largely or entirely unreconstructed, and others may backslide in respect to particular issues. Such persons are likely to advance proposals that would, if enacted into "law," be contrary to the General Will and to resist proposals that would express the General Will.

In short, Rousseau recognized that in all but the most ideal circumstances the possibility of disagreement is not the only problem left unresolved by radical democratization. An association as fully democratized as you please might nevertheless face attempts to use authority for morally unacceptable purposes. And some of those attempts might succeed.

But does not Rousseau's insistence on this point in effect give up the ground that he appeared to have gained in his attempt to reconcile authority and agency? Why should the decisions of the virtuous associates not be regarded by unregenerates as straightforward impositions on their individual interests and desires and hence on their agency? Why does the fact that a law accords with the General Will justify imposing it on others who, for whatever reason, do not favor it? Are not such impositions a violation of the agency of those who oppose them?

Rousseau will allow of no such characterization of the situation. He contends, rather, that those compelled to conform to the General Will have been "forced to be free." As Rousseau constructs the notion of the General Will, it is conceptually impossible for there to be a conflict between it and the *real* or *moral* will of any citizen *qua* citizen. If an individual finds himself inclined to oppose the General Will he thereby has conclusive evidence that his private will is threatening to triumph over his will as citizen. Behaviors resulting from such inclinations are thereby shown to be other than free, rational and moral. They are no more than effects caused by an upsurge of primitive, irrational and amoral passions—passions that have enslaved an individual who only appears to be free and rational (and who does not even appear to be moral). Thus when his virtuous associates compel him to act in conformity with the General Will, they force him to be free. Indeed it is wrong to say that "they" do so. For when he as citizen realizes that his private will is on the march, he himself as citizen will welcome and support the actions necessary to discipline and control it. It is in this sense that Rousseau claims the individual obeys himself alone, that his agency remains intact.

The difficulties with Rousseau's argument in this regard are too well known to require elaboration at length. True, there will almost certainly be circumstances in the affairs of any association in which some members will justifiably be compelled to act in ways that they would not choose to act. But the decision to employ compulsion cannot be justified in terms of its contribution to the freedom, rationality, or moral integrity of those who suffer the compulsion. Rousseau's attempts to reconcile authority and individual agency proceed by encompassing the latter under the former.[6] Any inclinations or behaviors that are contrary to the General Will are therefore dismissed as other than free, rational, and moral. Thus he "reconciles" authority and individual agency by emptying the latter category of those garden-variety instances of its exercise that create the difficulty which his "reconciliation" claims to solve.

12 Judging the Merits of the Actions of Authority Authority and the Authoritative

The Authoritative as the Criterion for Judging Authority

We may interpret Rousseau's argument as an attempt to combine elements of democratic, F-P, and S-P theories of authority. The democratic and formal-procedural aspects are merged in Rousseau's insistence on a radical form of participation. A proposal can acquire the authority of law only if it is adopted through a specified procedure—one involving the free and equal participation of all associates. The substantive and purposive element is his insistence that a proposal can be invested with authority only if its content satisfies some appropriate criterion or standard (i.e., in Rousseau's theory, that it serve the interests of citizens as such) not fully given by the procedures themselves. The democratic-*cum*-procedural and the substantive-purposive elements are connected by the contention that active involvement in the lawmaking process will enable associates to seek, to discover, and to act to serve the interests of the citizenry as such. If all associates do these things, authority and individual agency must be compatible because all rules carrying authority will be adopted and approved by each and every agent who is required to obey them. If many but not all associates do them, those who identify and act to serve the General Will are justified in requiring backsliders to accept and obey the rules that express the General Will. If we accept the notion of a true or real will they will be justified because the rules do no more than require the backslider to conform to his own true will. But even if we reject (as we should) this dubious notion, the virtuous are justified because the position they are taking satisfies the only defensible criterion of substantive correctness. The final possibility (and the one that Rousseau probably thought most likely to obtain) is that moral conduct will fail to materialize on a scale sufficient to sustain a political association possessed of authority. In this case associates will be obliged to do as well as they can in a world that is amoral at least to this extent.

Both the strengths and the complexities of Rousseau's construct (on this interpretation of it) may emerge more clearly if we recur to our distinction between authority and the authoritative. Rousseau believed that authority would be possible in the European societies of his day only if a moral transformation occurred among their populations. Let us interpret this contention as a version of the proposition that authority presupposes the authoritative. In societies as privatized and fragmented as Rousseau described, the emergence of widely shared values and beliefs would itself constitute a transformation of sorts. And we would certainly be warranted in talking about a transformation if the beliefs in question included Rousseau's idea that there is a common good that can be agreed upon and that authority must serve that common good. Rousseau may also have been correct that a vigorous participatory democracy is the surest means of sustaining a commitment to such values and beliefs.

Whether we agree or disagree with the last proposition, Rousseau was surely correct that we ought not to treat citizen participation in the making of a law as a *sufficient* justification for that law (and hence for the implication that citizens have an all-things-considered obligation to obey that law). The reason for agreeing with Rousseau on this point, a reason that is at least implicit in his distinction between the General Will and the Will of All, is that participation in the process of making laws places no limitations on the content of the laws that the process yields. Perhaps active citizen participation maximizes the likelihood of rules that merit approval and obedience. But even active, well-intentioned citizens (as with any other set of decision makers) sometimes do foolish and unfortunate things. If citizen participation is made a sufficient condition of rules that carry authority and entail all-things-considered obligations, it becomes impossible to deny the authority of any rule that the process yields and impossible to challenge the obligation to obey those rules.[1] Rousseau fervently wished for a society in which the actual will of all citizens and the General Will would coincide in every case. But he held back from making an identification between the procedural requirement of participation and the criteria of defensible use of authority.

His position in this regard accords with a view that we have argued throughout, namely, that more-than-procedural criteria for judging the substantive merits of rules must be included among the elements of a practice of authority. As with any version of this position, his argument raises the question of just which criteria, over and above citizen participation or any other formal or procedural rule, should be employed to determine whether proposed rules deserve to be invested with the authority of law and deserve to be obeyed if so invested. As a next step in pursuing this question, we further explore the possibility that Rousseau's notion of the General Will can be interpreted in terms of our concept of the authoritative.

As we are using the concept, "the authoritative" in a society consists in values and beliefs that the members actually accept and hold. These beliefs and values provide criteria for judging rules and proposed rules. The criteria are not themselves ordinarily at issue—in one respect cannot be at issue—when deciding the merits of particular rules. There is, in short, a "givenness," a "facticity," about the authoritative; a givenness that allows it at once to provide generalized support to a practice of authority and to supply criteria by which to judge the merits of particular rules. Because judgments of any sort presuppose criteria of judgment, it is difficult to see how, in the absence of some such set of values and beliefs, associates could decide how to assess and respond to the rules of their practice. Thus the content of the authoritative provides the requisite criteria for judging the actions of authority. And if the authoritative is in fact (as we have stipulated in our use of the concept) widely accepted among the members of the practice, its use as the source of criteria would not appear to derogate from the agency of those members.

Owing to these very characteristics of the authoritative, however, reliance on it as the exclusive source of criteria for judging the exercise of authority creates a serious difficulty. If we identify "General Will" and "the authoritative," Rousseau can be read as contending that rule formulations are entitled to authority just insofar as they are expressions of the authoritative (including as a part of the authoritative the requirement that rules be adopted through a suitably democratized procedure). But if all acts of authority are themselves expressions of the authoritative— rather than formulations to be tested in part by criteria that the authoritative supplies—then on our reading of Rousseau's argument it will be impossible for members of the association to find grounds on which to dispute or object to those acts. Instead of distinct phenomena standing in a sometimes supportive and complementary, sometimes conflicting relationship, authority and the authoritative are merged, thereby making impossible appeals from one to the other. Thus members who accept the substance of the authoritative values and beliefs as the proper criteria for judging acts of authority are locked into a conceptual and a sociopsychological whole against which appeal and dissent are impossible.

The problem here goes very deep. (It should be emphasized that it is one of the great merits of Rousseau's theory that reading him brings us up against the problem so forcefully.) Let us restate the elements of the problem as they have emerged thus far. (1) Authority is impossible in the absence of some version of the authoritative. (2) Commitment to the authoritative and to the practice of authority that its beliefs and values support is most effectively sustained in associations involving widespread and active participation in the processes of decision making by authority. (3) Active participation may contribute importantly to the merits of the decisions of authority, but the possibility of unregenerates, backsliding and well-intentioned mistakes in the use of authority cannot be eliminated. Hence participation cannot itself assure that the decisions of authority will be meritorious and it cannot be a sufficient criterion for assessing the merits of those decisions. (4) Decisions of authority that accord with the authoritative will, for that reason, be judged meritorious by most members of the association. (5) If the content of the authoritative and the content of decisions that carry authority (rules) are *identified,* it becomes impossible for dissenters to appeal to the authoritative in objecting to actions of authority and impossible for them to appeal to authority for assistance in challenging aspects of the authoritative that they find objectionable.

As we are interpreting him, Rousseau's response to the difficulty we are alleging is to deny (at the level of theory) that it is any difficulty at all. Because the General Will–*cum*–the–authoritative is always correct, the views of anyone who rejects it are necessarily mistaken and must be rejected. For the same reason, actions of authority that accord with the General Will–*cum*–the–authoritative are thereby shown to merit acceptance and obedience, and anyone who dissents from or disobeys them must be "forced to be free" (or at any rate compelled to conform). In other words, as Rousseau uses the concept of General Will–*cum*–the–authoritative, the idea of dissenting from it is absurd on its face; and there can be no question of dissenting from actions of "authority" that violate the General Will–*cum*–the–authoritative because such actions have no authority. What we might call the organic quality or the "self-containedness" of the social or jural order, so far from a difficulty to be overcome, is one of the most important virtues of that order. In particular it is the virtue that permits, or rather guarantees, reconciliation of authority and individual agency.

Attractive as it may at first sight appear, this outcome is unacceptable. It creates a situation of the kind explored with sensitivity by Alexis de Tocqueville and J. S. Mill among others, in which cogent dissent from values and beliefs that are widely received is all but impossible. Indeed it compounds the difficulty of dissenting from widely received values and beliefs by merging authority and the authoritative.

But how could the outcome be avoided? If "the authoritative" has the characteristics (the standing) that we have attributed to it, dissent from it would appear to be a psychological and perhaps a conceptual impossibility. In Wittgensteinian terms, if the authoritative is the foundation, the bedrock, of a practice of authority, *must* it not turn back every attempt to question it?[2] Are we not in fact faced with the choice that Rousseau identified, that is between, on the one hand, a society with no established standards for the exercise of authority and hence one in which what passes for authority necessarily imposes on the agency of some of its members and, on the other hand, an "organic" or "self-contained" society in which there is no possibility of a cogent appeal against the established standards?

Transcendent Criteria for Judging Authority

Pursuit of this question will shortly bring us back to
F-P theory and the contribution it might make to the justification of authority. But first we should pause to consider an argument characteristic
of a number of S-P theorists, especially those committed to some version
of natural law, natural right, or some other allegedly transcendental truths
or principles. These theorists (Plato and Saint Thomas Aquinas are obvious examples, Roberto Unger is a recent one[3]) have taken the problem we
have now reached very seriously indeed. They may agree that some mode
of authoritative belief (or opinion, as they are more likely to call it) is
necessary to and therefore in fact always found in conjunction with viable
practices of authority, and they may recognize that the authoritative is in
fact called upon in assessing the actions of authority. But however important the authoritative may be from the perspective of, say, positive
sociology or jurisprudence, it is almost certainly in the realm of belief or
opinion, not knowledge. Thus these theorists find altogether credible the
idea that the authoritative might itself be defective and that authority will
have to correct it. They resolve the conundrum that this argument appears
to present by positing a set of norms or standards whose standing does not
(properly) depend on acceptance by the preponderance of associates and
which can be acted upon by philosopher-kings or some other elite who
know and appreciate the significance of those norms. They posit appeals,
in other words, not merely from authority to the authoritative, but also to
some external, transcendent principles and the *an* authorities concerning
them. "Self-containedness" is a quality that a political order could be
allowed only if and only in the sense that the authoritative and the exercise of authority had come to coincide perfectly with natural law or right,
divine revelation, or whatever other body of transcendental truths or
principles they believe to be available.[4]

S-P theories with a natural law or natural right foundation, then, claim
to provide a criterion for judging both the acts of *in* authority and the
content of the authoritative by which such acts are (in fact) ordinarily
judged. The standing of this criterion, it is contended, is independent of
the belief system of the practice or practices in which it is employed, is
therefore not implicated in or corrupted by any defects of those practices,
and thus provides a basis for dissenting from both the belief system and
the actions of authority.

There are, however, well-known and decisive difficulties with this argument. Some of these are epistemological in character, having to do with
the basis and standing of the claims that there are truths or principles that
are transcendent and yet substantive (practical synthetic *a priori*'s, in
Kantian terms) and that these truths or principles can be known and

applied with certitude by persons possessed of the right characteristics or qualifications. But even if the standing of the truths and principles could be demonstrated in a philosophically satisfactory manner, those demonstrations would have to be available to associates caught up in the problems that the truths and principles are alleged to resolve. If they are not so available, it is far from clear why associates should pay any heed to them or to justifications for actions of authority that invoke them. Indeed it is far from clear how the truths and principles could play any role in a practice of authority. As we noted in our earlier discussion of surrender of judgment to *an* authorities, *an* authority relationships (which, as Plato's theory makes clear, is what *in* authority relationships become on this understanding) disintegrate—or deteriorate into something else, for example, compulsion or manipulation—if the B's are excluded from judging the merits of the propositions and performances of the A's. Advanced as a solution to problems of "self-containedness" in a political association, S-P theories with a natural law, natural right or other transcendental basis so "objectify" judgments concerning authority and the authoritative as to leave them logically impossible or necessarily unacceptable to anyone with a concern for individual agency.[5]

The difficulty in question, then, goes deep indeed. For both practical (i.e., "sociological") and normative reasons the actions of authority must have the support of those to whom they apply, and hence must congrue with beliefs and values that are in fact widely shared among the latter. Yet the fact that the actions of authority have such support is not sufficient to justify them. To treat that fact as sufficient constantly threatens to leave some B's without grounds on which to object to actions of authority.

There is no fully satisfactory solution to this difficulty; the difficulty can be minimized and controlled but not eliminated. But before drawing this conclusion in final form we must note contributions that F-P theory, in conjunction with democratization, might make toward keeping the difficulty within acceptable limits.

Formal Criteria for Judging Authority Formal-Procedural Theory Revisited

From the perspective of the position we have now reached, the most important feature of F-P theory is its insistence that *in* authority is constituted, defined and hence *limited* by formal rules. These rules are the basis of the distinction between *intra* and *ultra vires* acts. We have seen that this distinction cannot be drawn in the manner F-P theorists suggest, that is without reference to the substance and the purposes of the rules to which it is applied. For this reason it is clear that the distinction—and the F-P theory that depends so heavily upon it—cannot entirely resolve the difficulties we are considering. If the substantive considerations that go into the *intra-ultra vires* distinction are drawn from sources established within the society, the problems that arise when authority and the authoritative are identified will make their appearance. If those considerations are drawn from putatively transcendent sources, then one will face the difficulties that are a familiar feature of natural law and natural right theories.

An association marked by F-P type characteristics, however, need not face these problems in the same form in which they would arise in a radical democracy ruled by the Will of All or a Platonic utopia ruled by philosopher-kings. The difference, to shift from the somewhat dry terminology of F-P theory to the vocabulary more commonly employed in normative discussions of these matters, is produced when there is a serious commitment to the rule of law, perhaps to its close relation constitutionalism, and to the idea often intimately associated with both, namely that individual citizens should have certain rights against authority. To revert to a notion employed earlier, the differences are produced when an association is recognizably "civil" as we used that concept at the end of chapter 3.

Of these notions, the one closest to F-P theory in its sparest formulations (for example Hobbes' and especially Oakeshott's) is the rule of law. It is part of the very notion of a law (of its "internal morality" in Lon Fuller's well-known phrase[6]) that it must be public, general, and prospective. Commitment to these requirements presupposes some more or less explicit conception of the character and purposes proper to the association. There will be occasions in the life of any association when it will be attractive to punish actions that were lawful, or could not have been known to be unlawful, at the time they were taken, to use legislative authority to impose harms or benefits on named individuals, and so forth. Associates genuinely committed to the rule of law (and to constitutionalism and individual rights) will believe that succumbing to such attractions renders the association unacceptable to them. To this degree, at least, the rule of law, constitutionalism and related devices are not independent of the authoritative.

Nevertheless, the principles of the rule of law, constitutionalism, and the idea of individual rights are, *comparatively speaking*, formal in character. Commitment to them can be sustained along with a diversity of objectives and purposes and is compatible with a considerable array of rules. Because of their comparative formality these principles and ideas will not settle whether an association should integrate its several ethnic groups or self-consciously promote ethnic distinctiveness and pluralism;

whether to permit abortion on demand; whether to conscript for military service or rely upon a volunteer army; whether to employ taxes on income, sales taxes or both; and so forth through the major issues that present themselves for resolution in contemporary political associations. By the same token, disagreement over such questions need not (though it may and sometimes has) shatter agreement on the importance of the comparatively formal principles and rules.[7]

As noted in respect to "due process of law," however, these principles, and particularly the rule-of-law principle, are not so formal as to be empty, are not compatible with so wide an array of laws that they are useless in judging and restraining authority. If the rule-of-law principle is indifferent to the choice between an income tax and a sales tax, it clearly prohibits the collection of a tax of any sort before a tax law has been adopted and it clearly requires that rates, mode of payment, penalties for nonpayment and so forth be publicly announced and not varied arbitrarily from person to person. Although hardly sufficient to assure an acceptable system of taxation, these are significant limitations on the use of authority. They provide the A's with guidelines as to how their authority may be used and they provide B's, including those dissenting from aspects of the authoritative, with recognized bases for their objections.

It must be stressed yet again that these guidelines and limitations are not somehow external to the association; are not somehow independent of the values and beliefs, the objectives and the purposes of the members of the association. Rather, commitment to the guidelines and limitations is *among* the values, beliefs, purposes and objectives that have standing as authoritative within the association. But the comparatively formal character of the rule-of-law principle has sometimes allowed it to play a distinctive role. Associates can cogently, even conclusively, object to proposals and actions without winning controversies over their substantive merits. Whatever the advantages of censoring pornographic publications, those who publish them cannot be arrested or punished if no law prohibiting such publications had been passed when the magazine left the presses; however unpatriotic the activities of certain civil servants, to legislate away their position in the government service would be to pass a bill of attainder; as clearly guilty as the defendant may appear to be, he must be acquitted because the "evidence" against him is not admissible under the rules of criminal justice.

An analogy might help to clarify what we are, and are not, contending here. The analogy is with the role of comparatively formal principles and rules of inquiry such as laws of logic, tests of statistical significance, procedures for avoiding recurrent types of bias, and so forth. Even these most formal (seemingly transcendental) rules and principles come into play, have a meaningful use, only when they are employed in specific investigations conducted by assignable investigators under particular conditions and circumstances. To varying degrees, moreover, their interpretation and use alter with changes in subject matter, investigators and the purposes of the investigation. (Note that many social science departments prefer to teach their own courses in scientific methodology, statistical analysis and like subjects because they believe that these techniques and devices must be adapted to the distinctive characteristics of their subject matters.) Nor are these principles and rules an unmediated gift of God, Nature or Reason. They are themselves the subjects of specialized modes of inquiry—logic, statistics, philosophy and methodology of science—that have worked, and continue to work, important changes in their formulations, interpretations and more or less widely accepted uses. As we emphasized in chapters 3 and 4, there is no such thing as a principle or a rule apart from the roles it actually plays, the uses to which it is actually put, in some human practice(s) or activity(ies).

As vital as these qualifying remarks are, relatively formal principles and rules do achieve distinctive standing, do in fact play a distinctive role, in numerous disciplines. Persons who seek entry into disciplines and professions are expected to develop a degree of mastery of—indeed to display a commitment to—the principles and rules of inquiry that are accepted in it. (Just as members of some political associations are expected to understand and accept the rule of law, the constitution, and bill of rights.) Again, clear violations of such principles and rules are ordinarily regarded as straight our errors or mistakes. (Just as actions that are clearly unconstitutional or otherwise *ultra vires* therefore lack authority and are to be rejected.) Such mistakes may or may not vitiate the work in which they occur, but in either case they will be treated as mistakes that ought to be corrected. These first two characteristics would of course be impossible if it were not for a third, namely that there is commonly (though by no means always) *more* agreement concerning the formulations and uses of such principles and rules than about the issues, conclusions, explanations, theories and so on that the principles are used to explore and support. Laws of logic, tests of statistical significance and their ilk can be *brought to* investigations in ethics, in demography, in high energy physics, can be employed without arousing controversy among practitioners knowledgeable in the field. (Just as the rule of law, the constitution, the established individual rights, can be and sometimes are *brought to* debates about this or that public policy.)

In these several respects comparatively formal principles and rules for the conduct of inquiry stand to inquiry itself as comparatively formal principles and rules governing authority stand to the conduct of authority.[8] In both cases formal principles provide participants with grounds of judgment that are neutral to at least some of the controversies over substantive issues and actions (and parties to those actions) that they are used to judge and assess. The term "comparatively" in this account must be given a good deal of emphasis. Formal principles and rules are products of interactions among participants in a discipline or an association. For this reason there is and can be no assurance that any of them will achieve sufficient standing or play the distinctive role we have been discussing. For the same reason, such principles and rules undergo change and from time to time become the very focus of controversies that animate the discipline or association.

In the present context the important point concerns the advantages that accrue to the extent that formal principles achieve the distinctive standing we have been trying to delineate. These advantages, which are displayed in the histories of a number of the most notable and notably civil practices of *in* authority, relate directly to the difficulties we found to be (as it were) left over when the democratization of authority has been added to the authoritative.

Such formal principles can be viewed, in the well-known phrase of Charles McIlwain, as providing for appeals from "the people drunk to the people sober."[9] (They do not provide an appeal from the people, drunk or sober, to some transcendent principle or principles.) Most of the questions and issues that present themselves, day to day, for resolution in a practice must perforce be dealt with largely in terms of considerations drawn from the context in which they arise. The immediate interests and desires, objectives and purposes of the individuals and groups that are concerned, the economic conditions, the expected consequences of this as opposed to that decision or policy, actions previously taken on related issues, and so forth supply the materials out of which responses will be formulated, a debate conducted and a decision reached. We should add that a practice in which the policies and rules and their consequences frequently prove to be alienating to any substantial number of associates shows itself to be in a kind of crisis—shows itself to lack widely shared values and beliefs that allow its members to debate and to resolve topical issues in ways that do not drive one another to revolt or despair. In McIlwain's metaphor, a people that is always drunk is a people bereft of any recourse against its own conduct.

But it would only be in the imaginary world of Rousseau's ideal societies that members never find themselves dismayed, distressed or outraged by actions of authority. And it is in circumstances of such disaffection that the availability of McIlwain's appeal is most important. If the society is democratic, the appeal may first take the form of a demand for evidence that the controverted actions do in fact command wide support. This sort of appeal itself depends upon formal principles, those which specify the procedures by which the presence or absence of wide support is to be ascertained. If such support is demonstrated but segments of the society remain disaffected, the latter may contend that the (to them) unacceptable action conflicts with the authoritative, that it violates commitments that have evolved and been sustained over time and through the course of resolving a wide range of more immediate, more topical questions. If formal rules and principles are well established (as has been true of the rule-of-law principle and some of the principles of constitutionalism and of rights in a number of societies), appeals to them are a special case of appeals to the authoritative. If such an appeal is well grounded in established principles and rules such as the rule of law or the provisions of a constitution or bill of rights, making it ought to halt the action. It is for this reason that such appeals are the clearest instances of appeals from "the people drunk to the people sober." Despite the support of both A's and B's for the action, dissenters may be able to hold off its ill consequences without convincing its proponents that it is substantively undesirable. There will follow an interval in which supporters might "sober up" and during which dissenters may be able to persuade supporters that the action or policy is indeed undesirable.

Clearly, formal principles and rules are no panacea for the problem of finding criteria for judging the actions of authority or for the related but deeper problem of maintaining an acceptable relationship between authority and individual agency. There is no assurance that such principles and rules will in fact achieve the standing and play the sort of role that we have been discussing.[10] And where such a development does occur, the principles and rules can have no more than a comparative formality, no more than a relative independence from or neutrality in respect to the issues and controversies that bring them into play. Appealing to them is not simply the same as advancing yet another argument concerning the merits of the disputed policy or action, but neither does it leave argumentation about merits altogether behind.

For these reasons and because in its own way commitment to formal principles and rules is itself a substantive commitment, the availability of formal principles and rules that define and limit authority cannot insure against deep dissatisfaction with authority—dissatisfaction that may convince those who are required to conform that they cannot continue to subscribe to the practice of authority without abandoning their agency. Individuals and groups outraged in this way may well conclude that the formal principles and rules (which, after all, will in their view have been shown to be at least compatible with unacceptable actions and policies) form part of their problem and must be displaced.[11] For anyone who has reached such a conclusion concerning a particular association, the availability—even to the extent that they are genuine—of formal limits on authority will do little to qualify their belief that continued subscription to the practice of authority is incompatible with their freedom, reason and moral integrity.

13 A Justification for the Practice of Political Authority

We have reviewed the most familiar and in our judgment the most plausible of the understandings, arrangements and devices that have been proposed as means to reconcile authority and individual agency. Briefly, they are: the idea that associates must in some sense voluntarily subscribe or consent to authority; the idea of realms of action into which authority does not enter; the idea of democratizing authority in various ways and to varying degrees; the idea that the actions of authority, substantively speaking, will deserve acceptance and obedience only if they are congruent with values and beliefs that are widely shared among associates; and finally, the idea that authority should be limited by comparatively formal principles and rules.

These proposals are by no means irrelevant to solving the problem we have been examining in part 2. A practice of authority in which some one of the numerous variants and combinations of these ideas has been accepted and implemented will surely be less objectionable to persons who value their agency than practices which do not include them or give them only nominal standing and use. Those modern practices of political authority that have won the most willing—or, perhaps, the least unwilling—subscription of their members have included some combination of them.

We comment further on the positive value of these proposals below. But even the most enthusiastic acceptance and vigorous implementation of these proposals could not guarantee against situations in which some B's regard some of the obligations they have *qua* B's as unacceptable (and hence against situations in which—assuming that some B's refuse to discharge obligations they regard as unacceptable—the A's can bring about "compliance" with one or more X's only by coercing one or more B's). If we take the recognition of the authority of rules to entail an obligation to obey them, this conclusion could be "avoided" only by a conceptual maneuver (of the kind attempted by Rousseau) which assimilates the criteria of whether a rule has authority and the criteria for determining whether an act conforming to a rule was done freely, rationally and in a manner consistent with the moral integrity of the actor. But all such maneuvers, all such assimilations, "resolve" the problem only by emptying the concept of individual agency of its independent significance; they "resolve" that problem by denying—in the face of a plenitude of reason and evidence to the contrary—that it is a problem.

Does it follow that anarchists are correct? Are we to conclude that authority can be justified only if we forego or deeply subordinate our concern with individual agency? If the conclusion stated in the previous paragraph is correct, justifications of authority must recognize—and countenance—the possibility that practices of authority will sometimes conflict with the agency of their subscribers. If the reality or even the serious prospect of any such conflict is unacceptable, then Robert Paul Wolff is correct when he says that the idea of justified authority must be "consigned to the category of the round square, the married bachelor, and the unsensed sense-datum."[1]

As the formulation just quoted makes clear, Wolff's conclusion that authority and agency (autonomy) are incompatible is in no part a finding based on examination of instances of the practice of authority. Nor is the conclusion an assessment of the probabilities that this or that outcome will result from one or another possible arrangements of the features of such practices. It is a "deduction" drawn from analysis of the concepts "authority" and "autonomy." The conclusion of that deduction is not probabilistic or contingent, it is necessary and universal. Moreover, if morality is impossible apart from autonomy, the conclusion that authority is morally unacceptable is equally necessary. On this view there can be no question of significant variations in the frequency, intensity or gravity of the conflict between authority and autonomy. Equally, any notions of more or less objectionable restrictions on autonomy, any idea of "weighing up" or "striking balances" between the benefits of authority and those of autonomy, are excluded *a priori*. The question posed above, *whether* we can accept "the reality or even the serious prospect of any conflict" between authority and agency, is a question that answers itself. Indeed it is a question that shows itself to be based on a morally vicious misunderstanding.

Having rejected Wolff's neo-Kantian conceptualization of autonomy, we can scarcely accept inferences dependent upon it. We have insisted that recognition and respect for the agency of individual members is a condition of a practice of authority. Participants in a practice of authority must recognize one another as agents—as persons who engage in self-actuated, intentional, purposive and rational conduct. But agency can be more or less full, the possibilities for it can be more or less extensive, and our assessments of practice should be influenced by such comparative judgments. This way of conceiving of the matter allows judgments that are excluded *a priori* by the absolutist, all-or-nothing understanding advanced by Kantian and neo-Kantian conceptions. Given that a practice of political authority recognizes and respects its participants as agents (given, that is, that it is a practice of authority), we can ask whether it allows sufficient scope to agency to be justified *qua* practice. We might find practices that Kant would regard as justified because respectful of autonomy in his sense are not justified. And we might find that practices which Wolff rejects as incompatible with agency are justifiable.

A practice of political authority that accepts and implements the ideas and devices examined in chapters 11 and 12 would undoubtedly satisfy the minimal condition just discussed. Even restricted forms of democratization are incomprehensible apart from the idea that participants (*qua* participants in the practice) should, at least sometimes or in some respects, be in a position to engage in intentional, purposive and rational conduct. (This is why social scientific theories that interpret voting and other forms of political activity in purely causal terms—that is as explainable without residue by some set of causal forces impinging on the individual actor— are deeply inimical to the idea of democracy.) The same must be said of the idea that the actions of authority should respect the beliefs and values of the members of the practice and—though the connections here are more complex—of the idea that authority should be limited by comparatively formal rules and principles.

In short, given that the practice of authority need not be incompatible with the ideas and devices discussed in chapters 11 and 12, it follows that the practice of authority is a possibility in the sense that this among its necessary conditions can in principle be satisfied. (And it is, I think, safe to add that there have been and are now political associations that did or do accept and more or less implement the ideas and devices in question, and hence that there have been and are now practices of political *authority*. We return to this question in chapter 14.)

The question is whether there can be a practice of political authority that respects and conduces to individual agency to an extent sufficient to warrant the conclusion that the practice is in principle justifiable. The conclusion that there can be no guarantee against conflicts between authority and individual agency is a powerful negative consideration in this regard. It counsels that we cannot justify a practice of political authority—and hence that no person can properly subscribe to such a practice—without realizing that such conflicts may in fact occur. Knowing this, can we nevertheless construct a defensible justification for the practice? In the remainder of this chapter we set out (albeit with a certain reluctance and with important reservations) an affirmative answer to this question.

Political Authority and Other Deontic Practices

The principal step in this program will be to broaden our perspective on the considerations examined thus far and especially on the conclusion that there is no way to guarantee against conflict between political authority and individual agency. We begin the effort by returning to a comparison (introduced in chapter 9) between the practice of authority and other practices with pronounced deontic characteristics.

Consider such practices as promising and contracting. If I promise to meet you for lunch at 12:30, I thereby put myself under an obligation to do so even if, when the time comes, I find the arrangement unattractive or inconvenient. If I contract to purchase your air conditioner on a certain date and for a certain price, the onset of a period of cool weather or the unexpected availability of the same model at a lower price does not relieve me of my obligation to fulfill that contract. Having acted under the established rules governing these practices at $T1$, I have thereby acquired obligations to do or to refrain from doing certain actions at $T2$.

Consider also the related practice of rights. If B accords A a right to X, and if A chooses to exercise that right, B cannot object to A's doing X and cannot act in ways that prevent A from doing X. Having accorded A a right to do X, the actions properly open to B, the ways in which B can exercise his agency, are henceforth limited by A's right.

Shall we infer that the practices of promising, contracting and according rights are incompatible with agency? The argument Wolff makes against political authority (in his *In Defense of Anarchism*), as he himself recognizes, appears to carry this implication. He concedes that citizens might promise to obey the commands of authority, and he even allows that if they do so "the government does indeed have a moral right to command." But he insists that such a promise would "forfeit the autonomy" of anyone who made it.[2] The argument is not elaborated in detail, and it may be that Wolff would restrict it to the particular class of promises he actually discusses. But the argument is powerfully reminiscent of Thoreau's well-known dictum (a dictum that has been attractive to many anarchists) according to which "the only obligation which I have a right to assume is to do at any time what I think right,"[3] a maxim that militates not just against promises to obey authority but against all institutions and arrangements in which what it is right for me to do is settled, at least *prima facie*, by the combination of authoritative rules and the fact that I have acted under those rules at a previous moment in time. What would "I promise to do X" or "I recognize your right to do X" mean in a society consisting in individuals who lived by Thoreau's maxim?

This conclusion is sharply at variance with widely received thinking.

The practices of promising and according rights are commonly—and rightly—viewed as means of making agency more efficacious than it could possibly be if such practices were not available. By contrast with the capacity for more or less controlled physical movement that allows a person to act upon other objects (including other persons treated as objects), the exercise of personal agency characteristically involves interactions with other persons whose interests and desires, intentions, purposes and objectives have to be, more or less, coordinated with and accommodated to one's own if the actions are to have any prospect of success (indeed, if they are to be the kinds of actions they purport or set out to be). Practices and institutions such as promising and rights sometimes facilitate such coordination and accommodation. In this perspective the sort of autonomy that is implied by Thoreau's formula—and by Wolff's argument—looks suspiciously like the useless if not positively self-destructive "autonomy" of Hobbes' state of nature.

We should not pretend that promising, contracting and rights never conflict with or derogate from the exercise of individual agency. As valuable as they are, we occasionally find ourselves caught in the toils of their rules. Previous commitments bind us to actions that we now find not merely inconvenient or unattractive but seriously harmful to ourselves or to others that would be affected. But the practices we have been discussing are not without features that participants can draw upon to minimize the likelihood of such developments and to control their effects when they do occur. Some at least of these features are analogous to characteristics of the practice of authority—analogous in ways that are instructive concerning the issue before us.

Promising, contracting, making wills and testaments, according and respecting rights, and so forth reflect the values and beliefs shared in the societies in which they are found. The same is true of understandings concerning the conditions under which individuals are expected to keep commitments that they have in fact made. Wives in Europe and North America do not commit themselves to perform *suttee* on the deaths of their husbands, and if a wife had promised to do so no one would expect her to keep the promise when the terrible moment arrived. Some contracts are legally invalid on their face because contrary to established public policy, proposed rights that conflict too sharply with the values of the society are simply not accorded, and so forth. Moreover, contracts, promises and even rights that are generally accepted and respected contain an implicit *ceteris paribus* clause that exempts their makers and grantors from performance or wholly or partially excuses them for nonperformance if the consequences of performance prove to be unexpectedly and excessively severe. In these ways the potential conflict between participation in these practices and individual agency, while not eliminated, is kept within bounds that have proven acceptable to most participants. Participants recognize and may regret that such conflicts occur, but their continued participation in the practices, even in circumstances when the conflict is particularly marked, need not reflect, is not in fact thought to reflect, abdication of their agency.

The potential for conflict between political authority and individual agency is no doubt greater than in the case of promising, contracting and most other practices with pronounced deontic characteristics. In promising and contracting all of the agents involved agree to the substance of any obligations they undertake. In practices of authority, the A's can assign obligations to the B's the substance of which the B's have agreed to only (if at all) indirectly or distantly. In other words, the content of the obligations that arise from acceptance of the practice of promising can be controlled by individual participants to a greater degree than the content of the obligations that result from subscription to a practice of authority. What is more, those in political authority commonly have means of enforcing performance that promisors and promisees as such rarely if ever possess.

As above discussions have emphasized, however, at least some of the features that ameliorate difficulties with promising also operate in the practice of political authority. Membership in a practice of authority can rarely be said to be based on the sort of explicit, paradigmatically voluntary acts of consent or agreement that are the usual conditions of promising and contracting. There is nevertheless an important if not very precise distinction between a practice of authority that has the generalized and continuing acceptance of most of its members and a tyranny imposed and maintained by power and force.[4] An important part of this distinction concerns the acceptance and implementation of the ideas and devices reviewed in chapters 11 and 12. In an association in which some or all of the latter are accepted and more or less effectively implemented, the practice of political authority will merit at least some part of the justificatory force of the considerations noted in respect to promising and contracting. Participants will know that decisions altogether unacceptable to them or to others are a possibility that can never be eliminated: indeed they will know that that possibility will almost certainly become a reality at various moments in the affairs of the association. But their reflections as to whether authority is an acceptable feature of their association will be influenced not just by that possibility but by the fact that, on a more or less continuing basis, they find the two compatible and even mutually supportive. They do not give over or systematically subordinate their agency in order to obtain some advantage or good to the realization of which their agency is irrelevant. But neither do they operate with a conception of their agency according to which the least adjustment to established rules or to the thought and action of others—whether persons in authority or otherwise—is incompatible with it. Their agency is something that they have, exercise and preserve in the course of—among other things—the rule-governed relationships and interactions that make up the practice of authority.

These remarks bring us to a further and more controversial characteristic that may mark the thought and action of the members of a practice of political authority and—to the extent that it does mark them—may contribute importantly to maintaining an acceptable relationship between authority and individual agency. In terms of the comparisons we have been making, the characteristic in question is analogous to what we called the *ceteris paribus* clause that is a feature of promising and contracting. In negative terms, associates will *not* understand or be expected to treat subscription to political authority as entailing those conceptions of "surrender" of individual judgment that were considered and rejected in chapters 5 and 6. In particular, citizens will not be expected to forego concern with the merits of rules that have acquired authority. Such concern will be welcomed and encouraged, will be treated as integral to the authority relationship. This encouragement will extend to the kind of concern with merits that focuses on whether sequences of rules that are strongly objectionable to an individual citizen will be obeyed by that citizen. It is undeniable that widespread, continuous and well-intentioned (as opposed to merely criminal) disobedience of rules will mark the demise of a practice of authority (just as widespread, continuous and well-intentioned promise breaking will almost certainly mark the demise of a practice of promising). But from this undoubted truth it does not follow that recurrent and widespread (indeed, continuous and universal) readiness to consider the possibility of disobedience will do so. Nor does it follow that recurrent instances of disobedience of a recognizably civil character will undermine a practice of authority. Readiness to consider civil disobedience and occasional acts of such disobedience may relieve severe conflicts between authority and the agency of individuals and help to keep the exercise of authority within the limits that must be maintained if it is not to degenerate into tyranny or collapse into disorder.

Political Authority and Citizenship

We began this chapter by underscoring what in our view are some undeniable and undeniably unattractive characteristics of the practice of political authority. The perspective in which we have since been trying to view those characteristics cannot alter the characteristics themselves and is not intended to deny their undesirability. Our suggestion thus far has been twofold: first, some of the most salient of the undesirable characteristics of the practice of political authority also mark other practices and arrangements that are widely and indeed readily accepted; second, some at least of the understandings and devices that ameliorate the undesirable characteristics of practices such as promising operate in the practice of political authority as well. Perhaps the appropriate inference from these suggestions is William Godwin's response that promising, contracting, according rights, and so forth should be viewed with much greater skepticism than they in fact are. But this inference would require a notion of agency or autonomy that is deeply and properly suspect.

In slightly different terms, the practice of political authority has characteristics which, while undoubtedly undesirable, are neither as distinctively nor as severely undesirable as might appear. Although hardly a reason for hymning in praise of authority, if this suggestion is well taken it contributes to a balanced and differentiated assessment of the practice that is our concern.

But why should we accept the practice at all? If the best that can be said for it is that it need not be as severely destructive of agency as some have suggested, why not reject it entirely? Is there nothing of a positive sort to be said on behalf of its place among us?

We conclude this chapter by arguing that the practice of political authority can yield certain distinctive and distinctively important advantages to a human association. But before setting this argument out, two preliminary comments are in order. The first is that the argument is an argument "in principle," not "in fact." It suggests that certain important advantages can in principle be realized from a practice that is recognizably a practice of political authority. (That is, our more positive argument will not depend upon assuming away the characteristics that are arguably generic to the practice as it has commonly been conceptualized.) But we do not argue that those advantages have in fact been realized to an optimum or even a particularly satisfying degree in known historical instances of the practice. As a response to most if not all of what has been accepted as political authority in human history, the judgment that "it is not as bad as might be thought" is about the most that could be sustained. It is only proper to add that this sweeping judgment will be elaborated slightly but nowhere adequately defended in these pages.

The second preliminary comment is simply that the more positive argument that follows is intended to be consistent with the criteria for assessing authority that were set out in chapter 10. We do not intend to justify political authority in terms of benefits to the realization of which the agency of those benefited is dispensable or irrelevant. An abbreviation for the more positive justification that we will offer is that political authority is a necessary condition of numerous and important modes of individual agency and strongly contributive to the efficacy of a good many other such modes. More specifically, and of obvious importance in a study of political authority, a practice of authority is a condition of political modes of action—those commonly associated with the notion of citizenship—that have been celebrated (albeit by no means continuously or universally) from Aristotle to Arendt.

Authority is clearly a necessary condition of (not just compatible with) certain modes of action in many of their manifestations. The most obvious cases are those modes that are available only to someone who occupies an office of *in* authority. But to justify authority on this ground would be only slightly removed from saying that authority is justified because it is a condition of its own exercise.

A somewhat more interesting possibility is provided by an example already discussed, the action of voting. Voting can be viewed as the exercise of authority (in an extended sense of "authority") and the suffrage as a way of democratizing a practice of authority by distributing authority more or less widely. But ordinarily we think of having the suffrage as having a right. Having this right, and taking the actions that constitute exercising it, are possible only where there is some sort of election or balloting, and the latter are possible only where there are rules that settle such questions as who votes and by what procedures, how outcomes are determined, and the like. There may be cases in which such rules have developed and achieved authoritative standing through processes not involving promulgation by designated authorities. In the great preponderance of familiar instances, however, such rules are formulated and established by the latter process. Elections may help to reconcile authority and the agency of the B's, but authority is itself a condition of elections being held. If elections are a condition of a genuinely political association, authority is thereby also a condition of such association.

The point here can be applied much more widely. A considerable array of the modes of action most familiar to us occur—and can only occur—in contexts constituted in part by rules that are promulgated, interpreted and applied by *in* authorities. I can make a contract, write a will, bring a suit, petition for the redress of a grievance, and so forth only if there are rules that define and establish these modes of actions and the procedures that must be followed in order to take them. Again, rules of this sort might develop in a society (for example that of the Fox Indians) in which there are authoritative values, beliefs, and ways of doing things but no *in* authority; but these are hardly the circumstances in which we ordinarily encounter them. Thus the practice of *in* authority can positively enlarge the possibility of individual agency by creating forms of action that rarely if ever exist in its absence.

Yet more generally, if authority is a condition (a constitutive feature) of the state and other formal organizations, it is also a condition of an entire array of modes of action that only occur in such organizations. An anarchist might nevertheless argue that the availability of these modes of action is inadequate compensation for the restrictions authority necessarily imposes on its subscribers. But it cannot be denied that authority is a condition of these modes of action, and it is beyond doubt that a number of practices of authority have generated a considerable variety of such modes of action. Some at least of these modes would figure in most conceptions of what constitutes citizenship, that is of a main dimension of a political existence. For anyone attracted to the tradition of thought, running from Aristotle to Arendt, according to which citizenship is a distinctively human and distinctively valuable element of life, this consideration will be a major argument in favor of authority.[5]

A related point deserves mention in this connection. Several of the devices that can ameliorate the tension between authority and agency— elections, the rule of law and other comparatively formal limits on authority, legal rights against authority—are themselves dependent upon authority. They too are rule-constituted devices, and in the most familiar of their instances the rules that create and define them are adopted by authority. Thus authority itself is used to create devices—and the possibilities for political action that those devices open up and protect— which limit and may help to control authority. Authority is an integral factor in its own limitation and control and hence in the possibility of its own justification.

The second feature of authority that deserves a place in a more positive justification for it concerns its contribution to the production or realization of various aspects of justice, security, stability, the effective use of scarce resources, and so forth. As noted, this argument has been used to justify authority *despite* the admission that authority and agency are incompatible. Participants have been invited to regard the increased availability of various goods as more than adequate compensation for the loss or substantial diminution of their agency. On this view of the matter the production of such goods provides authority with the same kind of justification that a system of slavery receives when the masters are benevolent enough to accord various benefits to their slaves. From an existential (as opposed to a principled) perspective, this may be no insignificant matter. Under circumstances that have been all too common in human affairs it may be the only matter of existential significance to the slaves or to the slavelike subjects of those masters. The argument can hardly pass muster as a principled defense of the practice of authority.

But the foregoing is not the only formulation of the teleological argument and its contribution to the justification of authority. A further possibility is as follows: if or to the extent that a practice of authority has those characteristics which (according to our argument) open up the possibility that it will be compatible with agency, its capacity to contribute to the realization of various goods becomes a further reason for accepting it, perhaps even a reason for positively valuing it. Under the conditions just specified it might be valued because it contributes to the realization of a range of valuable goods without at the same time undermining or seriously conflicting with the freedom, rationality and moral integrity of those who benefit from those goods.[6]

The point can be put yet more positively. The goods that authority serves may be such that their availability (1) presupposes respect for agency or (2) enhances the efficacy of the agency of those who benefit from the goods. The first is almost certainly true of those aspects of justice in the name of which authority has frequently been justified. On most conceptualizations of justice, a practice that did not respect the agency of participants could not be said to yield or to contribute to justice. On anything approaching a teleological view of justice, moreover, the second comes into the picture as well. From Plato forward, teleologists have argued that life in a just society, even life as a just person in company with other just persons, enhances the agency of those who live such a life. Because authority is manifestly a necessary condition of legal justice, and may contribute importantly to social justice and justice in other wider senses, authority (1) presupposes and (2) may enhance agency.

There is a yet wider argument that the goods which authority makes possible actually enhance agency. The argument has played a prominent role in the movement from classical to contemporary or welfare state liberalism. It goes as follows: The actions of a suitably democratized and otherwise constrained practice of authority, so far from impeding individual freedom, rationality and morality, can "hinder the hindrances" that otherwise would limit and constrain the freedom of great numbers of people. At its worst authority is no more than one of many sources of constraint and imposition with which the individual agent must cope. And if it is suitably ordered and employed it can be used to eliminate or at least to minimize a number of the others. Laws that contribute to goods such as relative security of person, equitable distributions of wealth, education, and health care, efficient use of material resources, and so forth are not to be justified *despite* the constraints and impositions that their enforcement involve, but (at least in part) *because of* the ways in which they enhance the agency of all or a greatly increased proportion of subscribers. Authority has undoubtedly created and contributed to social and economic inequities and inequalities that have been barriers to the effective agency of large numbers. It will surely continue to do so. But it can also be used to remove such barriers and otherwise to create conditions conducive to a wider and more efficacious agency. To the extent that the arrangements and procedures by and through which authority acts to do these things are themselves *compatible with* such agency as presents itself in a society, the justification for it becomes much more powerful and persuasive than it could otherwise be. More particularly, the argument that it can contribute importantly to the quality of the political lives of its subscribers acquires a not inconsiderable cogency.

14 The Theory and the Practice of Political Authority

We find that the answer to the question with which we began this part is a kind of "yes." Whatever its other merits and disadvantages, the practice of political authority can, in principle, be arranged and conducted so as to respect and in certain respects to augment the agency of those who participate in it.

This conclusion carries at least one important practical implication. As a rejection of unqualified philosophical anarchism, it blocks categorical refusals to subscribe to authority and the obligations that authority entails. If compatibility with individual agency is the fundamental test of the acceptability of authority, and if the practice of authority can in principle meet that test, then the question of how to assess and act toward instances (or putative, declared instances) of the practice cannot be settled *a priori*.

Do the justificatory arguments presented in the previous chapters have further implications for thought and action in and in respect to practices of political authority? This final chapter will be devoted to some of the issues that make up this broad question about theory and practice. Examining these issues, we should say at once, will not yield an imposing list of action imperatives. It may reinforce and help to elaborate arguments we have been developing in this part and in part 1.

In chapter 4 we criticized and rejected essentialist positions according to which authority *is* what a suitably developed theory of authority makes it out to be. These positions are correct in denying that authority is "brute"—that it is simply given by some array of facts which "speak for themselves." But proponents of this view fail to appreciate that practices of authority are historical phenomena which can and do "speak for themselves" because their participants share a conceptualization in which speaking is done and in which a certain constellation of values, beliefs, rules, offices, and so forth *is* a practice of authority. A theory of authority grounded in familiarity with such conceptualizations can criticize and even correct them in certain respects. But if there were no such shared conceptualizations—no such practices—there would be nothing for a theory of authority to be a theory about. Authority "is" what a theory of authority makes it out to be only in the sense of "theory" in which we might say that the conceptualization shared among participants in a practice itself constitutes a kind of theory.[1]

Our entry onto the terrain of justificatory theory, however, poses difficulties for the foregoing understandings of the theory-practice relationship and forces us to consider a stronger case for a kind of essentialism. The argument for the species of essentialism in question goes as follows: if rule X carries authority for B, then that rule provides B with a weighty reason for obeying X (a kind of reason ordinarily called an obligation). In this sense at least the practice of authority has a normative character. Given this character, it would be puzzling, if not contradictory, to contend both that B has an obligation to obey X and that the practice in which X has its authority and from which it takes that authority cannot be justified. It appears that the expression "justified authority" is a redundancy, the expression "unjustified authority" a contradiction in terms. A practice that is not justified cannot itself provide good reasons (obligations) for obeying its rules; hence it cannot be a practice of authority. Justified authority is the only kind of authority there could be. Now if the justificatory theory of authority developed in this part is the correct theory, it would follow from this reasoning that a practice of authority is justified only if it meets the requirements of that theory:

Practice of authority = justified practice of authority (def)
Justified practice of authority = practice of authority that meets the requirements of the above (that is the correct) justificatory theory
Practice of authority = practice that meets the requirements of the above justificatory theory Q.E.D.

In short, the fact that authority is a normative practice necessitates a theory by which to judge whether putative practices of authority warrant that designation; and the notion of such a theory is essentialist in that the theory states necessary conditions of a practice of authority. Rather than a theory of authority being, as we suggested just above, contingent upon actual practices of authority, the reverse is true. There can be no practice of authority in the absence of a theory by which putative practices may be judged and identified. The theory of authority is not responsive and responsible to practices of authority, it dominates such practices.

We begin our examination of the (philosophically familiar) position just sketched (an examination that will occupy the larger part of this concluding chapter) by considering the practical implications that it appears to carry. Of course the argument by itself has only the practical implication already noted, namely that unqualified anarchism is mistaken. Any further implications require minor premises stating whether this or that practice satisfies the requirements of the theory. Practices that satisfy those requirements are therefore justified and their rules carry obligations for participants; practices that do not satisfy the requirements are not justified and do not themselves generate obligations. Establishing such minor premises requires empirical examination of whatever particular practice is in question.

Not having conducted such examinations, we are not in a position to make a well-grounded determination about any particular alleged practice. For purposes of exploring the argument just set out, we nevertheless permit ourselves the following modest assertions: the overwhelming preponderance of known political associations that have claimed or now claim authority did not or do not come close to meeting the requirements of our justificatory theory. Those few associations which (in comparatively recent periods of their histories) satisfy those requirements in certain respects also violate them with great regularity. Let us proceed on the assumption that these assertions are more or less correct. If so, we appear to arrive at the striking conclusion that the great preponderance of political associations have had no authority and the remaining few no better than highly qualified claims to it. On this reasoning we have to agree with Rousseau that the moral relations distinctive of a practice of authority—most especially that participants ordinarily have an obligation to obey *intra vires* rules—have not obtained and do not obtain in most known political associations and obtain only in attenuated form in a small number of associations. In short, if we conjoin our justificatory theory with what after all is a not implausible historical generalization, the combination yields startling practical implications.

Clearly, something has gone wrong with this reasoning. In respect to all but a few political associations, the conclusion is not wrong, it is absurd. Ivan the Terrible may or may not have had authority in his self-denominated office of tsar. But it would be ludicrous to answer the question by inquiring whether Ivan's newly baptized tsarist regime satisfied the requirements of our justificatory theory. One might say that it would be ludicrous because it is so obvious that Ivan did no such thing—that he did not respect individual rights, encourage democratic participation, maintain the rule of law, treat civil disobedience with appropriate understanding, or do any of the other things that indicate recognition of and respect for the agency of members of a practice. In fact, it is ludicrous for the deeper reason that the requirements set by our theory (indeed many of the concepts in which those requirements are stated) had no standing in the Russia of Ivan's day. Of course *we* might (indeed we should) say to one another that Ivan's claim to authority lacked justification because the institutions, arrangements and accepted patterns of conduct in his regime did not satisfy our theory. Such judgments do sometimes play a role in *our* affairs. But Ivan's authority (or its absence) was among sixteenth-century Russians, not among us. We do not have to accept the criteria that were employed by sixteenth-century Russians for purposes of deciding about authority among ourselves or for purposes of making our own assessments of sixteenth-century Russian arrangements. But if we are trying to determine whether Ivan had authority in sixteenth-century Russia, we must ascertain the criteria that had standing among sixteenth-century Russians and we must determine whether sixteenth-century Russians thought those criteria were satisfied. (Of course, investigation might establish that sixteenth-century Russians did not have any notion of authority and hence that the idea of judging whether Ivan or anyone else had authority was unknown among them.)

Have we now run to a particularistic position at the opposite extreme from the kind of essentialism we have been considering? Is each practice of authority *sui generis* such that it can only be judged in terms internal to it? In order to explore the matter further, we permit ourselves to assume the truth of additional empirical generalizations. True, the justificatory criteria proposed by our theory had no standing in sixteenth-century Russia (not to mention many other times and places in which they had no standing!). But they (or some reasonably close approximation to them) do have standing in a number of the political associations of our own time. The moral centrality of a vital individual agency and the rule of law, more or less democratic modes of participation, respect for individual rights, even a degree of acceptance of civil disobedience, as means of insuring such agency, are accepted and valued in the northern European democracies, the United Kingdom, Canada and the United States, Switzerland, New Zealand and Australia, and perhaps a few other places. Moreover, participants commonly connect these arrangements and ideas with political authority in that acceptance of and respect for them forms at least a part of the criterion of a legitimate government as opposed to a tyranny or despotism.

If correct, these generalizations suggest that our theory is *relevant to* judging whether the associations listed above have justified authority. It is relevant to such judgments, as it is not to judgments about Ivan IV, because (we are assuming) the requirements the theory sets have standing in the societies in which the authority in question is claimed. Although manifestly not a detailed description of the authoritative values and beliefs of any particular association, the theory (we propose to assume) specifies, orders, and elaborates upon the relationships among values and beliefs which, in varying formulations and manifestations, have authoritative standing in a number of associations.

If this reasoning is persuasive, two conclusions of substantial practical import follow, one from the reasoning itself, another with the addition of a not implausible (in our opinion) empirical generalization already mentioned. The first conclusion is that the theory provides associates in the states listed with an ordered formulation of questions they ought to ask and criteria they ought to employ as they assess their practices (or alleged practices) of authority. If associates find that those practices adequately satisfy the criteria given by the theory, they will have good grounds for according authority to the rules of those practices and for treating that authority as an ordinarily conclusive reason for obeying those rules. Associates will also have good grounds for seeing to it that such disobedience as they find justified remains recognizably civil in character.

The second conclusion that appears to follow from our reasoning, however, is that the decisions just mentioned must be negative, that associates ought to decide that, despite claims and even some appearances to the contrary, there is no justified political authority in these societies. If our theory provides the appropriate decision criteria, and if it is true that the putative practices of political authority in societies that accept those criteria regularly fail to satisfy them, then associates must draw the conclusion just indicated. They—we—must decide that the conclusion Rousseau drew in the eighteenth century remains correct in our own day; political authority is in principle a justifiable human practice, but at present that practice is nowhere actualized in justifiable form.

The attractions of this conclusion are not likely to be lost on anyone who combines some experience with the workings of the political associations we have mentioned with genuine concern for the values we have been discussing. We have not investigated the operations of these practices in the detail that would be necessary to put this conclusion on a firm basis. But it would be difficult to deny that, in actuality, these associations fall very short not only of some ideal requirement of entire, unqualified compatibility between authority and individual agency but also of the considerably less stringent requirements proposed by the present argument.

Despite the—to us undeniable—appeal of this "Rousseauist" conclusion, there are formidable objections to accepting it. For present purposes the most important of these objections is that the preponderance of the members of these societies pretty clearly reject the Rousseauist conclusion in respect to their own political associations. Explicitly by word and deed and implicitly by actions taken and avoided they demonstrate that they not only accord authority to their government but understand and find acceptable the implications of doing so. The Rousseauist conclusion flies in the face of these facts.

We now reach the most difficult and important conceptual issues that arise concerning the theory-practice relationship that we are exploring.

These issues concern not only the distinction between authority and justified or legitimate authority but the problem of "self-containedness" discussed in chapter 12. Indeed they concern our argument about the relationship between *in* authority and the authoritative, the understanding of authority as forming a practice, and the rejection of transcendental theories that we find to be implied by both. In the first part of the ensuing discussion of these several issues we will continue to assume that the disagreement between "the Rousseauist" and the citizenries of the associations we have in mind is not at the level of the criteria by which judgments about authority should be made. Both protagonists in the following "dialogue" know in at least a rough sort of way what distinguishes authority from related practices and relationships (such as, for example, power or coercion) and both accept and employ roughly the same criteria of justification. In other words, the disagreement we want first to consider concerns how to decide whether criteria of justification are satisfied by the putative practices of authority in question. But we will also have to attend to the wider questions mentioned just above.

Our Rousseauist might contend that the citizenries had made a relatively straightforward sort of mistake, a mistake that is at bottom an error of observation or perhaps identification. Their mistake is like that of an amateur rock collector or wildflower enthusiast who, despite possessing and accepting the authoritative field guide, does not look closely enough at his specimens and hence mistakes one species for another. A more careful observer (the Rousseauist, the professional geologist or botanist) points out that the specimen in question fails to satisfy the criteria of the species that the amateur has erroneously fastened upon it, in fact possesses the identifying marks of some other species.

Interestingly, however, the Rousseauist is likely to find himself employing conceptualizations that have no analogue in the language of geologists and botanists. The latter will simply say, "No, that's not an avalanche lily, it's a glacier lily." But the Rousseauist, in addition to or even in place of saying, "No, that's not a case of justified authority, it's only a case of power," might well say, "That's not a case of *legitimate* authority" or "That's a case of *illegitimate* authority." (Or perhaps, "That's a case of *de facto* but not *de jure* authority.") These familiar locutions appear to concede a measure of significance to the judgments of citizens that the botanist will not concede to the amateur specimen hunter.

Our Rousseauist is likely to construe this concession along the following lines. "This putative practice of authority does not in fact satisfy the appropriate justificatory criteria. But because the self-designated subscribers to the practice believe (mistakenly) that it does satisfy them, the practice has (thereby) acquired something that looks a good deal like justified authority (something that looks a good deal more like justified authority than an avalanche lily looks like a glacier lily). I will mark that something," he might go on to say, "with the concept 'illegitimate' authority, thereby recognizing its similarity to genuine or justified authority but at the same time denying it the standing of such authority. And I will then set about to disabuse the citizenry of their mistaken belief."

This construction on the part of our Rousseauist is cogent and defensible. But there are complications with it and substantial objections to it that must be considered. An objection especially pertinent to our present concerns might go as follows: "If by their words and deeds the members of an association attribute justified authority to it, that association *thereby* acquires the standing of possessing justified authority. As with the 'authorizations' by which clients accord lawyers the authority to represent them, such words and deeds, such subscriptions, do not recognize or identify authority, they create or accord it. They are not identifications of a phenomenon that has its reality (including in "its reality" its being a something-in-particular, not an anything-whatever) independent of those words and deeds, they are the acts that create and partially constitute the phenomenon. The Rousseauist notion (that the words and deeds of a citizenry about the authority of its government can be mistaken in the same way that the statements of the amateur geologist can be mistaken) is simply a confusion, simply a misunderstanding about the logical character and consequences of those words and deeds."

We explore this objection further by giving additional consideration to the concepts "legitimate" (*de jure*) and "illegitimate" (*de facto*) authority. The objection suggests the same conclusion we considered in respect to "justified" and "unjustified" authority, namely that the first of these concepts involves a redundancy, the notion of legitimacy adding nothing to the meaning of "authority" itself, while the second is a contradiction in terms, "illegitimate" canceling out "authority" and vice versa. If authority is accorded and partly constituted by a certain class of the words and deeds of subscribers, then when those words and deeds are present no logical space is left for notions like legitimate and illegitimate. A language *is* what the ensemble of its native speakers make it by speaking as they do; there is no criterion apart from their collected linguistic performances by which to judge whether their performances are correct. Analogously, a practice of authority *is* what the ensemble of subscribers or participants make it by their words and deeds; there is no criterion independent of the latter by which to judge its legitimacy, genuineness, and so forth. Thus the maneuver we attributed to the Rousseauist is blocked.[2]

The force of this objection to the Rousseauist position cannot entirely be denied. What we have just called the partly constitutive character of the values, beliefs, statements, actions and so forth of subscribers has been a central feature of our entire theory of authority. If no subscribers accord authority to a set of rules, institutions, etc. (that is if there are no subscribers), then there is no authority. It is equally clear that the Rousseauist's denial that a practice has legitimate authority cannot of itself alter the fact that subscribers believe that it does and that they act on that belief.

But we are every bit as committed to the cogency of some version of the Rousseauist position. If that position is excluded altogether, the whole idea of a critical justificatory theory of authority is excluded as well. On such a view the reflections in the previous chapters would be pointless. The question is whether there is some way to formulate the Rousseauist position and the objection to it so as to recognize and accommodate what is correct in each.

It is tempting to deal with the problem by using H. L. A. Hart's distinction between the internal and external points of view.[3] The citizen's statements and actions are made and done from within, made and done without calling into question, the authoritative belief and value system of the society or association. They reinforce that system and indeed constitute it in the sense that the system consists in the continuing flow of such statements and actions. Our Rousseauist, by contrast, speaks and acts from a standpoint external to that system, from a standpoint that calls that system into question. Thus the two statements simply go past one another and can be true (or justified) together.

There is at least one interpretation and application of Hart's distinction on which the conclusion just stated is indeed correct. If we treat the belief that the practice in question does have legitimate authority as itself forming a part of the authoritative, then the citizen's statements will be made from the internal point of view, the Rousseauists' from the external one. But this will be true simply because we have built such acceptance into the concept of citizen as we are using it in this stretch of our discussion and have excluded it from our concept of "the Rousseauist." And for this very reason such a use of Hart's distinction merely restates the problem without contributing to its resolution.

There is an equally eligible application of Hart's distinction according to which both the citizen and our Rousseauist speak from the internal point of view. Both assert that they accept that deeper set of beliefs and values which yield the criteria by which claims to justified *in* authority are to be judged. Their difference concerns whether *this* putative practice of authority in fact satisfies those criteria. On this application of Hart's distinction the external point of view would be exemplified not by our Rousseauist but by someone who claimed that Ivan IV lacked justified authority because he did not satisfy the criteria proposed by our justificatory theory—or by someone who denied the authority of the U.S. government because it does not satisfy the criteria advanced by the theory of Sir Robert Filmer.

It appears, then, that we have to deal with the problem in what might be called a more pragmatic manner. The difference between the citizen and our Rousseauist is that the citizen's statements express a widely shared judgment against which the latter's statement is a dissent that has thus far won little or no acceptance. The constitutive effect of a citizen's statements, though dependent on the fact that they proceed from his acceptance of beliefs and values that have authoritative standing, does not result sufficiently from this among its properties; rather, those statements must express a particular judgment that is also widely shared among members of the association. If the judgment ceases to be widely shared, continued expressions of it by this or that individual person will no longer have constitutive effects. Instead, they themselves will come to have the standing of "Rousseauist" views in the sense that they express a dissent from received judgments. By the same token, if our Rousseauist persuades the preponderance of a citizenry that his view is correct, he will cease to be a "Rousseauist" and his views will become "correct" in the sense that the putative practice of authority will have lost the bases of its justification and legitimacy.

It might appear that this argument turns authority into a "merely subjective" matter in the sense discussed in chapter 1; it allows anything whatever to be or to become a justified practice of authority merely because a sufficiently large proportion of any populace accords it that standing. But this would be a misinterpretation of the argument. If this were the case, it would also follow that neither Rousseauist nor any other dissenting statements could have more than a causal bearing on the standing of the practice. Rhetorically or psychologically effective presentations of such statements might *cause* citizens to abandon their support for the practice. But such statements could not *convince* citizens to do so because the beliefs of the citizens would not and logically could not rest on any sort of evidence or reasoning.

The question whether a practice has justified, legitimate authority, to begin with, does not arise under just any conditions whatever. Both those formal features of authority identified by F-P theory and the substantive criteria given by the authoritative have indeed changed substantially from time to time and place to place (the latter much more so than the former). But they do not change with any great rapidity; and at any moment in time they constrain what can present itself as a question about authority and what will be received as an apposite answer to such a question.

This is why our Rousseauist's statement that a practice of authority is illegitimate can stand as well formed and cogent and yet fail as an attack on the standing of a practice. It can be well formed and cogent (and hence troubling to participants who are aware of it and moderately self-critical concerning their acceptance of authority) because it is formulated and expressed in language and grounded in values and beliefs shared among participants and between them and the Rousseauist. Arguing from within the shared language, values, and beliefs, our Rousseauist finds a grounding for his contention that a particular judgment—namely that the practice in question satisfies the relevant criteria—is in fact mistaken. His statement may nevertheless fail to upset the practice because the latter does not depend exclusively on whether it satisfies the authoritative criteria in some objective, indisputable sense but also depends on whether the preponderance of participants in the practice make and act on the judgment that it does so. Such a judgment *is* just that—that is a judgment grounded in evidence and reason. It is not a mere inclination or opinion that can be held on any (or no) ground whatever and hence is logically invulnerable to question or dispute. But a practice of authority is a complex, many-faceted phenomenon, and judgments concerning it are governed by criteria that are difficult to apply (much more difficult to apply than, for example, the criteria that govern the identification of wildflowers). Hence there is a basis both for grounded, reasoned judgments concerning it and for grounded, reasoned disagreement concerning those judgments.

The position we are arguing, then, is somewhere between the pure Rousseauist's and what might be called collectivistic subjectivism. But that position accounts for what is correct in each of those positions. Our Rousseauist contends (1) that authority and justified, legitimate authority are coterminous. He further contends (2) that the question whether a putative practice of authority is in fact such a practice can and must be decided on objective grounds, that is by determining whether the practice satisfies the one and only set of criteria appropriate to the decision. Our "collectivistic subjectivist" agrees with the first of these propositions. But he rejects the second and instead contends that authority is entirely constituted by the "performative" actions and utterances of participants in the practice—that is that we find authority if and when (only if and only when) subscribers have created it and that any authority that we find *is* whatever subscribers have made it. The words and deeds by which subscribers create authority may be guided by the criteria that the Rousseauist advocates. But this is an altogether independent and contingent matter that has no bearing on whether they have created a practice of authority (and hence on whether the practice they have created is justified, legitimate, etc.).

Our Rousseauist is correct in his contention that the question whether a practice has justified authority is a question susceptible of reasoned discussion and decision; he is correct that there are criteria by which that judgment is properly made and that there are procedures by which to determine whether a given practice satisfies those criteria. Because he is correct on these points his arguments for or against ascribing justified authority to this or that practice can be cogent, well-grounded arguments that deserve the consideration of participants (and any others interested in judging the practice). He is mistaken on two points; first, that there is and can be one and only one set of criteria for judging *all* practices of authority; second, that satisfying that set of criteria is a necessary and a sufficient condition of a practice being justified. It is not a sufficient condition because the participants in the practice must judge, and must act on the judgment, that the criteria are satisfied. It is not necessary because, as noted, while a practice must satisfy some set of criteria, there is no single set of criteria that all practices must satisfy.

Our collectivistic subjectivist, in turn, is correct that any practice of authority is partly constituted by the words and deeds of its subscribers. Accordingly, he is also correct that the authority of a practice cannot be established or disestablished by applying criteria that have no standing among its subscribers. But he too is mistaken on two vital matters. The first is that any words and deeds whatever (so long as they are words and deeds of self-designated subscribers) are adequate to constitute a justified practice of authority. The words and deeds must be recognizably about authority as opposed to other things—the population of China, the atomic weight of lead, the distribution of power in the society—and they must be the expression of beliefs that have authoritative standing in the society or association. His second mistake is to think that established practices of authority are not susceptible to cogent, well-grounded challenge and criticism by nonsubscribers, that challenges that come from such non-subscribers are necessarily inapposite.

These conclusions provide at least a partial answer to the question of the relevance of our justificatory theory to (actual or putative) practices of authority known to us historically. The theory has a decidedly limited bearing (which is not to say no bearing) on the great preponderance of those practices. This is because the theory (we continue to assume) is an ordering and an elaboration of values and beliefs that have or had little or no standing in the societies of which the preponderance of those practices were or are a part. Studying the latter through the categories provided by our theory may help us to discern what they were *not*. Hence it can help us to make the kind of assessment that takes (usually implicitly) the form "Given what *we* are, what we value and disvalue, believe and disbelieve, we should be glad—or sad—that we did not live in that time and place"—a kind of assessment, of course, which may affect our attitudes and perhaps our actions in respect to the arrangements that obtain in our own time and place. But if we treat those categories as an account of what authority was and was not, is or is not, the theory can only hamper our effort to understand the practices we study.[4]

The theory can have a more positive bearing on our *understanding* of those relatively few practices that (we continue to assume) accept the beliefs and values from which the theory proceeds. The theory is not a detailed account of any instance of such a practice, and hence it can hardly provide a sufficient analysis or evaluation of any such instance. But to the extent that it succeeds in identifying, in abstract terms, the significance of those beliefs and values for authority it may assist students of particular practices to understand the workings of arrangements, institutions and processes that are intended by their subscribers to serve those beliefs and values.

The more important point, however, concerns the bearing of our theory on our assessments of and our conduct in relation to those practices of authority that we have had primarily in mind in formulating the theory. It cannot itself tell us whether a particular practice is justified, and it cannot instruct us in detail concerning the day-to-day decisions and actions that we take as participants in such a practice. The most obvious reason that it cannot be put to these uses is that the theory is at much too general a level to provide such guidance. A goodly dose of what has traditionally been known as casuistry is necessary to bring the abstractions of the theory into contact with the particulars of this or that practice. We explore this matter of casuistry a bit further because doing so may both further clarify the theory-practice relationship and support our argument that authority can contribute to distinctively political modes of agency.

On Rousseau's argument the need for casuistry—and the possibility of well-grounded dispute concerning casuistic questions—is all but eliminated. The requirements that must be satisfied for a practice to have and maintain justified authority not only can but must be fully delineated by that part of normative political philosophy which deals with the General Will. If an individual dissents from that delineation, he thereby demonstrates a kind of moral failure and his political associates must set him straight. If a political association deviates from that delineation, it thereby abdicates its claim to justified authority and its citizens not only may but (morally) must renounce their obligations to it.

Rousseau's argument makes at least three crucial assumptions. The first is that moral or more generally normative questions, or at least that considerable subset of normative questions that arise in determining the content of the General Will, can be answered in a manner that excludes the possibility of well-grounded disagreement. It assumes, in other words, the possibility of an objectively correct, an incorrigible, and hence a transcendental axiology. The second is that such an axiology can in fact be established among all or at least the great preponderance of the members of an association. It presupposes that the correct axiology and what we are calling the authoritative body of values and beliefs can be made to coincide. Finally, it presupposes that the axiology-*cum*-authoritative belief and values system is pellucid in its application to and implications for questions that arise in the day-to-day processes of rule making and rule implementation.

There are philosophical reasons for doubting the plausibility of these assumptions. The first and most fundamental of the assumptions posits that fugitive commodity known as a necessary moral truth (or rather a body of mutually consistent necessary moral truths). And yet, to mention but one further difficulty, these necessary moral truths are to be freely adopted and acted upon by the citizenry, adopted and acted upon in a manner consistent with the integrity of their personal agency. The combination of these assumptions may well be unintelligible. For present purposes, however, the more pressing difficulty resides in the strongly antipolitical character of the position that results when these assumptions are combined in what purports to be a theory of political authority.

The most obvious respect in which the position is antipolitical is familiar to us from criticisms of the closely related arguments of Plato in the *Republic* (closely related, that is, to Rousseau's position as we have described it here). Having reduced moral and political issues to matters of necessary truths, Plato has nothing but contempt for the kinds of argumentation, disagreement, and out-and-out conflict which, since Aristotle, have so often been regarded as a distinctive characteristic of moral and especially political life. In this perspective Rousseau differs from Plato only in his insistence that the entire citizenry can and must grasp and act upon the truths that form the essentials of a practice.

In the present context, the point to be stressed is that this understanding is inimical not only to politics but to authority as a part of political life. Platonic and Rousseauist positions have sometimes been viewed (perhaps by Plato himself but not by Rousseau) as substituting authority for politics;[5] as requiring that decision making by those in authority entirely supplant or exclude the participation of other members of the association and the disagreement and conflict that is the invariable concomitant of such participation. On the present argument, however, this view is incoherent. It is incoherent because justified authority would itself be an impossibility under the conditions posited by the view. Authority itself presupposes subscribers who make the judgment (disciplined by a shared concept of authority and grounded in shared values and beliefs) that the rules which form and which issue from the putative authority provide them (the subscribers) with a weighty reason for accepting and obeying those rules. Such a judgment can only be made by persons who regard themselves as and are treated with the respect owed to agents. The Platonic theory excludes all those not in authority from such agency in respect to (what it mistakenly calls) authority. Hence it excludes authority. The Rousseauist theory appears to invite the exercise of such agency on the part of all members of the association and hence appears to allow of authority. But this is appearance only, not reality. It is appearance because the theory excludes the possibility of cogent, well-grounded disagreement concerning whether the (alleged) authority of rules provides agents with a reason for accepting and obeying them. Realizing that authority can provide such a reason (can be authority) only if there are shared criteria by which to judge rules, it mistakenly contends that *any* disagreement concerning the criteria or their application proves either that there are no shared criteria or that one or more of the disagreeing parties is morally deficient and deserves exclusion from the role of agent until he corrects the error of his ways. The result, of course, is that the authority of a rule *cannot* provide such a deviant with a reason for accepting or obeying it.

The result, to put the matter another way, is that authority can provide members of an association with reasons for accepting and obeying rules if and only if they accept those reasons in the sense not of agreeing that they are reasons but of agreeing that they are *the* reasons that have a bearing on the action in question. And this argument in turn entails the result that "authority" is restricted to circumstances in which there is unanimity among the membership concerning the substance of every decision and action taken. The operation of authority is restricted to circumstances in which there is nothing for authority to do except to provide those already in agreement among themselves with a bogus justification for imposing their will on persons who disagree with them (bogus because, on the assumptions of the theory, the proffered justification cannot be regarded as a justification by those to whom it is presented). Authority is redundant among those who already agree and impossible between those who agree and those who do not. In short, the practice of authority is an impossibility.

On the present theory, by contrast, possibilities for (though not the certainty of) accommodating and coping with reasoned agreement and disagreement are built into the very notion of a practice of authority. The authoritative beliefs and values in which the practice is grounded provide the comparatively stable and widely accepted criteria which are conditions of reasoned judgment concerning issues that arise in and concerning the practice. The availability of these criteria, together with the established rules, procedures, and offices that make up authority, creates the possibility (though, once again, not the certainty) that day-to-day issues can be raised, controverted, and decided in a manner that deserves to be called reasoned in character. More specifically, these conditions create the possibility that members of the practice can agree and disagree over the substance of rules and can know in what their disagreements and agreements consist. Yet more important in the present context, the presence of these conditions creates the possibility that members can disagree over rules and nevertheless agree that those rules present them, as agents, with the weighty reason for action afforded by authority. The reasons for the substance of the rules are not likely to be the only possible reasons concerning them (are not likely to be the only statements entitled to be regarded as reasons concerning them); but even those who do not find them entirely convincing can (logically) find them to be reasons that support the rules. Thus the rules present themselves to members in their character as agents, in their character as free, rational and moral persons rather than as degenerates or unregenerates in the grip of some passion that is irrational and a- or immoral in character. Hence it becomes possible (though not necessary) for them to decide, as agents, to obey the rules despite disagreeing with their substance. It also becomes possible for them to decide to disobey them in a recognizably "civil" manner, that is in a manner that recognizes and respects their authority and seeks to overturn them without attacking or endangering the practice of authority from which they have emanated.

We must now enlarge our discussion to address wider questions that arise about the place of the authoritative in the justificatory theory of authority. We have contended that the criteria for assessing a practice of authority and its rules are given by values and beliefs that are in fact widely accepted by the subscribers or potential subscribers to that practice. Now it might be agreed that in fact authoritative values and beliefs can and do provide such criteria. (We leave aside the implications of this argument for discredited "state of nature" notions according to which authority creates, *ab initio,* the authoritative.) But it will be objected that this argument, especially given the explicit rejection of transcendental norms or principles that accompanies it, does entail collectivistic subjectivism at an only slightly deeper level. We can look to the authoritative to assess and to justify or disjustify a practice of authority, but there is nothing to which we can look to assess the authoritative. The values and beliefs that make up the authoritative in any society or association are invulnerable to cogent or well-grounded objection. They are in effect the prejudices of that society. As with all prejudices, they may or may not change and they may or may not be attractive to outsiders. But they cannot be deliberated or deliberately challenged because, by hypothesis, there are no criteria in terms of which to deliberate or to challenge them. In the case at hand, the authoritative standing of the value of human agency provides a criterion for assessing authority. But nothing can be said, the objection runs, in defense of according such significance to agency. If the South Africans or the Brazilians or the Ugandans do not accord agency such standing, the French, Swiss, Canadians, and so forth who do accept it cannot cogently or even meaningfully criticize them and the Ugandans, Brazilians, et al. cannot cogently criticize the Canadians, Swiss, etc.

We have in effect been presenting the merits of this objection in much of part 2 and in the several discussions of the authoritative throughout this work. Stated in general terms, its merits rest on the combination of a general feature of reasoning and a fact about known human societies. The general feature of reasoning is that A cannot convince B of X if he argues for X exclusively from premises that are unacceptable or incomprehensible to B. The historical fact is that the value and belief systems of known associations, societies, cultures, and civilizations have differed importantly one from the other—have in some cases differed so radically as to create deep difficulties for cogent and effective argumentation (even communication) across associational, societal, cultural, and civilizational boundaries.

We count it among the advantages of our argument concerning the place of the authoritative in the justificatory theory of authority that it recognizes and provides a theoretically derived place for these undeniable facts. But we need not run to a transcendentalism that is philosophically dubious as well as destructive of the possibility of authority in order to find a basis for rejecting the conclusion in the form in which it appears in the objection we are considering. If we imagined value and belief systems that were so entirely unique as to be mutually inaccessible, we might appear to have imagined circumstances about which the conclusion would be unqualifiedly correct. But while we can conduct such an experiment in imagination in the entirely abstract terms just employed, the very terms of the experiment exclude assigning any content whatever to more than one (that is our own) among the posited systems of value and belief. The experiment would yield a vision not of collectivistic subjectivism but of collectivistic solipsism. Which is of course to say that the objection we are considering could not arise.

The objection can arise because we have sufficient access to, which is to say that there is sufficient commonality among, known value and belief systems to permit us to identify differences among them and to ask ourselves which of them is preferable. Our ability to make such identifications and to ask this normative question by no means guarantees that we will be able to arrive at a universally accepted answer to that question. But the conceptual resources that permit us to raise the question also allow us to deliberate it in a mutually intelligible and (given some further requisites that hardly need mentioning) intelligent manner. If we ask ourselves why we should accord respect for agency such significance in assessing the practice of authority (or in assessing other of our arrangements and institutions), we can formulate an answer in part by making comparisons with societies, cultures and so forth which did not or do not do so. We can formulate an answer, that is, by drawing upon the rich resources bequeathed to us in the record of reflection and action in respect to authority. Answers formulated in this way have manifestly worked an immense influence on human practice. Some among us, regretting the vast diversity, the abundant confusion, and the seemingly intractable conflict that remain, persist in the quest for an answer that would obviate all such contingency. Skeptical and, yes, not a little apprehensive about their project, we are at least entitled to insist that instantiating the difference between a mere prejudice and a well-formed argument or a well-grounded belief does not wait upon the success of that project.

The understanding of the practice of authority that we have been developing materially abets the justification that can be offered for it—particularly its justification as a practice that may contribute to political agency. Earlier we suggested that authority can make such a contribution because it itself creates and supports distinctive statuses and roles and hence possibilities for distinctive modes of action. We have now suggested further and more general respects in which a practice of political authority may encourage and sustain these and a host of other modes of action. It may do so in part because of its relationship to the authoritative, because of the way in which that relationship supplies criteria necessary to both reasoned agreement and reasoned disagreement. And it may do so because it yields reasons for action that are neither separable from nor entirely reducible to the reasons for the substance of this or that rule. In F-P terms, a practice of authority creates the possibility that a political association can take certain types of action despite disagreement among its members. In the present terms, a practice of authority creates the further possibility that in so acting a political association can not only respect but enhance the freedom, rationality and morality of its members. Hence the possibility also arises that a political association possessed of authority may act widely and purposively without destroying the agency of its individual members—without requiring its members to choose between the benefits that such collected action may provide and their character as agents. In yet more positive terms, the invitation to enter and to participate in a practice of authority is itself a part of the invitation to engage in political life, an invitation to pursue human ends in a manner befitting human agents.

But it would be altogether wrong to end on the note just struck. The foregoing discussion is an attempt to explore, at a theoretical level, the possibilities cast up by the practice of political authority as the most distinctive features of such a practice may be discerned in a number of notable political associations. We must stress yet again that to our knowledge these possibilities are nowhere realized in anything approaching a full or fully satisfying manner. Along with the achievements that have been realized there stands a historical record of abuses and distortions that abundantly warrants the judgment that political authority is a dangerous institution. Understood in the manner we have been discussing, a practice of authority provides an ordered and focused setting for collected political and moral action, a setting that facilitates meaningful, reasoned exchanges and interactions among persons apt to disagree without itself (*qua* practice) dictating or determining the outcomes of such exchanges. In actuality, however, even the most impressive instances of the practice regularly and indeed systematically discourage and deflect the participation of whole categories of people, suppress arguments and modes of action that have perfectly good grounding in the values and beliefs of the society, impose rules that serve the narrowest private interests of those in offices of authority, and employ threats and coercion against citizens whose conduct is, by the criteria of the present theory, innocent or positively exemplary in character.

There is, of course, no single explanation for the recurrent pattern of affronts and outrages that is so salient a part of the history of authority. Nor can an adequate explanatory scheme be derived entirely from materials internal to the theory of authority itself. A practice of authority does not, as it were, sail in a sea that is entirely of its own making. Its workings can be and regularly are powerfully affected not only by the authoritative and its changing content but by numerous other developments that are largely beyond its own control (attacks and threats of attack by foreign states being no more than the most notorious case in point). Knowing even this much, it would be dangerously naive to adopt a sanguine attitude toward the practice.

There are, however, plenty of features of *in* authority itself that help us to understand the regularity with which practices thereof have violated the norms and run roughshod over the values and beliefs which, at a theoretical level, give plausibility to the argument that it can be a justifiable human institution. In our judgment the most important of these is a characteristic that is absolutely central to both *in* and *an* authority and that contributes mightily to creating and maintaining the intimate empirical relationship that the former has almost always had with the exercise of power and the use of coercion. The characteristic is rooted in the crucial notion that the authority of a rule is itself a reason for accepting and obeying that rule.

On the present account of authority this among its features is inseparable from the requirement that there be reasons for the substance of any
rules that are adopted. But our account allows that the B's need only be
satisfied that there are such reasons, not that they find the reasons given
convincing. And it allows that where this and related requirements are
satisfied the B's ordinarily have an obligation to obey the X and an obligation to make any disobedience recognizably civil. Moreover, the requirement that there be reasons for rules, in addition to being undeniably
controversial at the theoretical level, is difficult to satisfy under the best of
circumstances and is by no means regularly satisfied in actual practice.
Yet the authority of a rule provides all subscribers with an obligation to
obey it.

Until such time as a practice has more or less visibly collapsed, those
holding offices of authority will have enormous advantages in any controversies, disagreements or conflicts that may develop. Even if we leave
aside the perquisites and power that tend to accumulate around positions
of authority, the A's will be in a position to accuse, with a degree of
plausibility, all those who reject or resist their decisions of a kind of
wrongdoing. Hence they will also be in a position plausibly to demand the
support of other subscribers in punishing or otherwise suppressing that
wrongdoing. It requires no very deep, systematic, or even complex skepticism to realize the risks that are run in according one set of human
beings such advantages over any other set of human beings.

Notes

Introduction

1. George Armstrong Kelly, *Hegel's Retreat from Eleusis* (Princeton: Princeton University Press, 1978), p. 222.

2. For example, those that induced Aristotle, as impressed as anyone in our tradition with the importance of the *telos* of a phenomenon, to do his definitional thinking in terms of material, formal, and efficient "causes" as well as final ones.

3. See esp. chap. 1 of my *The Practice of Rights* (London and New York: Cambridge University Press, 1976).

4. Michael Oakeshott, *On Human Conduct* (London: Clarendon Press, 1975), p. 128.

5. Ibid., pp. 150–51.

6. Actually, Oakeshott allows that there is a certain species of authority which can only be understood in terms of teleological considerations. This is the authority of what he calls the "enterprise association" or *universitas,* as opposed to the "civil association" or *societas* to which the passages in the text apply. I discuss the two types of association and their authority in chaps. 2 and 3.

7. I will also identify the propositions characteristic of S-P theory and from time to time make comparisons between the two types of theories. But I nowhere explicate S-P theory systematically or in detail. From the perspective of its undeniable historical prominence (Plato, Saint Thomas and virtually all Thomists and neo-Thomists, numerous early modern natural law theorists, modern social theorists of a functionalist bent, are almost without exception properly classified as S-P theorists), this procedure produces a decided imbalance in the present discussions. My reason for allowing this imbalance to remain (in addition to the fact that I am not writing a history of thinking about authority) is the conviction stated above, namely, that F-P theory is clearly superior and that explicating it in some detail will contribute to my analytic objectives as such an explication of S-P theory would not do.

8. See Kelly, p. 204. Kelly goes on to suggest that Hegel achieved, in advance as it were, a synthesis of these opposing positions; see pp. 204–22.

9. The arguments I make through use of the concept of the authoritative

involve some of the more complex issues in social theory and in the philosophy of action. Formation of the conceptualization was influenced by Max Weber's various discussions of shared values and beliefs, by Émile Durkheim's notion (in his *Division of Labor*) of the *conscience collective* and more especially his later (*Suicide* and *The Rules of Sociological Method*) *représentations collectives* and by reformulations of these ideas by later sociologists and anthropologists. I have not, however, discussed the history of the idea and I have left for another occasion the task of demonstrating in detail that my use of it is compatible with the emphasis I give to individual agency and action. I try to show why the conceptualization is important to a theory of authority, and I deploy it in attempting to develop such a theory. These caveats, however, are not intended to deflect criticisms directed at my use of "the authoritative." Rather, I await critical reactions in this regard with especial interest.

Chapter 1

1. What Max Weber called charismatic authority only appears to be an exception to the last statement. Many of the instances that Weber discusses under this heading may be better regarded as cases of leadership than of authority; rather than obeying or regarding themselves as under an obligation to believe the statements of such figures, followers are swept along by the force of the leaders' personalities. As Weber himself emphasizes, however, charismatic authority is *an* authority and becomes *in* authority only when it has been "routinized," that is when obedience is owed first and foremost to the office not to the personal qualities of the individual who holds it. Weber discusses these distinctions at a number of places in his work; see esp. *Economy and Society,* ed. Guenther Roth and Claus Wittich (New York: Bedminister Press, 1968).

2. Henceforth I will employ the following abbreviations: A=the agents or agencies, the rules, procedures, and arrangements, that are *an* authorities or that have *in* authority; X=the content of the authority of A or of the rules promulgated, interpreted, etc., by A; B=the person or persons for or over whom A has authority; Y=the content of the obligations, duties, or other attributes that the B's have by virtue of A's authority.

3. One of the things I am saying here is that no form of authority is "brute" or "natural" in the sense of being extraconventional, that is, independent of human artifice, choice, and agreement. But putting the matter this way is trivial because it does little or nothing to distinguish authority. It might also be noted that the following discussions of shared values and beliefs, both in this chapter and in chaps. 3 and 4, might profitably be viewed in the context of Ronald Dworkin's criticisms of legal positivism; see his *Taking Rights Seriously* (Cambridge, Mass.: Harvard University Press, 1977), esp. chaps. 1–5 and the literature cited there.

4. Walter Miller, "Two Concepts of Authority," *American Anthropologist* 57 (1955): 271–89; see esp. p. 272.

5. Ibid., p. 282.

6. See esp. Fred Gearing, *The Face of the Fox* (Chicago: Aldine Publishing Co. 1970).

7. It may be useful to restate the foregoing discussion of the similarities between *in* and *an* authority in terms of what a number of writers have described as the structure or basic logic common to nearly all uses of "authority." Richard T. De George's schema is typical of a number of such accounts. "A is an authority for B over field C in virtue of D." Authority, De George argues, is always "a relation or relational quality" and it always involves a "bearer" (A), a "subject or subjects" (B), a "field" (C), and a justifying "quality" or "attribute" (D). In the case of *in* authority as I have analyzed it thus far, A is a rule or set of rules that sometimes sets up an office occupied by a person or persons; B is (are) the person(s) who accept or subscribe to A (who undertake obligations and "surrender" judgment to A); C is A's jurisdiction; and D is the set of values and beliefs, including the authoritative, held by B in virtue of which A has authority. In the case of *an* authority A is (usually) the person who has distinctive knowledge or expertise; B is the set of persons who accept that A has such knowledge or expertise and who "surrender" judgment to A; C is the subject matter or activity about or in which A has knowledge or expertise and within which the B's "surrender" judgment; and D is the set of values and beliefs by virtue of which the B's judge that A is an authority in C. For De George's analysis, see his "The Nature and Function of Epistemic Authority," in *Authority: A Philosophical Analysis*, ed. R. Baine Harris (University: University of Alabama Press, 1976).

8. In part 2, I argue that Rousseau took this course and that his having done so is the source of serious difficulties in his normative theory of authority.

This is also a convenient juncture to emphasize the point, implicit in the above discussion at least since mention of Thomas Masaryk, that the *in-an* distinction is analytic, not phenomenological. A single individual can simultaneously possess both *in* and *an* authority and the two may support and even strengthen (or weaken) one another. Perhaps the most striking instances of this combination come from religious life. Pope John, for example, held an office of *in* authority. But his capacity to exercise the authority of that office effectively was undoubtedly enhanced by his standing as an authority on questions—especially moral questions—which arose during his reign. This point is important both to understanding the dynamics of the exercise of authority and as a rejoinder to the objection that there are species of authority, for example, religious authority, that cannot be analyzed through the *in-an* and F-P-S-P distinctions (and through the formal schema I have adapted from De George). Dynamic interaction between *in* and *an* authority, whether mutually supportive or otherwise, may be more common in regard to religious than to other modes of authority, but we can say this only because the analytic distinction applies to both.

9. I shall not work out the particulars of the applications of these contentions to *an* authority or the authoritative. Very briefly, 1 and 3 are no problem because the enlargement the first refers to is an enlargement to include concern with *an* authority and the authoritative, and the considerations advanced in support of the third apply to the authoritative in a quite straightforward manner. Thus if there is a problem about applying these three contentions to *an* authority or the authoritative, it concerns their compatibility with 2. Can A be said to be an authority for someone who, whether cogently or otherwise, rejects either the criteria of judgment or the claim that A has satisfied them? The disposition to say this about *in* authority stems partly from the obvious ways in which it is a feature of an association and hence readily survives rejection by individual members. The same can be said about the authoritative. But to what extent is *an* authority a property of an association? It requires established identifying criteria, and it is very commonly the case that such criteria are given by widely shared beliefs. But while there is nothing odd about saying that Jimmy Carter is in authority over citizens of the United States who reject, even for cogent reasons, the proposition that he has it, it would be decidedly odd to say that Sir Kenneth Clark is an authority on art history for someone who thinks that his works on the subject are rubbish. Sir Kenneth is widely recognized as an authority on the subject. But this fact does not carry the same force as the fact that Jimmy Carter occupies an office that is widely accepted as a source of *in* authority. These points will prove to have an important bearing on the questions of "surrender of judgment."

Chapter 2

1. Few works on authority are entirely devoid of the propositions characteristic of F-P theory. But a small number of theorists have developed these propositions with particular clarity and have tried to form them into coherent and distinctive constructs. Historically the most important figure here is Hobbes. Among more recent writers who have elaborated versions of an F-P theory, the most important is Michael Oakeshott. Hence his recent works on the subject, particularly his elegant *On Human Conduct* (see above, intro., n. 4), are the main source of the present account. Important statements have also been made by Hannah Arendt (see esp. *On Violence* [London: Allen Lane, Penguin Press, 1970] and *On Revolution* [London: Faber & Faber, 1963]); Richard B. Friedman ("On the Concept of Authority in Political Philosophy," in *Concepts in Social and Political Philosophy*, ed. Richard E. Flathman [New York: Macmillan Co., 1973]; and "An Introduction to Mill's Theory of Authority," in *Mill: A Collection of Critical Essays*, ed. J. B. Schneewind [New York: Doubleday & Co., Anchor Books, 1968]); Richard Peters ("Authority," in Flathman, ed.; and *Authority, Responsibility and Education* [London: George Allen & Unwin, 1959]); Robert Peabody, *Organizational Authority* [New York: Atherton Press, 1964]); and of course by

Max Weber in those parts of his work that are concerned with what he called rational-legal authority (*Economy and Society* [see above, chap. 1, n. 1]). It must be emphasized, however, that the category "F-P theory" is of my own devising, not one that is employed by the writers in question. There are important differences among the theorists just listed and I am no doubt distorting their views by treating them as contributors to a single mode of theory.

2. See, for example, Hobbes, *Elements of Law*, ed. Ferdinand Tonnies, 2d ed. (London: Frank Cass & Co., 1969), pp. 114, 172, 185–86; *Leviathan*, with intro. and notes by C. B. Macpherson (Harmondsworth: Penguin Books, 1968), pp. 218, 303–12, 323; Friedman in Flathman, ed., pp. 124–29; Oakeshott, esp. pp. 149–56, 164, 189; Weber, 2:652.

3. Friedman in Flathman, ed., p. 126. If I understand the intention of Friedman's argument, he might better have written "is precisely not to approve or to disapprove of that action itself."

4. Ibid., p. 141. Friedman's use of the term "dissociate" calls to mind Joseph Raz's argument, which we will take up below, that rules which carry authority should be understood as "exclusionary reasons" for doing the action the rule requires, that is, as reasons that exclude consideration of other reasons for or against the action and hence leave B to act in conformity with the rule. See Joseph Raz, *Practical Reason and Norms* (London: Hutchinson & Co., 1975); and "On Legitimate Authority," in *Philosophical Law*, ed. Richard Bronaugh (Westport, Conn.: Greenwood Press, 1978).

5. See Friedman, ibid., pp. 141–42.

6. Oakeshott, pp. 55–56.

7. Ibid., p. 58 and 58n.

8. Ibid., pp. 116–17.

9. It is doubtful that Oakeshott's theory of authority in enterprise associations can be characterized as an F-P theory. As with the interpretation of the *in* authority–*an* authority distinction that I considered in chap. 1, his contention that the "civil"-"enterprise" distinction is categorial seems to mean that in his view there is little more than terminological similarity between the uses of "authority" in the two modes of association. If this is the case, it would of course be surprising if both concepts could be understood in terms of a single theory. Later I discuss this question and the difficult matter of the relationship between these two constructs or, as Oakeshott calls them, "ideal characters" and empirical instances of human associations.

10. The passages quoted are from Oakeshott, pp. 152–53. There follows an inventory of closely related misunderstandings of the obligations entailed by authority.

11. Ibid., p. 108.

12. Ibid., pp. 153–54.

13. Ibid., p. 124.

14. Ibid., p. 150.

15. Ibid., p. 125.
16. Ibid., p. 128.
17. Ibid., p. 129.
18. Ibid., p. 130.
19. Ibid., p. 139.
20. Ibid., p. 141.
21. Ibid., p. 143.
22. Ibid., pp. 141–43.
23. Ibid., p. 131.
24. Ibid., p. 133.
25. Ibid., p. 136.
26. Ibid., pp. 137–38.
27. We must recognize that these considerations enter Oakeshott's theory because he does not indulge the sort of simplifications about all but self-interpreting rules that are common in the works of theorists of the so-called *Rechtstaat*. It should be stressed immediately, however, that many of the characteristics of the process of interpretation and application of rules that Oakeshott recognizes in respect to the judge also obtain, in the first instance as it were, in the activities of associates who must decide whether the actions they contemplate will constitute adequate subscription. Only a tiny part of the interpretation and application that goes on in a system of rules is or could be done by courts. When this fact is recognized, the significance of the qualifications that the discussion of adjudication enters in the construct is substantially increased.
28. Ibid., pp. 142–43.
29. Ibid., p. 143.
30. Ibid.
31. Ibid., p. 144. He concedes that such qualities and characteristics commonly become associated with ruling because of the need to staff and manage bureaus and departments and in general to insure the "wherewithal to exercise their authority." But "in doing so rulers are not ruling; they are merely joining to the exercise of their office an ordinary transactional engagement . . . (ibid.). These relations are not with associates of the civil association as such. They are private, not public, relationships (ibid.).
32. Ibid., pp. 159–60.
33. Ibid., pp. 169–70.
34. Ibid.
35. Ibid., pp. 164–65.
36. Ibid.
37. Ibid., p. 162.
38. Ibid., p. 180.
39. Hobbes, *Elements of Law* (see n. 2 above), p. 152.
40. Oakeshott, p. 152.
41. See ibid., esp. p. 206, for an explanation of the logical status of an ideal character.

42. Ibid., p. 181.
43. Ibid., pp. 191–93.
44. Ibid., p. 78.
45. Ibid., p. 6.
46. For my views on issues about inquiry and theory construction, see Richard E. Flathman, *The Practice of Rights* (see above, intro., n. 3), esp. chap. 1.

Chapter 3

1. Because I have discussed related issues in a previous study, and do not wish to simply repeat arguments there advanced, it may be well to give a brief statement of the relationship between the following discussion and the earlier effort (see Richard E. Flathman, *Political Obligation* [New York: Atheneum Publishers, 1972], esp. chap. 3). Much of the earlier discussion was concerned with theses to the effect that various types of rules and the obligations that they (or rather some of them) generate are or should be inaccessible to reasoned assessment and discourse, are or should be outside the realm of reflective, deliberate choice and action. This issue simply does not arise concerning the versions of F-P theory under discussion here. Certainly no reader of part 1 of Oakeshott's *On Human Conduct* (see above, intro., n. 4) would ascribe any such thesis to him. But Oakeshott and other F-P theorists have presented what seems to me to be a misleading account of the sorts of deliberation involved in and the range of choices presented to actors in a system of rules invested with authority. In attempting to amend this account I will draw on some of the considerations concerning rules and rule-governed conduct that I found relevant to dealing with the issues taken up in *Political Obligation*.

2. Recall in this connection Oakeshott's view that we know rules when we encounter them. This is doubtless true in the sense that it is hard to imagine a competent speaker of almost any language who did not command the concept of a rule. In this perspective such competence is what Oakeshott would call a postulate not only of civil association but of all practices. Perhaps analysis of this postulate would contribute as much to the theory of practices as consideration of the several other postulates examined in part 1 of *On Human Conduct*.

3. Cf. Wittgenstein's remark that a rule cannot be obeyed just once, that a rule and obeying a rule is a custom or practice (*Philosophical Investigations*, I, 198).

4. Of the F-P theorists I have examined, Oakeshott is the only one who explicitly emphasizes the indeterminacy of rules. But the tendency to treat rules in isolation from the activities in which they figure, which is a pronounced feature of all versions of the theory save Weber's, all but guarantees that the theory will carry this implication. In this as in other respects, Oakeshott is simply the most self-conscious and consistent proponent of the theory.

5. Even the strictest F-P theorist must recognize this in the limited

sense that a statement cannot be a rule with *in* authority unless it carries certain credentials that it can only acquire from an association or practice that includes offices of authority. The presence of an office of authority is a feature of the context or the practice in which the concept of a rule with *in* authority has application. But if we left our specification of context with this point, it would appear that the A's promulgate rules exclusively because they have been accorded the authority to do so. It would appear this way because we would have put nothing into our account in terms of which we could understand why the A's chose to promulgate a rule, which is of course to say that we could not account for the fact that A's chose to pass this as opposed to that rule, to pass it now rather than two years earlier or later, and so forth. And the only thing we would be able to say about the meaning of the rule (as opposed to the meaning of the words in which it consisted) would be that it carried authority. Which would be to say precisely nothing about its meaning.

6. *Philosophical Investigations,* I, 89.

7. Ibid., I, 84–85.

8. Ibid., I, 198.

9. Ibid., I, 107.

10. We should note in passing that the intentions in question are only most commonly, not necessarily, the explicit, avowed intentions of an assignable person or set of persons who promulgated the rule. Sometimes understandings, generally held assumptions, recurrent patterns of conduct (that is, descriptions thereof), acquire the standing of *in* authority rules not through formal enactment at a determinate moment in time but through a (usually) gradual and informal process of belief formation and acceptance on the part of associates. In this kind of case it will often be impossible to identify an intention on the part of assignable persons to make X a rule. But even here we can speak of the belief that X is (now) a rule and of the intention, on the part of assignable persons who hold that belief, to treat it as a rule.

11. The pro-attitude might only be held on balance or all things considered rather than unqualifiedly. For example, if A's intention is to promulgate rule X, he must desire, want, and so forth to promulgate it. But he might at the same time regret that circumstances are such that promulgating X seems to be the best or the least bad thing to do in them. There is also a further complication that is sometimes marked by a distinction between A's intention to do X and the further intention with which A does X. For example, A might promulgate rule X because he expects that doing so will spark a revolution that will bring down a government of which he is a part but which he secretly detests. He intends X, and he has a pro-attitude toward it in the sense that he believes that it will serve a purpose or satisfy a desire of his. But the intention with which he promulgates X is to bring down the government.

12. Thus, as already noted, there is no sense to the idea of adopting or recognizing a string of nonsense syllables as a rule. Nor is there any sense

to the idea of adopting or recognizing as a rule an X which, though having a meaning, has no meaning as a rule. "My pen is running out of ink" is no more eligible to become a rule than is "bookshelf red happy were ashtray."

13. See P. F. Strawson, *Meaning and Truth* (London: Oxford University Press, 1970). Strawson calls the two types of theory, respectively, "formal semantic" and "communication-intention."

14. In the terminology of the Austinian "speech-act" variant of communication-intention theory, *in* authority rules are always perlocutionary, not just illocutionary; see J. L. Austin, *How to do Things with Words* (Cambridge, Mass.: Harvard University Press, 1962).

15. The above argument is intended to represent the logical core of a process that manifests itself in its most dramatic form in those systems that include substantive limits on what can be an *in* authority rule (such as those imposed by the Bill of Rights of the U.S. Constitution). Anyone familiar with the work of guardians of such limits—for example, the U.S. Supreme Court or the Constitutional Court of the German Federal Republic—knows that considerations of desirability commonly figure prominently in their deliberations about the constitutionality of legislative enactments. Faced with the question whether an enactment is entitled to the authority with which legislators intend to invest it, these courts obviously must have what I have called minimal knowledge of the meaning of the enactment. And while judges may try, with varying degrees of vigor and success, to distinguish between what they think is desirable and what the legislators think is desirable, they cannot satisfy this need for minimal knowledge without attending to questions of desirability. My argument, of course, is that the need to test one *in* authority rule against constitutionally superior rules only makes especially manifest a feature of any and all attempts to identify in authority rules.

16. Supra, p. 60.

17. Of course, the notion of the goals or purposes of an activity can be viewed as just as problematical as the notion of a rule and following a rule. Does every activity or practice have identifiable goals? Only one, or a plurality? If a plurality, do the several goals form a hierarchy? What, if any, is the relationship among the goals of several different activities in which the same actors may participate? Does the claim that G is the goal of a practice entail that all participants knowingly pursue it? Wittgenstein evidently feels free to introduce the notion of a goal without taking up these questions. He is trying to clarify the idea of a rule and following a rule as they work in day-to-day affairs. He finds that this idea connects with the idea of a goal and that bringing out the connection helps to clarify "rule." Because he is using "goal" in an untechnical way, he can make this connection without pausing to analyze "goal." But this does not mean that he thinks "goal" is a primitive or unanalyzable concept or that questions such as those just mentioned are of no importance. In another context he might well take up the concept of a goal.

18. It is worth stressing again that little is to be gained from appeal to the distinction between the conditions of an action and the substantive objectives or purposes of that action. One can say that the substantive purpose of drivers, bus riders, and so forth is to get where they are going, that the bus lane rule establishes an adverbial condition under which they pursue that purpose, and that the purpose of legislators in framing and promulgating the rule is no more than to establish such a condition. Saying this takes such point as it has from the fact that neither this nor very many other traffic regulations would make sense if associates did not have and did not pursue the general purpose of getting where they are going and from the further fact that they could pursue that purpose under a considerable variety of conditions. But it is equally possible, and a good deal more plausible, to say that the purpose of drivers and bus riders is to get where they are going as rapidly and as safely as possible and that it is the purpose of legislators to frame rules that assist them in doing so. In addition to the fact that establishing and maintaining adverbial conditions is itself a purposive activity, what from one perspective can be viewed as adverbial conditions can just as well be viewed as part of the purpose of the action itself.

19. 261 U.S. 525, 1923.

20. 300 U.S. 379, 1937.

21. My use of expressions such as "are open to" and "commonly encountered in" with respect to the idea that *in* authority rules are to be obeyed without reference to their merits and consequences will be regarded, and not only by F-P theorists of the Oakeshott persuasion, as understatements so serious as to constitute egregious errors. Richard B. Friedman, for example, allows that *in* authority rules have substance and purpose and can be assessed in terms of their merits (see "On the Concept of Authority in Political Philosophy," in Flathman, ed. [see above, chap. 2, n. 1]). But he insists that it is part of the notion of authority that associates have an obligation to obey rules simply (exclusively) because of their formal credentials. Similarly, Joseph Raz not only allows that important subclasses of what he calls "mandatory norms" have substantive and purposive characteristics but argues that those characteristics constitute "primary" reasons for (or against) action, that is (roughly) that they are reasons for action independent of the fact that they have formal standing as rules (*Practical Reason and Norms;* and "On Legitimate Authority," in Bronaugh, ed. [see above, chap. 2, n. 4]). But he insists that the formal properties of mandatory norms (rules) themselves constitute them as "secondary" ("exclusionary," "protected") reasons for action that ordinarily exclude consideration of any "primary" reasons that may conflict with them. And he agrees with Friedman's view (albeit without mentioning the latter's argument) that this is a characteristic of mandatory norms as such and hence (since rules that carry authority are a subclass of mandatory norms) a part of the very notion of a rule with authority. I return to the arguments of Friedman and Raz in chaps. 5 and 6.

22. These points hold for the "second part" of the definitional thesis (which concerns the obligations entailed by the recognition of the authority of A or X) as well, but there is a complication here that I will do no more than notice at this juncture. The complication concerns the contention that there is a conceptual relationship between "in authority" and "obligation" such that B's recognition that A or X has authority for him itself entails that he has some obligation or obligations in respect to A or X. Leaving aside comparatively minor questions about X's in respect to which it is difficult to formulate an obligation (for example, rules that accord a so-called power to B's—for instance, the power to make a will), this contention is correct as an account of the ordinary uses of "authority" and "obligation." The important question concerns the conditions, if any, under which B can break or at least mediate the conceptual connection, can concede the authority (for him) of X but nevertheless cogently deny or qualify the implication that he has the corollary obligation. Some versions of the theory of civil disobedience, for example, involve the argument that there are circumstances in which B can recognize the authority of a law or command X and yet cogently deny that he has an obligation to obey X. Of course, F-P theorists from Hobbes forward have insisted that the connection is direct and categorical. They deal with the often agonizing practical problems that this position seems to create by saying that there are circumstances under which B might justifiably decide not to discharge the obligation he has. I have discussed aspects of this question in *Political Obligation* (see n. 1 above), esp. the final chapter, and will return to it in the context of the present investigation in chaps. 5 and 6 and 10–13 below.

Chapter 4

1. Arendt presented versions of this argument in various of her writings. The most direct and unqualified formulation of it is in her "What Was Authority," in *Authority,* ed. Carl J. Friedrich, *Nomos* 1 (Cambridge, Mass.: Harvard University Press, 1958). Essentially the same article, entitled "What Is Authority?" may be consulted in Hannah Arendt, *Between Past and Future* (New York: Viking Press, 1961).

2. A related argument seems to be implicit in the diffuse ramblings of Robert Nisbet's work, *Twilight of Authority* (London: William Heinemann, Ltd., 1976). Whereas Arendt had a disciplined and carefully discriminated understanding of *in* authority, however, Nisbet uses the term as a kind of catchall for the things he admires. His contention that authority has declined or disappeared has less in common with Arendt's position than with the lamentations of disaffected political reactionaries —lamentations that are sounded about as regularly, and with about as much support, as the plaint that we are inundated by authority.

3. Oakeshott (see above, intro., n. 4), p. 154; emphases added.

4. See Richard B. Friedman in Flathman, ed. (see above, chap. 2, n. 1), esp. pp. 142–46.

5. Oakeshott, p. 74.

6. This is not a historical study. But we must be careful not to confuse ahistoricity and antihistoricity. A duly self-conscious ahistorical study will respect and preserve a place (or rather places) for historical study. The most likely fate of attempts at antihistorical studies is the writing of bad history.

7. See Joseph Raz, in Bronaugh, ed. (see above, chap. 2, n. 4), pp. 12–13.

8. Not all participants need share the same language, but it must be possible, through translation among the languages of the society or association, for all or nearly all participants to understand the concept of authority and to understand the rules, commands, and so forth of which the practice consists. No single language is shared, for example, among all the people of Switzerland, but translation among the several established languages satisfies the above condition. (Is it, incidentally, insignificant to the theory of authority that this work of translation is now typically done by lower-level officials or employees and does not carry with it any substantial *in* or *an* authority?)

9. The most specific such applications with which I am familiar are in the works of Hugh Dalziel Duncan. See, for example, his *Communication and Social Order* (New York: Bedminister Press, 1962); *Symbols and Social Theory* (New York: Oxford University Press, 1969); *Symbols in Society* (New York: Oxford University Press, 1968). In addition to Max Weber, Duncan is heavily influenced by such theorists as G. H. Mead, C. H. Cooley, Erwin Goffman, and especially Kenneth Burke. The major works of these latter writers, although only intermittently and obliquely concerned with *in* authority, are continuously concerned with the authoritative and may be profitably consulted in this connection.

10. Ludwig Wittgenstein, *Philosophical Investigations,* I, 141. See also Wittgenstein's treatment of statements such as "Here is one hand, here is another," "The earth existed for a long time before my birth," and "I have never been far from the earth's surface" in his *On Certainty.* Such beliefs might be said to be dispositional as opposed to occurrent.

11. There is an exception to the above remarks that I partially discussed in chap. 1. An X can have authority or be authoritative in a society or association even though particular B's reject or are unaware of its standing as such. Thus, B may be criticized and even punished for thought or action that does not conform to X's that are so established, even though he is unaware of their standing. This process presumes that some substantial number of the members of the society or association are aware of and accept the authority or the authoritativeness of the X and that B could become aware of its authority if he looked into the matter. Moreover, if a B does not respect the X, when he is criticized or punished the other participants will make it known to him that the X has authority or is authoritative in the association.

12. For more detailed discussion of these views, see my *Political Obligation,* (see above, chap. 3, n. 1), esp. intro. and chaps. 4 and 5.

13. For further discussion of this example, see my *The Practice of Rights* (see above, intro., n. 3), esp. chap. 9.

14. For further discussion of these and related distinctions, see my *Political Obligation*, esp. chap. 3; and my *The Practice of Rights*, esp. chap. 5.

15. The genesis of attitudes toward rules has been explored by a number of social psychologists, the work of Jean Piaget on the subject being the most influential. See especially his widely cited *The Moral Development of the Child* (New York: Free Press, 1965).

16. There are a great many studies that can be viewed as treating empirically of the authoritative as we are using the terms. A few of those that are particularly suggestive are: Reinhard Bendix, *Work and Authority in Industry* (New York: John Wiley & Sons, 1956); and *Kings or People* (Berkeley and Los Angeles: University of California Press, 1978); Michael Crozier, *The Bureaucratic Phenomenon* (Chicago: University of Chicago Press, 1964); J. D. Greenstone and Paul E. Peterson, *Race and Authority in Urban Politics* (New York: Russell Sage Foundation, 1973); Eugene Genovese, *Roll, Jordan, Roll: The World the Slaves Made* (New York: Pantheon Books, 1974); Max Gluckman, *Politics, Law and Ritual in Tribal Society* (Oxford: Basil Blackwell, 1965); Herbert Leuthy, *France against Herself* (New York: Meridian Books, 1955); Eric Nordlinger, *The Working Class Tories* (London: Macgibbon & Kee, 1967); Simon Ottenberg, *Leadership and Authority in an African Society* (Seattle: University of Washington Press, 1971); and of course preeminently the works of Alexis de Tocqueville and Max Weber.

Chapter 5

1. Richard B. Friedman, in Flathman, ed. (see above, chap. 2, n. 1), p. 29.

2. See Joseph Raz, *Practical Reason and Norms;* and "On Legitimate Authority," in Bronaugh, ed. (see above, chap. 2, n. 4). I shall discuss Raz's views in chap. 6.

3. See Yves Simon, *A General Theory of Authority* (Notre Dame, Ind.: Notre Dame University Press, 1962); Carl J. Friedrich, "Authority, Reason and Discretion," in Friedrich, ed., *Authority* (see above, chap. 4, n. 1); and *Tradition and Authority* (London: Pall Mall Press, 1972).

4. See esp. George Cornewall Lewis, *An Essay on the Influence of Authority in Matters of Opinion* (London: John W. Parker, 1849). On the views of Lewis, Mill, and the jurist John Austin, see Richard B. Friedman, in Schneewind, ed. (see above, chap. 2, n. 1).

5. I ignore cases in which A may be said to have privileged or even incorrigible knowledge, for example, A's statements about his own present or future intentions.

6. Robert Wolff, *In Defense of Anarchism* (New York: Harper & Row, Harper Torchbooks, 1970), p. 15.

7. A mode of conduct, indeed a way of life, that some moral philoso-

phers who are especially tender about personal autonomy have not shrunk from recommending. For a recent example of this, in which the kind of concern about facts and consequences that is characteristic of utilitarianism is itself said to threaten autonomy, see Bernard Williams' essay in Williams and J. J. C. Smart, *Utilitarianism: For and Against* (London: Cambridge University Press, 1973).

8. Or rather, aspects of a generic form of confusion aside; I return to other aspects of this same confusion in chap. 7 when I take up the relationship between authority and power.

9. Elizabeth Anscombe, "Authority in Morals," in Flathman, ed., p. 158.

10. Ibid., pp. 185–89.

11. See P. H. Nowell-Smith, "On Legitimate Authority: A Reply to Mr. Raz," in Bronaugh, ed.

12. Joseph Raz, in ibid., p. 10. But cf. his account of advice, p. 15.

13. See C. W. Cassinelli, "Political Authority: Its Exercise and Possession," in *Contemporary Political Theory,* ed. Anthony de Crespigny and Alan Wertheimer (New York: Atherton Press, 1970).

14. Friedman, in Flathman, ed., p. 129.

15. Cassinelli, in de Crespigny and Wertheimer, eds., pp. 77–78.

Chapter 6

1. Joseph Raz reaches essentially the same conclusion. See Raz, in Bronaugh, ed. (see above, chap. 2, n. 4), p. 28.

2. Ibid., p. 25.

3. Ibid., p. 27.

4. Raz insists, oddly, that the mother's order is both a primary and a secondary reason, and he calls the combination of the two a "protected reason." Indeed, he insists that all "mandatory norms" are protected reasons. Quite apart from other difficulties discussed below, it is astonishing that he should treat the mere fact that a rule is a mandatory norm—for example, the fact that it is invested with authority—as itself a primary reason (in his sense) for action. If Johnny's mother orders him to gorge himself on apples until he is sick to his stomach, is that really a primary reason for Johnny to do so? Would it, apart from the fact that it was an order issued by someone with authority over Johnny, have any weight whatever on the balance of primary reasons? And if it is the fact that it is an order that gives it standing as a primary reason, what has happened to the distinction between primary and secondary reasons?

5. Joseph Raz, *Practical Reason and Norms* (see above, chap. 2, n. 4), p. 64.

6. See ibid., pp. 36–45, and Raz in Bronaugh, ed., pp. 18–19.

7. Raz, *Practical Reason and Norms,* p. 42.

8. Ibid., p. 43.

9. Ibid., p. 40.

10. For related criticisms of Raz's other examples, see D. S. Clarke,

Jr., "Exclusionary Reasons," *Mind* 86 (April 1977): 252–55; and the review of *Practical Reason and Norms* by R. G. Frey, *Philosophical Books* 17 (October 1976): 135–37; and that by C. H. Whitely, *Philosophical Quarterly* 26 (July 1976): 287–88.

11. Raz, *Practical Reason and Norms*, p. 36.

12. Indeed, though the terminology "exclusionary rule" may be distinctive to Raz, the idea that certain principles and rules prohibit giving any weight whatever to certain types of reasons for action is commonplace in antiutilitarian moral philosophy. Examples are Robert Nozick's rights as "side-constraints" and John Rawls' argument that the alleged benefits of slavery are simply not to be considered in setting up a just social order. See Nozick, *Anarchy , State and Utopia* (New York: Basic Books, 1974), pp. 28–35; and John Rawls, *A Theory of Justice* (Cambridge, Mass.: Harvard University Press, Belknap Press, 1971).

13. On this point, see Raz in Bronaugh, ed., p. 8.

14. On this feature of rights, see my *The Practice of Rights* (see above, intro., n. 3), esp. chap. 3.

15. Perhaps authority is, at least in this respect, an "essentially contested" concept. Note, however, that to agree to this much would also be to agree that the interpretations of "surrender of judgment" that we have been considering are not conclusively established. Hence it would also be to agree that alternatives to those interpretations, including alternatives that legitimate the judgments of B's *qua* B's about the merits of X's, are not conclusively excluded by logical or conceptual considerations.

16. See Hobbes, *Leviathan* (see above, chap. 2, n. 2), chap. 14.

17. In fairness to Raz it should be noted that his conceptualization has features that will accommodate this result. One such feature is his notion of "scope-affecting reasons," that is, reasons that determine the range of first-order reasons that an exclusionary reason excludes from consideration. See *Practical Reason and Norms*, esp. pp. 46ff. Another is his argument that neither mandatory norms nor any other type of rule is an "ultimate" reason for action. All rules "have to be justified on the basis of fundamental values" (ibid., p. 76). Without exploring the exegetical question in detail, these features of Raz's apparatus, though welcome from the present perspective, blur the distinction between primary and exclusionary rules.

18. There is by now a very large literature on civil disobedience. A satisfactory entry point into it is provided by the readings collected by Michael P. Smith and Kenneth L. Deutsch, eds., *Political Obligation and Civil Disobedience* (New York: Thomas Y. Crowell Co., 1972).

19. Herbert J. Storing, "The Case against Civil Disobedience," in *On Civil Disobedience*, ed. Robert A. Goldwin (Chicago: Rand McNally & Co., 1968). It might be noted in passing that the civil disobedient need not find Storing's metaphor altogether unsupportive of his views. A degraded woman is admittedly a woman for all of that. But it does less than honor to womankind to act as if there is no difference between degraded women

and other kinds. The root trouble with the metaphor, however, is twofold. First, it falsely suggests that civil disobedients in fact think something that they insistently deny, namely, that authority, which does the slapping, is degraded. For the metaphor to fit, womankind would have to respond to the insult. Second, it ignores the fact that most proponents of civil disobedience counsel the action not in response to single isolated instances of unjust or otherwise objectionable laws, but to a recurrent pattern of such laws.

20. The membership of this subclass, and indeed of the entire class of participants in the practice, has been variously defined. In most of the actual or putative practices of authority known to me the membership of both has been quite narrowly defined. The great preponderance of persons living in the territory of the society or association were (are not) treated as free, rational, and moral beings who act on or who are entitled to be given reasons for action. They were (are) not participants in the practice of authority, they were (are) treated as recipients or objects of the effects produced by that practice. They were not to wonder why, they were just to do or die. I am not, in other words, building democratic or egalitarian notions into my account of authority. (I do build such notions into the justificatory theory that I develop in part 2.) The point is that all those who are viewed as participants must be accorded, indeed are thereby accorded, the standing of agents capable of exercising and acting on reasoned judgments.

Chapter 7

1. The quoted passages are from: G. E. G. Catlin, "Authority and Its Critics," in Friedrich, ed. (see above, chap. 4, n. 1), p. 129; Sebastian de Grazia, "What Authority Is Not," *American Political Science Review* 53 (June 1959): 321; Roberto Michels, "Authority," *Encyclopaedia of the Social Sciences* (New York: Macmillan Co., 1930); Talcott Parsons, "On the Concept of Political Power," in *Political Power,* ed. Roderick Bell, David W. Edwards, and R. Harrison Wagner (New York: Free Press, 1969), pp. 263ff.

2. See, for example, Hannah Arendt, *On Violence* (London: Allen Lane, Penguin Books, 1970), pp. 41ff.; Michael Crozier, *The Bureaucratic Phenomenon* (Chicago: University of Chicago Press, 1964), esp. pp. 58ff. and passim; Bertrand de Jouvenel, *Sovereignty* (Chicago: University of Chicago Press, 1957), esp. pp. 32–33 and passim; and *The Pure Theory of Politics* (New Haven: Yale University Press, 1963), passim; Richard B. Friedman, in Flathman, ed. (see above, chap. 2, n. 1), passim; Carl J. Friedrich, *Tradition and Authority* (see above, chap. 5, n. 3), esp. pp. 45–78; H. L. A. Hart, *The Concept of Law* (London: Oxford University Press, 1956); Oakeshott, *On Human Conduct* (see above, intro., n. 4), esp. p. 150; and esp. "The Vocabulary of a Modern European State," *Political Studies* (June–September 1975), pp. 212–13; Yves Simon, *A General Theory of Authority* (Notre Dame, Ind.: University of Notre

Dame Press, 1962); Peter Winch, "Authority," in *Political Philosophy*, ed. Anthony Quinton (London: Oxford University Press, 1972).

3. Bertrand Russell, *Power* (London: George Allen & Unwin, 1938), pp. 35, 10–11.

4. For an inventory of some of the uses of "power" that are hard to distinguish from "force," "energy," and so on, see Hanna Pitkin, *Wittgenstein and Justice* (Berkeley and Los Angeles: University of California Press, 1972), esp. pp. 276–79.

5. See Robert A. Dahl, "The Concept of Power," in Bell et al., eds.

6. Peter Bachrach and Morton S. Baratz, *Power and Poverty* (New York: Oxford University Press, 1970), p. 21. The pertinent chapters of this book are also available in Bell et al., eds.

7. Ibid., p. 21.

8. Talcott Parsons in Bell et al., eds.

9. In this and other respects Parsons's account merges power and authority in a manner that misconstrues both.

10. Matthew Crenson, *The Un-Politics of Air Pollution: A Study in Non-Decisionmaking in the Cities* (Baltimore: Johns Hopkins University Press, 1971). Quoted in Steven Lukes, *Power: A Radical View*, © British Sociological Association (London: Macmillan Press, 1974), p. 43.

11. Ibid., p. 39.

12. Ibid., p. 39.

13. Ibid., p. 41.

14. Ibid., p. 55.

15. Ibid.

16. H. L. A. Hart, *Punishment and Responsibility* (New York and London: Oxford University Press, 1968), p. 176.

17. Hart discusses strict liability at numerous junctures in both *Punishment and Responsibility* and *The Concept of Law* (see n. 2 above). The discussions are well marked in the indexes of both works.

18. My discussion of strict liability and negligence permits me to clarify at least a part of Lukes' puzzling use of the notion of conscious and unconscious actions. In general, the notion of a conscious action might be thought a redundancy, the notion of an unconscious action a contradiction in terms. However that may be, the idea of "due care" stands in a very uneasy relationship to the idea of an unconscious action. How exactly would I go about taking due care to identify the consequences of an action that I do not know I am taking? If Lukes were using "unconscious" in anything like its usual senses, the idea of due care would be excluded by it. Some considerable number of pages after he has introduced the notion (see Lukes, pp. 51–52), however, we learn that he is using it in quite technical, quite restricted senses. One of these is to convey exactly what a judge intends when he finds an accused guilty of manslaughter by negligence, namely, that the person had neglected to inform himself of the more or less readily discoverable consequences of the action he prepared to take and in fact took. Note, however, that of such a person we would

ordinarily say that he was "unaware" of the consequences of his action. Would we say that he was "unconscious" of those consequences? Not unless we had some idiosyncratic theoretical objective in view.

19. Mention should be made at this juncture of a minor controversy in the recent literature as to whether the Y which A holds before B can be a benefit that B will have to forego if he does not do X, as well as a hurt, harm, or other disadvantage that he will suffer. This issue has been partly resolved by Peter Blau. Blau points out that if A has regularly been supplying B with some good and then threatens to withhold it if B refuses to X, B will think of A's action as threatening a harm or disadvantage (see Peter Blau, "Differentiation of Power," in Bell et al., eds., pp. 293–94). But the more important point concerns the potential significance to B of any benefits that A offers. If B is in a deprived or even a no more than minimally satisfactory situation and A presents the prospect of a genuinely significant improvement, the thought of foregoing the benefit and leaving his situation unchanged will commonly be viewed as a negative sanction and A's action as an exercise of power over B. On the other hand, if the prospective improvement in B's circumstances is marginal, it is probably better to treat A as offering an inducement, not as exercising power. Wealth in respect to a particular valued good is a likely basis for power over those who are poor in respect to that good, but it is not much of a basis for power over the wealthy. For these reasons, there is a case for restricting "power" to cases in which the Y has the character of a harm or hurt, to cases involving the threat of a negative sanction. We might call inducements that have this character "threatening inducements."

20. In personal conversation Professor Crenson has suggested that the executives of U.S. Steel often found it unnecessary to make explicit threats or even to announce their opposition to antipollution measures. Keenly aware of the harm U.S. Steel could do to the community, politicians, labor leaders, and so forth would anticipate the company's opposition to such measures and would themselves avoid arousing the ire of its officials by acting to keep the measures off of the city's agenda. Such cases fall outside my original schema in that A does not explicitly threaten any B. Clearly, however, B regards A as "threatening," a judgment no doubt based on experiences in which A not only employed threats but made good on them if B did not respond in the desired manner. I might add that such cases are instructive concerning the notion of individuals and groups who or which are politically, socially, economically, or otherwise "powerful" in a generalized sense. Of course, this notion is commonly employed as a catchall characterization for agents and agencies who regularly obtain their objectives—whether by persuasion, manipulation, authority, force, or whatever other method or device. But the adjective is better employed to characterize agents and agencies such as U.S. Steel in Gary, that is, those who (which) have the wherewithal sufficient not only to make convincing and effective threats but sufficient to get their way without putting such threats in explicit form.

21. In fact, even outside of the confines of the law of negligence we do say that A acted intentionally if he does not trouble to obtain readily available information about the effects of his contemplated actions. See G. E. M. Anscombe, "The Two Kinds of Error in Action," in *Ethics*, ed. Judith J. Thomson and Gerald Dworkin (New York: Harper & Row, 1968).

22. Hart, *Punishment and Responsibility*, pp. 182–83.

23. There is evidence that some of what now seem to be its manifestly repugnant consequences were positively valued in some quarters. There are nineteenth-century lithographs in which black smoke belching from factory chimneys is so depicted as to leave no doubt that the artist regarded it as beautiful.

24. I say "appears to think" because Lukes accepts both and does not ask whether their logics conflict with one another.

Chapter 8

1. *Iliad,* esp. 1.180–240.

2. See esp. R. B. Brandt, *Hopi Ethics* (Chicago: University of Chicago Press, 1954).

3. As with her stipulations concerning "authority," Arendt's restriction of "power" to "action in concert" is clearly at variance with established uses of the concept and there would be no particular point in eschewing the use of the concept in respect to interactions among individuals. As usual with Arendt's departures from ordinary usage, however, this one is in the service of an important idea and repays careful attention.

4. Hannah Arendt, *On Violence* (see above, chap. 7, n. 2), p. 46.

5. For some interesting examples, see Michael Crozier (see above, chap. 4, n. 16), esp. the discussion of "Case 2, the Industrial Monopoly"; and Simon Ottenberg, *Leadership and Authority in an African Society* (Seattle: University of Washington Press, 1971), esp. pp. 171ff. These examples are of particular interest because they involve instances in which *in* authority has been sustained for considerable periods of time despite the fact that those who hold it have virtually no power.

6. Note that if one accepted both Arendt's account of power and her view that authority has disappeared from the modern world, one would have to say that power had also disappeared from the modern world.

7. See, for example, G. E. M. Anscombe, "On Brute Facts," *Analysis* 18 (1958): 69–72; J. R. Searle, *Speech Acts* (London: Cambridge University Press, 1969), pp. 50–54.

8. Richard B. Friedman, in Flathman, ed. (see above, chap. 2, n. 1), p. 126.

9. There is no evidence that he distinguishes between force and power, but if his remarks apply only to force as we are using the term here, that argument is of no interest in the present context.

10. Note that it can still be said that the necessity of actually administering a punishment, just as with the necessity of making good on the threat issued by a person exercising power, is proof of a kind of failure of

264 Notes to Pages 158-67

authority. Strictly, B ought to do X simply because it carries authority. Unlike the case of power, however, the necessity of administering a punishment is proof of a failure on the part of B, not of A. B has an obligation to do X, and his failure to discharge it properly brings punishment into play. Put another way, whereas the need to make good on threats shows that, to that degree, A is (or was) without power over B, the need to punish only brings another dimension of A's authority into play.

11. In fact the doctrine has recently acquired, at least for me, a comparatively greater appeal owing to the increasing prominence of the view that we should replace punishment by various forms of therapy or other modes of "treatment." Herbert Morris' arguments convince me that if the choice were between the doctine of therapy and the Kantian-Hegelian doctrine that lawbreakers have a right to be punished we should opt for the latter. See Herbert Morris, "Persons and Punishments," *Monist* 52 (October 1968): 475–501.

12. Although I cannot judge its historical verisimilitude, Genovese's *Roll, Jordan, Roll* (see above, chap. 4, n. 16) is a persuasive development of this theme in the context of a system that has been taken to present the very paradigm of power relations in which virtually all of the acceptance and support must have come from the A's.

13. To return to the speculation indulged concerning Arendt above, note that in principle this could happen even in a class society so long as the class divisions were not drawn so as to exclude the disadvantaged class from participation in the institutions and processes in and through which action in concert takes place. The fact that a class of persons is systematically disadvantaged (in terms of their distinctive interests) might prove to be irrelevant to whether they would value power and its exercise. What matters is not whether you win or lose, it is that you get to play in the game. But while it is possible that Arendt had some such view in mind, the more plausible interpretation is that she was so convinced of the value, to the A's, of action in concert that she simply did not pay much attention to the fact that power is exercised over some person or group.

14. Cf. Karl Marx's comment on life in Indian villages: "[W]e must not forget that these idyllic village communities, inoffensive though they may appear, had always been the solid foundation of Oriental despotism, that they restrained the human mind within the smallest possible compass, making it the unresisting tool of superstition, enslaving it beneath traditional rules, depriving it of all grandeur and historical energies" ("The British Rule in India," quoted in Robert A. Nisbet, *The Sociological Tradition* [New York: Basic Books, 1966], p. 68).

15. It may also serve to misdescribe, misconstrue, and exaggerate the plight of the disadvantaged. As insensitive as it would be to deny that conventionally established role definitions were (and remain) harmful to women who accepted them without question, there remains a vital distinction between the circumstances of such women and that of, say, slaves in the antebellum United States, blacks in South Africa, Jews in

Nazi Germany, the Ibo in Biafra, and so on through a long list. There remains, in other words, a vital distinction between people who are satisfied with, even happy about, their life situation—however mistaken observers may think those assessments to be—and people who are continuously outraged and made constantly and very consciously miserable by acts of violence, coercion, and power of which they are intensely aware but that they are unable to resist.

Chapter 9
1. See H. L. A. Hart, "Are There Any Natural Rights?" in Flathman, ed. (see above, chap. 2, n. 1), esp. pp. 445–48.

Chapter 10
1. This is a simplification if only because of the many variants of anarchism. But it also continues the simplification already indulged, namely, overlooking the fact that theorists who have rejected anarchism have held widely disparate views as to why and to what extent we should accept authority.

2. The classic statements of this position in the literature of political philosophy, wherein it is applied to questions about the value of authority, the grounds of obligation, and a number of other recurrent issues, are to be found in T. D. Weldon, *The Vocabulary of Politics* (Baltimore: Penguin Books, 1953); and Margaret McDonald, "The Language of Political Theory," in *Logic and Language,* ed. Antony Flew, 1st ser. (Oxford: Basil Blackwell, 1951). For a more cautious and refined statement, see Hanna F. Pitkin's two-part article, "Obligation and Consent," *American Political Science Review* 59 (1965): 990–99, 60 (1966): 39–52.

3. I have criticized the position in my *Political Obligation* (see above, chap. 3, n. 1), esp. pp. 90–111; I will not repeat that discussion here.

4. The above remarks take support from the prominence of notions strongly akin to what we are calling agency in leading theories of rights and of justice. Examples would be H. L. A. Hart's argument that if there are any natural rights then creatures capable of choice have a natural right to equal freedom, Joel Feinberg's formulation of the notions "respect," "dignity," and "claiming" in his account of the distinctive value of rights, the dominant place of liberty (and the moral psychology that surrounds it) in John Rawls' theory of justice, the idea of "action" in Alan Gewirth's theory of egalitarian justice, and the concept of a right to equal concern and respect as developed by Ronald Dworkin. In addition to the papers by some of these writers in Flathman, ed., (see above, chap. 2, n. 1), see John Rawls, *A Theory of Justice* (see above, chap. 6, n. 12); Alan Gewirth, *Reason and Morality* (Chicago: University of Chicago Press, 1978); and Ronald Dworkin, *Taking Rights Seriously* (see above, chap. 1, n. 3).

5. The above remarks are not intended to suggest that any very high percentage of the states and other political associations that have claimed to have authority justifiable by the criteria I have been discussing have

been warranted in that claim. Nor are those remarks meant to imply that the bulk of modern populations believe that the states under which they live are warranted in such a claim. A distressingly large proportion of actual states manifestly are (and always have been) despotisms that satisfy neither the criterion of voluntary association nor any other notably eligible normative standard. The bulk of the populations do not accept and obey the authority of these states because they believe it to be justified; they submit to their force and power—force and power that the states are able to generate because some more or less substantial minority of the populations in question believe that it is in their interest to sustain that force and power. The proposition that the preponderance of modern populations accept the idea that political authority can be justified is based, rather, on the evidence that so few have adopted any version of the anarchist argument that authority can *never* be justified.

6. The discussions of the individual in the state of nature in Hobbes, Locke, and Rousseau are only the best-known cases in point. For a dramatic recent instance, see essay 1 in Oakeshott's *On Human Conduct* (see above, intro., n. 4).

7. J.-J. Rousseau, *Social Contract,* esp. 2.1 and 3.15.

8. In addition to the works by Oakeshott and Nozick already cited in other connections, see Friedrich von Hayek, *Law, Legislation and Liberty,* 3 vols. (Chicago: University of Chicago Press, 1973–79), esp. vol. 2.

9. For a cogent critique of this position, see Michael Taylor, *Anarchy and Cooperation* (New York: John Wiley & Sons, 1976).

10. See esp. "A Plea for Excuses," in J. L. Austin, *Philosophical Papers* (London: Oxford University Press, 1961).

11. For a helpful introductory discussion of Kant's thinking here, see John Ladd's intro. to his ed. of Kant's *The Metaphysical Elements of Justice* (New York: Library of Liberal Arts, 1965). The two senses of "will" are discussed at pp. xxv–xxviii.

12. Robert Paul Wolff, *The Autonomy of Reason: A Commentary on Kant's Groundwork of the Metaphysics of Morals* (New York: Harper & Row, 1973), p. 223; see also pp. 49–50, 88–89, 132–33, 175–81, 185–86. Wolff does believe that action on chosen ends can and should be governed by reason and duty as specified by the Categorical Imperative, that is (on his reading), by the principle of consistency. This principle is formal in character and does not "rule any choices of policies *in.*" But given a context in which an agent or group of agents have adopted certain purposes and policies, some courses of action will be ruled *out* as inconsistent with choices already made or choices implied by purposes and policies already adopted. It is unclear to me how the formality of the Categorical Imperative overcomes or obviates the difficulty of bridging the gap between the noumenal and phenomenal realms.

13. See esp. Kant, *Metaphysical Elements of Justice,* ed. Ladd, pp. 84–89.

14. See Max Stirner, *The Ego and Its Own,* ed. J. H. Martin, trans.

Steven T. Byington (reprint ed., Magnolia, Md.: Peter Smith, n.d.).

15. In *The Autonomy of Reason* Wolff sketches a contractarian view according to which obligations must be grounded in commitments that *B* has actually made. He contends that "there is no special sort of commitment . . . which gives rise to a legitimate state" (p. 224). But he does distinguish between "ends which one posits by oneself, treating other persons as external to the process of choice, [which] give rise to what are commonly called principles of prudence," and those ends which one "posits collectively with other rational agents, through a process of rational discourse culminating in unanimous agreement, [which] give rise to what are commonly called moral principles." If in fact there are any obligations of the sort commonly called "political," they would presumably arise in the second of these two ways. The requirement of unanimous agreement would appear to render improbable any very large number of such moral principles–*cum*–obligations (especially given the nonrational character of the process of positing ends), and hence it looks as though Wolff is likely to remain, at least *de facto*, in the anarchist camp (cf. ibid., pp. 129–30, n. 12, and p. 178, n. 30). Readers familiar with the contractarian tradition, however, will not be astonished to find that the remark about unanimous agreement is qualified by invoking notions of "tacit" or "rational" consent. "I am persuaded that moral obligations, strictly so-called, arise from freely chosen contractual commitments between or among rational agents who have entered into some continuing and organized interaction with one another. Where such contractual commitments do not exist, cannot plausibly be construed as having been tacitly entered into, and cannot even be supposed to be the sort that *would* be entered into if the persons were to attempt some collective agreement, then no moral obligations bind one person to another" (ibid., p. 219). And again: "But most of the time persons find themselves associated in ongoing institutionally organized patterns of interaction which neither in fact nor in plausible fiction can be traced to an original contractual agreement. In such cases, limited or partial obligations exist, the scope and force of which correspond to the degree to which the quasi-contractual situation approximates to the pure case of explicit collective commitment" (ibid., p. 224). In fairness, it should be emphasized that these views are only sketched in the course of a commentary on Kant, not fully developed or defended.

16. See esp. Richard Wasserstrom, "The Obligation to Obey the Law," in Flathman, ed.

Chapter 11

1. Note that on the above usage one could favor the democratization of authority without being much of a democrat in major modern senses in which the term is used. For example, Aristotle's argument that citizens should rule and be ruled in turn is a proposal to democratize authority in the above sense, but it would be an outright mistake to treat Aristotle as a

democrat if the latter characterization is taken to mean someone who favors extending the rights and duties of citizenship to all or to any very high percentage of those who live in the territory of the polis.

2. The point in the text might be emphasized by noting that in a number of European countries the "electoral law" is regarded as both the expression and the guarantor of the legitimacy of the political order.

3. If we take these democratic beliefs and arrangements as forming a part of the authoritative in the countries alluded to, the proposition in the text becomes something close to a necessary truth. I return to this point and the substantial difficulties it poses later in part 2.

4. Rousseau, *Social Contract*, 1.6.

5. See Robert Wolff, *In Defense of Anarchism* (see above, chap. 5, n. 6), pp. 34–37.

6. In fact, Rousseau's notion of the General Will—which is the repository of authority—is a hybrid concept combining features of both "authority" and the "public interest" or "common good" as the latter concepts are ordinarily used.

Chapter 12

1. Note that F-P theory is formally comparable in its contention that the satisfaction of insistently nonsubstantive criteria conclusively establishes (indeed is the sole consideration relevant to establishing) that the rule is a law.

2. Wittgenstein, *Philosophical Investigations*, I,217.

3. See Roberto M. Unger, *Knowledge and Politics* (Riverside, N.J.: Free Press, 1976); and *Law in Contemporary Society* (Riverside, N.J.: Free Press, 1976).

4. Rousseau can and possibly should be interpreted as making an argument of this same type. If the General Will is treated as consisting in transcendent truths rather than as a body of values and beliefs that are (merely) widely accepted among a population his argument takes on this character. The exegetical question, of course, is not a major concern in our context. Whether Rousseau made the argument discussed in the text, that argument is important and requires our attention. (And if Rousseau made a transcendental argument, if the General Will stands for allegedly universal principles of freedom, equality, or the like, then the objections we make to such arguments apply to him.)

5. At a philosophically deeper level, the two kinds of difficulties with natural law and natural right theories merge into one. This is because the wherewithal for establishing the truths or principles which such theories purport to advance must themselves have standing in a practice or form of life.

6. See Lon M. Fuller, *The Morality of Law* (New Haven: Yale University Press, 1964).

7. It is of course true that constitutionalism and the device of individual rights have frequently been employed in settling such issues. This is done,

for example, by adopting constitutional provisions against an income tax or by according a constitutional right to abortion on demand. Such uses of constitutionalism and individual rights reduce their formality, minimizing the differences between the role played by them and the role of "ordinary" decisions of authority.

8. A number of other analogies might be employed in this connection. Among them would be formal rules of games, such as those governing the moves of the pieces in chess or the rank order of hands in poker, as compared with judgments about what move to make or what bet to place in this or that game, or the rules of musical notation and composition, as compared with judgments about what will produce the desired musical effect in a particular composition. Although these cases differ importantly from one another, they all involve a distinction between comparatively formal and relatively widely accepted rules and principles, on the one hand, and judgments concerning the substantive merits of particular decisions and actions, on the other.

9. Charles H. McIlwain, *Constitutionalism: Ancient and Modern,* rev. ed. (Ithaca, N.Y.: Cornell University Press, 1947), p. 146 and passim.

10. For a wide-ranging and often suggestive discussion of the conditions under which the rule-of-law principle is likely to achieve the requisite acceptance and respect, see Unger, *Law in Contemporary Society.* Unger's work is concerned, albeit from a very different perspective, with many of the same issues that have been under discussion in the present section.

11. For example, a not inconsiderable group of persons who had become radically dissatisfied with the conduct of the U.S. government in the 1960s and 1970s began to argue that established and relatively formal principles such as the rule of law and the individual rights of the First Amendment were contributing to the difficulty and ought no longer to be respected. For versions of this argument, see Herbert Marcuse, Robert Paul Wolff, and Barrington Moore, *A Critique of Pure Tolerance* (Boston: Beacon Press, 1969).

Chapter 13

1. Robert Paul Wolff, *In Defense of Anarchism* (see above, chap. 5, n. 6), p. 71.

2. Ibid., p. 57. Cf. pp. 29, 41, 69. As noted above, Wolff takes a very different position in *The Autonomy of Reason* (see above, chap. 10, n. 12).

3. Henry David Thoreau, *Civil Disobedience,* third paragraph from the beginning.

4. The precise sense in which the citizens of Sweden, New Zealand, Italy, and Canada have consented or agreed to the authority of the governments of those countries has proven to be difficult to formulate. But that these associations deserve to be called voluntary in a sense that the Soviet Union, Albania, and Uganda under Amin do not can hardly be debated.

5. As one who has been attracted to the Aristotelian view, the argument discussed above stands as the single strongest consideration that positively supports acceptance of authority (as opposed to considerations that refute or weaken familiar arguments against it). Engaging in the reflections reported in this book, however, has sharpened my personal awareness of the importance of authority to the argument for citizenship (especially in the Arendtian formulation of that argument). The first and to some extent lasting effect of this sharpened awareness was to mitigate somewhat my—perhaps merely native—suspicion of authority. But that suspicion remains strong, and hence the awareness in question has somewhat tempered my enthusiasm for the citizenship argument. Because citizenship presupposes authority, and because authority—however vigorous the citizenry—is a dangerous institution, citizenship cannot be an unalloyed good.

6. Of course, many of those who have defended authority in terms of its contribution to the production of various goods (especially "public" goods in the technical sense) have contended that a practice of authority that satisfied the conditions mentioned above would not be capable of producing the goods in question. Or more exactly, they have contended that a practice that satisfied those conditions would not be a practice of authority. But I have already responded to that contention.

Chapter 14

1. I have discussed this and various related meanings of the concept "a theory" in chap. 1 of *The Practice of Rights* (see above, intro., n. 3).

2. On this view, the words and deeds of the citizenry might be treated as a performative in the first person plural, a collective—or at least a collected—performative.

3. See H. L. A. Hart, *The Concept of Law* (see above, chap. 7, n. 2), esp. pp. 54–55, 86–88, 98–99. For a closely related distinction, see John Searle, "How to Derive an 'Is' from an 'Ought,'" in *Theories of Ethics,* ed. Philippa Foot (London: Oxford University Press, 1967).

4. It should perhaps be emphasized that the foregoing disclaimers do not apply to my discussions in chaps. 1–8. If they do not help us to understand a practice of authority, however remote it may be from the beliefs and values that make up our own practices, those discussions are inadequate and need revision.

5. See, for example, Sheldon S. Wolin, *Politics and Vision* (Boston: Little, Brown & Co., 1961), esp. p. 52.

Index

Abuses and usurpations, long train of, 117, 119, 120
Actions and acting, 53–56, 67, 102, 108–9, 123, 134–37, 140–41, 148–52, 157, 161–62, 168, 177–81, 246, 253–54, 261–62
Adjudication, 41–43
Adkins v. Children's Hospital, 66
Agamemnon and Achilles, 148–49, 164
Agency or autonomy, 2, 122, 124–25, 177–91, 194–95, 201, 205, 207, 212–20, 221, 225, 237–39, 240–41, 246, 258
An authority, 16, 17–20, 24–26, 81, 91–92, 94–102, 104, 116, 206–7, 247, 248; distinctively respectful attention and, 96–98, 100–101
Anarchism, 6, 8, 9, 73, 83, 84, 87, 89, 109, 118, 122–24, 155, 175, 176–78, 180, 214, 224, 226, 265
Anscombe, Elizabeth, 97–99, 100, 258, 263
Aquinas, St. Thomas, 206, 245
Arendt, Hannah, 6, 71–78, 86, 90, 126, 152–55, 160, 163–65, 167, 221–22, 248, 255, 260, 263–64, 270
Aristotle, 66, 221–22, 237, 245, 267, 270
Austin, J., 126, 257
Austin, J. L., 187, 253, 266
Authoritarian personality, 98
Authoritative, the, 6–8, 25–27, 29, 31–33, 50–51, 66, 70, 77–78, 80–81, 83–84, 85–88, 142, 146, 147, 149, 150–53, 155, 159–67, 202–12, 228–30, 233, 235, 239–40, 245, 248, 256, 268
Authority: advice and counsel versus, 104, 106, 109; children and, 98–99; commands to be obeyed and, 14, 93, 102–3, 168; concept of, 20, 72–73, 77, 82–83, 109, 116, 117–19, 123, 126, 128, 147, 151, 154–55, 176, 233, 237, 247, 249, 268; decision, choice and, 106, 122, 131, 179, 180,

186; *de facto* and *de jure*, 15, 31, 160, 161, 182, 230, 231; disagreement, conflict, consensus and, 27–32, 45, 73, 85, 88, 91, 195, 196, 237, 238, 241, 242; efficacy of, 155–59; ends or purposes of, 2, 3, 5, 15, 168, 169; equality, inequality and, 15, 27, 93, 99, 195, 196; essentially contested concept, 259; feature of associations or collectivities, 31–32, 248; freedom, reason, morality and, 15, 82, 100, 103, 104, 107, 118, 119, 124, 168, 169–70, 177–80, 183, 185, 189–90, 196, 201, 207–8, 212–13, 223, 234, 235, 238–39, 241–43; functional or other necessity of, 7, 15; justice and, 3, 91, 118, 122, 169, 170, 178, 222–23; justification and disjustification of, 7–8, 13, 76–77, 91, 109, 169–71, 175, 181–82, 213–24, 225, 226, 234–35, 242–43; legitimate and illegitimate, 15, 48, 158–59, 230–34; limits on, 193–94, 203–4, 206, 207–12, 215, 222; manifestly dangerous, 122, 170, 270; marks of, 19, 20, 52, 71; Marxist thinking concerning, 2, 126; merits, desirability, consequences and, 35–37, 41–47, 53, 61–70, 75, 88, 91, 99, 103–4, 106–9, 113–16, 119–24, 165, 168–69, 190–91, 254; personal or impersonal character of, 14, 17, 35, 169, 170; political, 17–18; politics and, 237–38; practical character of, 34, 102; practice of, 4, 7, 8, 9, 23, 72, 76, 100, 109, 116–25, 190–91, 207, 215, 219, 222, 224, 230, 234, 238, 241–42, 260, 270; puzzling character of, 13, 14; reasons for belief and action and, 8, 50, 80–82, 90, 94, 99, 101, 104, 106, 111, 112, 118, 121–22, 124–25, 127, 154, 156, 157, 164, 186, 242, 243; relational character of, 98–99, 102–3; religion and, 16, 24, 71, 72, 73; right, right-